"Avoiding academic jargon, Spindel writes convincingly about how her research has helped her to understand attitudes toward American Indians."

—*Publishers Weekly*

"Although a great deal has been written about the controversy of using fake Indians to get fans pumped up at football games, it took an entire book to give full vent to the subject. Carol Spindel does this admirably and evenhandedly in *Dancing at Halftime*, which dissects this controversy at the U. of I., where it is perhaps at its sharpest."

—*Chicago Tribune*

"Not only a well-written plea for greater interracial empathy, but also an interesting reflection on the uses and abuses of history, a subject that never goes away."

—*St. Louis Post–Dispatch*

"Yesterday's racism we recognize and we are embarrassed by it. Today's racism we often do not recognize until we read something like Carol Spindel's clear and fascinating message in *Dancing at Halftime*."

—Senator Paul Simon

"With clear and compelling language, Spindel shows us how the naive rituals of a previous era can become the insensitive orthodoxy of today. I can't imagine a more readable—or a more even-handed—exploration of the mascot issue. This should be required reading for anyone committed to building a new sense of community in the United States."

—Frederick E. Hoxie, Swanlund Professor, University of Illinois, and editor of *The Encyclopedia of North American Indians*

"Spindel displays considerable courage in tackling a controversial subject. A very personal account of the twentieth-century phenomenon of American Indians used as sports mascots, *Dancing at Halftime* also contains some fascinating history of early college football. The whole is strongly and beautifully written."

—Dee Brown, author of *Bury My Heart at Wounded Knee*

"Honest, insightful, and a well balanced analysis of this complicated problem . . . a 'must read.'"

—Vine Deloria, Jr., Professor of History Emeritus, University of Colorado and a Standing Rock Sioux tribal member

"I celebrate *Dancing at Halftime*, which brings Carol Spindel's wry and penetrating perception to this subject. As she well understands, it is a cipher through which one can read the deeper meanings not only of American history but of contemporary life today."   —Susan Griffin, author of *A Chorus of Stones*

Dancing at Halftime

Sports and the Controversy over American Indian Mascots

Updated and with a New Afterword

CAROL SPINDEL

NEW YORK UNIVERSITY PRESS

New York and London

NEW YORK UNIVERSITY PRESS
New York and London

First published in paperback in 2002.

© 2000, 2002 by New York University
"Minstrel Show," by Dennis Tibbetts reprinted by permission of
Dennis Tibbetts; Edgar Lee Masters, "Starved Rock," from *Starved
Rock,* originally published by the Macmillan Company. Reprinted
by permission of Hilary Masters.

Library of Congress Cataloging-in-Publication Data
Spindel, Carol.
Dancing at halftime : sports and the controversy over American Indian
mascots / Carol Spindel.
p.   cm.
Includes bibliographical references (p.   ).
ISBN 0-8147-8126-8 (cloth) — ISBN 0-8147-8127-6 (pbk.)
1. Sports team mascots—Social aspects—United States. 2. Indians of
North America—Social conditions—20th century. 3. University of
Illinois at Urbana-Champaign—Mascots.   I. Title.
GV714.5 .C27 2000
306.4'83—dc21   00-009148

New York University Press books are printed on acid-free paper,
and their binding materials are chosen for strength and durability.

Manufactured in the United States of America

10 9 8 7 6 5 4 3 2 1

About the title page illustration: Timothy Tiger, from "Feathers of the
University of Illinois Trustees" series, #6 "Illinois Spirit of Ignominy,"
13"H x 4 1/2"W x 1 1/2"D, copper, wood, Illinois soil, fabric, 1999.

For my father, Murray Asher Spindel, 1922–1999

Two of my father's lines steered my thinking as I worked on this book. The first was tossed at me after I had proudly recounted the news from my *Weekly Reader.* Always delivered in a tone of shock, it was: "Do you believe everything you read?"

The other, equally important for understanding this subject, was his guideline for choosing roadside motels in the old days before they became standardized. If the motel's sign proclaimed that it was "modern," he always drove on. "If they have to put it on the sign," he said, "you know it isn't."

Contents

Prologue

A friend of mine says Americans lack a sense of place. An environmentalist and geographer, he is a person who has grown up, been educated, married, raised a family, and buried a son on the same patch of prairie. The rest of us? We are nomads, nostalgic for the place where we grew up and unattached to the place where we live. This lack of attachment to place makes us, he maintains, neglectful stewards. We don't wince when ancient trees are cut to widen a street because they aren't the trees we played under as children. While the wrecking ball destroys historic buildings, we walk by—our grandmothers never shopped there. He would like us to quit pining for faraway places and attach ourselves, barnacle-like, where we actually live.

The horizon line on an autumn day, the silhouette of a grain elevator, the sound of corn growing—none of these quickens my pulse. When friends drop their voices to a hush about these things, I know they're real midwesterners. Perhaps my children will feel that way. They never remark on the wind like I do. They have never lived any place where the air is still.

Fourteen years ago the Harpies of Geographic Dislocation snatched me out of Berkeley, a place I had chosen, and set me down in the cornfields. I knew they were laughing, their wild hair whirling in the high-altitude winds, their long bony fingers cradling globes and sextants as they unrolled their topographic maps to search out the most unsuitable possibility. They had me cornered. Stay where I had chosen to live, or stay married and go where my husband could get a job. I moved to Urbana, Illinois.

Of course, in a Greek drama, you don't incur the wrath of the Harpies arbitrarily. You have to anger the gods through some act of arrogance. I, too, had asked for it in my own neoclassical and melodramatic way. My moment of tempting the fates took place in a yellow Volkswagen squareback on a road in Iowa over twenty years ago and had to do with the word "never," the hubris of which I did not comprehend in my twenties. I thought I was alone on that road, just small green corn plants for miles around, but I didn't know that the Harpies can hear you anywhere. As I drove away from Iowa City, after three years at the University of Iowa, I stuck my head out of the window of my yellow VW and yelled into the wind, "Good-bye, Midwest! I will *never* come back." Strands of my long brown hair caught between my teeth. Of course the Harpies waited just long enough for me to choose a piece of earth before they snatched me up, my stubby little roots dangling like naked tentacles.

For ten years I lived in Urbana like a tree in a large pot, anchored to my house and my neighborhood, to people but not to place. But the tenth winter, curiosity changed that. That winter I finally began to ask questions about the place where I lived. For starters, I simply wanted to understand why, at the university where I taught, a student dressed up as an Indian named Chief Illiniwek and danced at sports events. Even more than that, I wanted to know why the entire town pledged allegiance to this Indian chief.

You might ask how I could live in a place for ten years without giving this any thought. Easily. This halftime display, I assumed, had to do with football, which had nothing whatsoever to do with me.

This is not to say that I hadn't noticed the university's symbol, an Indian wearing a feather headdress drawn inside a perfect circle. There was no way to avoid it. A sports-loving giant with two ink pads, one bright orange, the other blue, must have stomped through in seven-league boots and rubber-stamped the round design on every flat surface in the side-by-side towns of Urbana and Champaign.

In silk screen he was emblazoned on T-shirts; in needlepoint, he decorated office walls and dens; in stained glass, he shone through the windows of doughnut shops. Thickly coated with resin, his face animated clocks. He loomed over me on restaurant awnings. He roared past me on the delivery vans of companies named Chief this or Illini that. He was on the front page of the newspaper nearly every day. Waitresses wore aprons embroidered with his face, craft shops sold patterns to re-create him in cross-stitch, and at the farmers' market you could purchase him on webbed lawn chairs or pot holders. Around the campus, the sidewalk was a mobile collage of his blue and orange image.

My son came home from preschool and told me that Chief Illiniwek had come to show-and-tell, carrying his Indian clothes inside a long plastic bag. Even then I didn't give this a second thought. And I certainly did not connect the ubiquitous circle or the student with the dry-cleaning bag to real American Indian people who live in the contemporary world and not in some historical and mythical dreamtime.

Until one day when I opened the *New York Times* (after ten years in Champaign-Urbana I still did not subscribe to the local paper) and read an op-ed piece by Michael Dorris, a writer whose work I admire. "People of pro-claimed good will have the oddest ways of honoring American Indians," Dorris began. "Sometimes they dress themselves up in turkey feathers and paint to boogie on 50-yard lines." My eyes pricked up, so to speak. Turkey feathers? Fifty-yard line? Clearly Dorris was talking about none other than Chief Illini-wek. "War-bonneted apparitions pasted to football helmets or baseball caps," he pointed out, "act as opaque, impermeable curtains, solid walls of white noise that for many citizens block or distort all vision of the nearly two million native Americans."

A few days later I reached toward the top shelf of a refrigerated display in the supermarket and suddenly stopped. Smiling down at me from the rock-hard box of butter was an Indian maiden with long black braids. I had been buying this brand for years. I had given more thought to whether my family should eat margarine or butter than I had to the image on the package. The girl kneeled, ready to please, her fringe draped neatly over her folded thighs. As I stood in that cold pale air with my hand open but empty, I suddenly realized that for ten years I had buttered my whole wheat bread with "white noise" while I refused, without asking myself why, to identify with the symbol of the University where I taught. Meanwhile, I had assumed that Native American struggles took place in some faraway place to the west or north of me.

That moment of supermarket epiphany took place during my tenth winter in the Illinois country. A long time to get around to asking some very basic questions about the town that had become my home, where I taught, wrote, lived, and where my two children were born. Michael Dorris's opinion was one I took seriously because I felt that he had a rare vantage point from which to view the chief's halftime dancing. Half Modoc, Dorris was raised as a white American because his Indian father died when he was very young. Trained as an anthropologist, founder of a Native American studies program, he was also a novelist whose characters had deepened my understanding of other lives. If Dorris considered it worth his while to think and write about Chief Illiniwek, shouldn't I, who lived and worked surrounded by him, give his halftime dancing a few moments of consideration?

Another day, as I sat in Wendy's eating hamburgers with my son, I pointed out the chief wallpaper next to our table. "I've heard that some Native American people don't like the idea of Chief Illiniwek," I told him.

"Yeah," my son said casually. "Like if David dressed up in my clothes and pretended to be me at school and then did something really stupid on the playground." As if the matter were settled, he returned to dragging his french fries through little ponds of ketchup to coat them, first on one side, then on the other.

His reaction amazed me. When I tried to make an equation between Chief Illiniwek, modern Indian people, and myself as viewer, I felt as if I were writing xs and ys with invisible ink while sitting in dense fog.

Certainly the chief was borrowed imagery, but wasn't borrowing what cultures did all the time? And weren't the hybrid forms that resulted the very thing that renewed our culture and made it lively and dynamic? Was it possible to stack up concrete blocks around images or ideas, to say that only some people could use them or that these people had to authorize their use? People borrow and blend and hybridize, they create new traditions no matter how you try to stop them. When they see a dance step they like or hear music that moves them, they incorporate the movements and notes into their own style. You can no more prevent this than you can keep a child from growing taller by placing a brick on her head.

I decided to assign the topic to my writing students and find out what they thought. They were enthusiastic about the subject but their essays repeated the same emotional arguments made in the campus newspaper by its student columnists. Isn't it harmless for the marching band to include a student dressed as an American Indian who dances to certain songs? Isn't it derogatory and racist? How do we remember the first Americans? Isn't that important? He's all right because he's authentic (a position the university held onto until 1990). This is a frivolous debate when there are people that are hungry, that are homeless—shouldn't we spend our time on more important things? Inevitably our discussions about Chief Illiniwek always circled back to a single swirling point: can it be wrong to represent an Indian if that representation is a positive one? If it inspires admiration?

The Illinois Indians, who Chief Illiniwek is intended to honor, suffered, in my students' essays, a postmodern crisis of multiple identities. "The Illinois Indians never existed," stated one essay. "The Illinois Confederacy lived here on these prairies until their land was taken from them and Chief Illiniwek was their leader," said another. "The Illinois Indians were killed in warfare with another tribe. The last survivors were outnumbered so they took refuge on a high cliff named Starved Rock and fought (the Iroquois, the Potawatomi) to the death." (The enemy varied from one essay to another). "The Illiniwek died of epidemics."

Who was right? As an immigrant to Illinois, I had no idea. But when I asked other faculty members or longtime residents, they didn't know either. Was Chief Illiniwek fiction, myth, or a collage of historic figures?

Down a tunnel in the basement of the library, through a narrow passage of file cabinets, I found the university archives. In this out-of-the-way spot with steam pipes running overhead, helpful librarians unearthed not potions to make me larger or smaller but old yearbooks and boxes of football programs from the 1920s, filled with advertisements for campus eating spots, raccoon coats, and Chicago ballrooms.

The university depicted in these photographs looked very different from the one I knew. In the 1920s and 1930s there were student theatricals with large casts of blackface minstrels, students dressed in rags for the annual hobo parade, and students wrapped in blankets holding Indian pipes as they initiated new members into an honorary society. Corn maidens and fairy queens danced at the May fete.

When I emerged from the tunnel and walked out of the library, everything around me looked different. Or rather, I should say that it looked just the same. But for the first time, when I looked at the brick buildings and right-angled streets, I had a sense of how a bustling campus had come to exist here, on this piece of prairie land. Along with students playing frisbee, I pictured the fairy queens around their maypole and the hobos passing in their costume rags, the boys wrapped in Indian blankets passing pipes as they sat around their fire. The names of the buildings I entered and the streets I drove down now referred to people who had become real to me. A few had been commemorated with stately edifices. Some had bronze plaques or busts. Others didn't fare so well.

C. R. Griggs, for example, who ended up with only a four-block side street, was the entrepreneur and lobbyist who rented a suite of rooms in the grandest hotel in Springfield and plied the legislators with oyster suppers, free theater tickets, quail dinners, and fine cigars. Urbana, whose bid was fourth in value out of four, was chosen as the site of the new land grant university. Clark Robinson Griggs never got the tree-lined avenue he deserved; the town wanted to pretend that Urbana was a natural choice. You won't find a bronze statue of him any-where on campus. But without his oysters and his glad-handing, and had he not wheeled and dealed in smoke-filled rooms, there would be no supercomputing center, no engineering campus, no performing arts complex, no massive library in Champaign-Urbana. If there were any justice, one of the new shopping cen-ters of discount stores, at the very least, ought to be named the Griggs Mall.

From the basement of the library I climbed to the fourth floor, where a col-lection dedicated to the history of Illinois was located. The more I learned about the Illinois Indians, and about other Indian groups who moved into this area in the course of their migrations across the country, the more I realized how little I knew. When I thought of westward expansion, I pictured covered wagons and Indians on horses. But in the center of the country, where I now live, Native peo-ple and the earliest European settlers traveled on rivers and lakes, and settled along their banks.

In school I'm sure I learned about the French explorers La Salle and Jolliet, and Father Jacques Marquette, the priest who traveled with Jolliet. Why then, when I thought about exploration and settlement, did I picture covered wagons and blue-coated cavalry? And when I thought of Indians, why did I see only barebacked riders with bows and arrows?

Daily, for the last decade of the century, the students at the University of Illinois and the townspeople of Champaign and Urbana have debated, in the most emotional terms, whether it is appropriate to have a student who dresses up as an Indian chief as a symbol of their sports teams. Were this discussion truly frivolous, it would have ended long ago. Certainly economics is involved. Sell-ing the Indian image brings in large profits for the university and for business owners. But many people who do not profit from Chief Illiniwek in any monetary way are passionately determined to retain him as their icon. It was the nature of this attachment that I set out to understand.

The story of Chief Illiniwek is about a specific place: the red-brick football stadium, the midwestern prairie on which the stadium was built. But fictional Indian chiefs are not unique to Illinois or the Midwest. At the present moment, there are over 2,500 schools with American Indian-based team names and mascots. Nor are college students the only ones debating the issue. School boards across the country are facing emotional confrontations over team names, designs, and halftime performances. The American Indian Movement estimates that at least six hundred schools have already decided to rename their teams and change their mascots.

Fans love the Washington Redskins, the Atlanta Braves, the Kansas City Chiefs, the Cleveland Indians, the Florida State Seminoles, the Chicago Blackhawks, and the Warriors and Chiefs of their hometown high schools. If sports is an American religion, these Indians are our gilded and carefully preserved icons. It is precisely because sports holds such a prominent place in American culture that naming a team after someone is such an honor, supporters of the names claim.

If we do a census of the population in our collective imagination, imaginary Indians are one of the largest demographic groups. They dance, they drum; they go on the warpath; they are always young men who wear trailing feather bonnets. Symbolic servants, they serve as mascots and metaphors. We rely on these images to anchor us to the land and verify our account of our own past. But as these Indians exist only in our own imaginations, they provide a solipsistic connection and leave us, ultimately, untethered and rootless.

Of all the imaginary Indians, Chief Illiniwek may be the most complicated. There is no doubt that he is genuinely revered by his followers. Furthermore, his appearance, the reproduction of his image, and the behavior of his fans are scrupulously monitored. There is nothing cartoonish about the round logo. Illini is not, in and of itself, a disparaging name. Other mascots have objectionable features: names like Redskins, Squaws, or Savages; cartoon images like Chief Wahoo; the tomahawk chop. But at the University of Illinois, the debate centers around the practice itself, around the fundamental question of whether it is appropriate to have an American Indian as a mascot. His fans say that Indians are overly sensitive and are imagining an offense where none is intended. Intended or no, his critics reply, Chief Illiniwek stereotypes and demeans Indian people. The same performance is described simultaneously as a gesture of admiration and as a racist insult. When they watch the same ritual, Americans are divided into two groups, who deduce wholly opposite conclusions about its meaning.

Spiraling backward and forward from halftime to Wild West shows, from a mock battle in a football stadium to the Little Bighorn, this book is an attempt to understand what each group sees when Chief Illiniwek slips out of the marching band and begins to dance. It is an inquiry into why we non-Indian Americans are so attached to fictional Indians who live in an imaginary past and a mythological present, an attachment that tells us very little about Indian people, but a great deal about ourselves.

Home Game

It is a warm Saturday afternoon in October, the afternoon of a home game, and about forty thousand Fighting Illini fans file into Memorial Stadium. The stadium will hold nearly seventy thousand, but the team is losing badly this year. Blue pants are topped with bright orange blazers and orange sweaters. The round circle logo of Chief Illiniwek's face is on the plastic drink cups they carry, on the stadium seats, on the blankets, and on their sweatshirts and caps. Two boys and two girls walk in laughing, all four faces painted half orange and half blue. On their cheeks are temporary tattoos—small round circles of Chief Illiniwek.

A group of students carrying signs marches from the center of campus and stands silently outside the stadium. "Racist Stereotypes Dehumanize," their signs say.

"Get a life!" yells a football fan as he passes them with his ticket. Others echo him. "Yeah, get a life!"

The marchers wear T-shirts and buttons with the round chief logo crossed out by a slash. "Imagine the Pope dancing at halftime," says one posterboard placard. "How would you like Jesus on a butt cushion?" asks another.

A second group of students, clad in bright orange T-shirts, are scattered throughout the crowd. They hand out round stickers that say, "Save the Chief." They are swamped by takers, who thank them warmly. Some fans shake theirs at the line of protesters as they pass.

The anti-chief students have a line of security surrounding them, trained students and activists who wear armbands. They also have literature to hand out, although most of the passing fans wave it away and keep walking. Between the protesters and the field full of RVs and blue and orange tents where pork chops sizzle on huge grills, members of the university police force stroll back and forth, watching the demonstration and the passersby closely.

Once the game starts and the fans are inside, the demonstrators march off yelling, "One, two, three, four, we don't want your chief no more!" and "Win the game, lose the chief!"—a recent addition to their repertoire.

All afternoon, yells echo over the town, a dull roar. When the Illini score, a cannon booms, the female cheerleaders are tossed high in the air, and an enormous orange flag is carried around the field at a run.

At halftime the Marching Illini step out onto the bright green astroturf. The sun glints off the brass instruments, and the braid on the navy and white uniforms gleams. The musical program, which is never repeated, is followed by a musical and dramatic ritual that is never altered, game after game, year after year. The band calls this medley the "Three-in-One." They march down the field to "The Pride of the Illini March." Then the band members sing the "Trio" portion:

We are marching for Dear old Illini.
For the men who are fighting for you.
Here's a cheer for our dear Alma Mater.
May our love for her ever be true. . . .

The band changes direction and begins to play "The March of the Illini," standing so their bodies spell out ILLINI. Chief Illiniwek, who has been hiding among the band members, emerges and dances down the field to what the band calls "an Indian-flavored march melody." BOOM-boom-boom-boom! BOOM-boom-boom-boom.

"Chieeeef! Chieeeef!" yell the fans in deep basso voices. The cries, echoing back and forth between the stadium walls, sound like booing. The chief, a university student dressed in beaded buckskin and a trailing turkey feather headdress, performs a vigorous, rhythmic dance that ends in acrobatic leaps. Legs split wide, he vaults into the air and touches his toes, fringe flying. The crowd cheers. Then he strides to the Illinois side of the field, raises his arms wide, folds them down, one over the other, lifts his chin as high as it will possibly go, and stands facing the fans. Many of them mime the gesture in mirror image. Quietly now, the crowd rises and sings the school anthem:

Hail to the Orange, Hail to the Blue,
Hail Alma Mater, Ever so true!
We love no other so let our motto be,
Victory! Illinois Varsity!

For many graduates, some of whom are proud to be second- or third-generation Illinois alumni, the halftime moment when Chief Illiniwek poses and they, along with thousands of other people, stand and sing, is a serious, even quasi-religious, ritual. This symbol and this moment have become part of their identity. They are Illini. It is a rare moment of American cultural fusion—the black and white football team, the Indian icon, and the huge crowd of mostly white midwestern Americans who identify with both. There are no big-headed mascots here, no caricatured T-shirts or sideline hijinks, no tomahawk chops or scalp 'em headlines. The appreciation for the beautifully crafted clothing, the dance, and the music is genuine. With so much good feeling, can this be racism?

The Controversy

At school board meetings, at universities, in professional sports, and on the editorial pages of widely read newspapers, objections are being raised to teams named the Warriors, Braves, Chiefs, Indians, and Redskins. Teams named after specific tribes such as the Apaches and Mohawks have also been criticized. Six teams—the Florida State Seminoles, the Fighting Illini at the University of Illinois, the Atlanta Braves, the Washington Redskins, the Kansas City Chiefs, and the Cleveland Indians—have been targeted by an organization of Native American activists, the National Coalition on Racism in Sports and the Media. Of all minority groups, only American Indians, they point out, are still depicted in stereotypes and caricatures.

In the 1970s, in response to student protests, the Dartmouth Indians became the Big Green, the Stanford Indians became the Cardinal (singular), Syracuse University retired its Saltine Warrior, also known as Big Chief Bill Orange, and University of Oklahoma retired its "Little Red" mascot. Since then, dozens of universities have replaced mascots based on American Indians. The Miami University Redskins in Oxford, Ohio, are now the RedHawks, in response to a request from the Miami tribe of Oklahoma; the St. John's Redmen are the Red Storm; and the University of Tennessee at Chattanooga has retired Chief Moccanooga. Marquette University's sports teams, which had Indian themes, have become the Golden Eagles. Eastern Michigan students and fans are no longer the Hurons. Hundreds of high schools have changed their team names and symbols. And at least two minor league baseball teams have transformed themselves: the Chiefs of Syracuse became the Skychiefs and the Akron Indians are now the Akron Aeros. Of all these teams, only Syracuse University seems to have struggled to find a new identity. The Saltine Warrior, an Indian chief invented in a hoax in the student newspaper in 1931, was replaced with a parade of unpopular mascot wannabes. The school finally settled on Otto the Orange in the 1990s.

Newspapers including the *Oregonian* of Portland, Oregon, the *Star Tribune* in Minneapolis, the *Akron Beacon Journal*, the *Seattle Times*, and the *Salt Lake Tribune* have established an editorial policy of not printing Indian-inspired team names. They refer to the Braves, for example, as the Atlanta baseball team. Two radio stations in Washington, D.C., have followed their lead. The Los Angeles School District gave its three public high schools with Indian mascots one year to come up with replacements. The policy was upheld by a court decision. Dallas, Texas, also mandated a change. State boards of education, civil rights commissions, or state commissions of Indian affairs in Minnesota, Michigan, Nebraska, Kansas, Maryland, South Dakota, and Wisconsin have asked schools in their states to rename their teams, retire their mascots, and redesign their logos. The New York State Education Board, after a two-year review, urged its public schools to make changes as soon as practically possible.

The owners of professional teams—the Braves, Indians, Chiefs, Blackhawks, and Redskins—insist that their teams are private businesses and refuse to bow to pressure. In Cleveland at the first game of each baseball season, Native Americans protest outside the stadium. "We are people, not mascots," their signs say. Twice, demonstrators have been arrested. They were shown on national television burning an effigy of Chief Wahoo, whose bucktoothed grin and big nose can be seen on the Cleveland team's uniforms and on the licensed pennants, hats, and T-shirts sold to fans. The teams also face legal challenges. Legislation has been proposed in Cleveland, Kansas City, and Washington, D.C., to deny public funds for stadiums if minority groups will be disparaged within.

Many American Indians refuse to pronounce the name of the Washington football team. To them it is the Native American "n-word." When the Washington Redskins played in the Super Bowl in Minneapolis in 1992, they were greeted

Indian-theme sports souvenirs. The child's T-shirt that spells "Illini" with Indian figures is probably from the 1940s. The button is from 1966, the Chief Illiniwek beer from 1984, and the boxer shorts from 1998. The other items were purchased in 1999. Photograph by Bea Nettles 1999.

by three thousand protesters, although the temperature was seventeen below. Later that year a legal proceeding was filed against them. Seven prominent Native Americans petitioned to have the team's trademarks canceled under a clause of the trademark law that says that disparaging or scandalous terms cannot receive federal trademark protection. They pointed out that the nation's capital city should not use a racial slur to name its team. Seven years after the petition was filed, three judges of the Trademark Trial and Appeal Board ruled for the petitioners and revoked the team's trademarks. The team has appealed the ruling.

The oldest and largest American Indian organization, the National Congress of American Indians, which represents about 250 tribes, has passed a resolution condemning Indian mascots. So have many other tribes and intertribal organizations. In support, the NAACP has issued its own resolution. Senator Daniel Inouye, the chairman of the Senate Select Committee on Indian Affairs, has asked that we not carry these names and stereotypes into the twenty-first century.

However, longtime fans and alumni resent being asked to give up an identity they're attached to. Fans (a nickname derived from the word "fanatic") assert that naming teams after Indians is a positive way to honor them. They say they admire Indian leaders and Indian ways. Many see the anti-mascot movement as proof that political correctness has gone too far.

Native Americans respond that the stereotypes endanger their children's self-esteem. Organizations of psychologists and educators agree. They point out the extremely high dropout and suicide rates among Indian youth. They also cite a 1999 Department of Justice study that found that Indians were more likely to be victims of a violent crime than any other racial group; in fact, the rate of crimes against Indians is two and a half times the national average; 60 percent of their attackers were white. Prejudice toward Indians has traditionally justified this violence and is still significant. Ideally, we would like other Americans to understand sovereignty, water rights, repatriation, and other complex issues that affect our community, prominent Indian leaders say. But as a first step, we would like them to acknowledge that we are human.

But not all American Indians are bothered by the mascots. The ousted chief of the Seminole tribe of Florida, James Billie, enjoys a positive relationship with Florida State University, where the tomahawk chop began. He supports the use of his tribe's name by the school's teams. A student dressed as Osceola, a Seminole war leader, who lived from 1804 to 1838, rides out on an Appaloosa horse named Renegade and opens every game for the 'Noles by throwing a flaming lance. There are American Indians protesting outside every Florida State game, including some Seminole people. They say the mascot looks like a Lakota who got lost in an Apache dressing room riding a Nez Perce horse. But a spokesperson for the Seminole tribe of Florida maintains that the issue simply doesn't apply to his tribe. Florida State's Indian imagery, he responds, is nothing like Chief Noc-A-Homa, "the smiling dumb Cleveland Indian," or the Washington Redskins.

The Atlanta Braves have finally retired Chief Noc-A-Homa, who sat in a smoking teepee in their stadium, running out when the Braves hit a home run to circle the tepee in a wild dance. They maintain that this sensitivity to how Native Americans are depicted entitles them to keep the name, tomahawk logo, and orchestrated "Indian" chanting. In Illinois, fans and alumni who support Chief Illiniwek feel that there is a difference between a demeaning caricature and a positive, although fictional, depiction. Like the Seminoles, they insist he is not a mere mascot, but an honored symbol. And while they concede that some stereotypes and team names demean Indians, Chief Illiniwek, they maintain, because he keeps a dignified distance from fans and follows a carefully choreographed script, honors the first inhabitants of the state.

At Illinois, Florida State, and the University of North Dakota, where the controversy is over the Fighting Sioux nickname, Indian mascots are part of a larger mythology about collegiate sports. "Honor" is a word that comes up frequently in discussions on these campuses. Although college basketball and football programs are essentially entertainment corporations attached to educational institutions, they are rarely discussed in those terms. Amateur athletics is treated with a deference that is rare in American life. Activists call on these schools to retire mascots for the sake of doing the right thing and to live up to their mission statements, which guarantee equal treatment for all students.

But professional teams like the Washington Redskins, the Cleveland Indians, the Kansas City Chiefs, the Atlanta Braves, and the Chicago Blackhawks have never promised to educate anyone. Their business is strictly entertainment and the goal of their management is to make a profit. Pro teams also promulgate myths about sports and about their special relationships to the cities in which they are located, myths that sports journalists often disseminate without question. This partly explains why sports mascots based on Indians have endured so long without a serious national debate about their appropriateness. Mascots don't live in the real world, but in the rarified imaginary space created by the overlapping bubbles of two of our most cherished American myths—sports and Indians. This double layer of mythology protects them; well-polished, transparent, it is completely invisible to most American eyes.

It's hard for outsiders to understand the obsession, but living in Champaign-Urbana means being pro-chief or anti-chief. The controversy that is breaking out in high schools all over the country and in Washington and Cleveland has been an accepted part of the cultural landscape in this midwestern college town for the past ten years. The current political movement to retire Indian mascots was started here by Charlene Teters in 1989.

Making up new names for the team is a parlor game at faculty dinner parties. The Byting Illini? Urbana is the birthplace of Hal, the independent-minded computer in *2001: A Space Odyssey*, so why not mascot Hals running around the field? The Illini Lightning. The Corn Borers. The Tornadoes? (Urbana was struck by one in 1996.) When a community group, Women Against Racism, sponsored a contest to come up with a new name and mascot and offered a thousand dollars prize money, there were eighty entries. The winner was Prairie Fire, a name the group is urging the university to adopt. Using bumper stickers (We're FOR Chief Illiniwek) and T-shirts (Racist Stereotypes Dehumanize), semantics (he's a symbol—no, he's a mascot), artwork, a film, letters to the editor, talks by visiting Native activists, street theater, and demonstrations, the students, staff, faculty, and alumni have kept up a ten-year debate about the halftime star and sports logo.

But the university administration and trustees have remained aloof from the debate. After voting to keep the Indian-theme performance in 1990, the board of trustees maintained for ten years that there was nothing further to discuss. They have received hundreds of letters on the subject (one trustee told me that mail runs forty to one for the chief). During trustees' meetings, there is a time period set aside for public comment, and opponents of the mascot often speak. Native Americans, both national activists and university students, have asked for roundtable discussions. But the trustees never respond to what is said in public comment sessions; they did not reply to the requests to sit down for talks; nor to a faculty vote recommending they retire the mascot. In January 2000, three national academic organizations, the American Association of Anthropologists, the Society for the Study of Indigenous Languages, and the Linguistic Society of America, passed resolutions censuring the university and resolved not to return to Illinois for meetings until the mascot was retired. Still, the trustees had no comment. They seemed convinced that if ignored, the tempest would eventually blow over.

In February 2000, when the university's academic accreditation came up for a ten-year review, the evaluation team was deluged with letters about the mascot and complaints about the trustees' handling of the issue. The accreditation organization, the North Central Association of Colleges and Schools, granted accreditation to the university for another ten years, citing its overall excellence. However, there were several conditions, all relating to the chief. A school's mascot is not usually an accreditation issue, but the evaluation team felt that, in this case, the symbol had educational consequences. In fact, eight pages of a 35-page report were devoted to the mascot question.

Forced to finally take the issue seriously, the trustees called for an open, respectful dialogue on the symbol. They declared that every single interested person would have a chance to voice an opinion about the chief. "Too little, too late," responded student activists. "Been there, done that. Where were you?" The university has made it clear that the board itself remains pro-chief. The trustees refuse to concede that the mascot is an educational issue, a stance that leaves many faculty members fuming. "A sham," some labeled the dialogue. Although the university maintains that the chief is not an educational issue, he certainly pops up in a large number of classrooms. The student who graduates from Illinois without having written one paper on the chief or taken part in a classroom discussion must be an exception. In fact, the debate is such a staple topic for papers that the librarians in the university archives keep a well-thumbed folder of information handy for the students who come to do research. Extracurricular clubs face the issue, too—if only to decide whether to put the logo on their posters.

The campus itself centers around the Quad, a rectangular lawn edged with the university's oldest buildings, a quadrangular heart for the collegiate body. The old brick buildings with columns look so Ivy League that a movie about Harvard was filmed there a few years ago. On Quad Day, held early in the fall semester, the sidewalks are lined with card tables and banners from organizations and social clubs. Some freshmen have already "rushed," hoping to be chosen to join one of the nation's oldest and largest systems of fraternities and sororities. Many are shopping among the campus ministries; upbeat Christian banners dominate the event. Still others are signing up to save wild rivers, usher at theatrical events, sing a capella, or joust with padded lances.

A few card tables away from each other, the anti-chief students are passing out a "disorientation guide" and the "Save the Chief" students, in orange T-shirts, are handing out free Chief Illiniwek buttons and collecting signatures. Before they have figured out how to use the online catalog to find books, freshmen encounter the idea of a stereotype and ponder the semantic distinctions between a mascot and a symbol. As if a giant game of tug-of-war is about to start on the Quad, they are expected to choose sides.

"Remove Chief Illiniwek. He is a racist image" printed on red ribbons in gold block letters is what the anti-chief students are offering along with their information. "It's racism pure and simple," they say. "When you single out one ethnic group and make them your mascot, that's a racist practice."

"A mascot is what they have at Wisconsin," a student I'll call Jim explains to me. He has debated publicly to keep Chief Illiniwek and he writes for a conservative-funded newspaper where the anti-chief movement is described with phrases like "fringe group," "radical left," and "stinks of political correctness." Jim's voice is firm. Every word is clearly enunciated. "A mascot runs around in a costume and does sideline antics. What we have is nothing like that." Jim and I agree to meet again to talk and he offers to bring other pro-chief students.

Tod, who joins us, is an Eagle Scout and a member of the Order of the Arrow, an auxiliary Scout group whose members study Indian tribes, dress in Indian clothing, and perform Indian dances. "We deal with Indian history and Indian personalities and Indian costuming in such a way that it's built into a larger picture of leadership, values, and tradition. It's something we hold very highly, research a lot, we try to communicate with tribes, try to authenticate this as much as possible. It's a brotherhood," he explains. Although he's young to have done so, he has already worked his way to the highest level of the Order of the Arrow.

Tod is also active in College Republicans. Perhaps it's the wool cardigan or his formal way of phrasing his thoughts or his deep voice—for some reason he seems more like an older uncle than a college student.

"For me," Tod continues, "Chief Illiniwek is a good way to remember what was once a great place for a proud people. It's a bygone era that very few white people ever saw. It internally destroyed itself through several different mechanisms."

I question Tod about these very few white people. It is my impression that by the time the Illinois were relocated from the state in the 1830s, Indians and whites had lived in close contact for about 150 years.

"But the culture was nothing like it had been," he replies.

I ask him what it is about the Illinois Indians he admires.

"To be brave, to have tenacity and will to endure whatever might lie ahead. Not to give in to outside pressure. Not to throw the towel in. They fought hard but ultimately, they were beaten."

Save the Chief Students Outside Memorial Stadium, University of Illinois. Photograph by Brent McDonald.

"He's certainly a worthy representation of who was here. He provides a little nexus between me and our Indian past." This is from the third student in the group, Matt. He looks more like the students I'm used to seeing. No straight-arrow Boy Scout shoulders here. He slouches, shrugs, fidgets, and speaks with a more tentative tone of voice.

I ask them if it isn't possible that the students could come up with a new symbol, something equally exciting.

"I'm not going to say they couldn't," Jim replies, "but I am not aware of any other campus in America that has anything like Chief Illiniwek. I don't think the students of the future will form as strong an attachment to a Bucky Badger-like mascot as they do to an honored symbol."

Matt walked around among the tailgate parties before a football game with a petition to retain the Chief. He was amazed at the response. People came forward not by ones and twos, but twenty at a time, demanding to sign. One group drives up from Tennessee; members of the group insisted they would stay home if the chief was retired. "We would be disassociating thousands of people, we would be destroying a link between the past, the present, and the future. These people wouldn't know what their university stood for any more."

"But what about Native American students who come to the University of Illinois and who feel demeaned by Chief Illiniwek?"

"It's not just about honoring a particular group of people," Jim replies. "If a Native American student doesn't feel honored, I guess I think that's unfortunate. It is something that deeply concerns me and that I devote a great deal of thought to. How can we rectify the situation? But at the same time I'd point out that it's about more than just honoring a certain group of people. The Native American students at the university don't have any claim. There is no one today who can claim that they are the descendants of the Illini. They were wiped out in conflicts with other tribes. There are no direct descendants of the Illini remaining."

Rather than debate this, I ask them if they think the character is a stereotype.

"If you go to Oklahoma any month of the year," Tod says, "you can find a celebration where people are dressed like that and dance. It's not something that we made up. It's real."

"Honestly," says Jim, swinging into his debate mode, "it almost insults the intelligence of your average Illini fan and university graduate to say that they look at the chief and think it's a perfectly accurate description of what every

Native American looks and acts like. I never felt that way. I never met the person who said that."

"There are stereotypes everywhere in our world. It's the way we deal with them that's important," Tod says.

Jim adds, "If we were in an educational vacuum, we might have a problem."

As I walk to the coffee shop near campus, I turn this conversation over. The threads are familiar ones, tangled together with our ideas about Indians in a mess of knots. I cast about for a loose end.

Internally destroyed itself by several different mechanisms. Wiped out in conflicts with other tribes. No direct descendants remaining. In other words, although some Native Americans have survived and live in the same contemporary world we do and even come to the same campus to study, they are not Illini. They are not legitimate contenders for the identity that is so important to these students. And it was not whites who wiped out the Illini. That was done by other tribes—or the very vague "internal mechanisms." Perhaps this is a euphemism for epidemics of European-introduced diseases.

When I suggest that early settlers and Illinois Indians knew each other well, I am told that "the culture was nothing like it had been." What is admirable is some pure and noble Indian culture, something that only the very first Europeans who set foot on the continent encountered with wonder. Ever since, Indian culture has become adulterated, diluted, and despoiled. White culture, European and American culture, is so decadent and dangerous that exposure to it turns these simple noble people into empty shells of humanity, addicted to alcohol, irresponsible, careless about their own future. Everything that is valuable about Indian culture belongs to the long long ago, before contact induced impurities and rot. This logic makes it possible for the student who is a Boy Scout to dedicate himself to learning traditional dances at the same time that he discounts the opinions of fellow students who are Native American.

The student also tells me that the character of Chief Illiniwek, the brave and noble Plains Indian chief in feather headdress who dances wildly, is real because he can be found at a powwow in Oklahoma. It is certainly true that at a powwow, we could see Indian men who dress up in flashy costumes and dance, not only for spiritual reasons, but for entertainment or to win prizes. They seem to have stepped off a Broadway stage. The steps they perform have been combined and adapted from various tribes. In comparison, Chief Illiniwek looks like a warrior of yesteryear. But is old-fashioned clothing worn as a costume inherently more real than a contemporary costume? And even if we decide it is, does that make the dancer who wears it more authentic? What counts for the most points in the authenticity ratings? Is it the clothing, the steps, or the dancer's genes? And finally, assuming that the powwow dancers are authentic because they are Indian, is it true what the student is saying—that their existence makes Chief Illiniwek *real*? In this case, reality is hard to pin down. Perhaps we should settle for asking whether these other dancers render him appropriate.

As we will see, Indians and whites both participated in Wild West shows; both contributed to the creation of "show Indians" who dress like Sioux and dance professionally. Show Indians live on in the movies. In areas where few American Indians live, there is a widespread belief that this show Indian culture is the only real Indian culture. Many non-Indians ignore or discount anything Indian that does not resemble the show Indians they recognize. In response, wanting to be acknowledged as Indians, many Indian people from other tribes have adopted aspects of Plains Indian dress so they can at least look the part. And at intertribal powwows, Plains music and dance dominate.

The question of who is an Indian is a complicated one surrounded by a swirl of uncertainty and insecurity. It often undermines any discussion of imaginary Indians and Indian mascots. It would be helpful if we could settle it at the outset. But how? Is it a question of blood and genes? A certain percentage of Indian blood, the famous blood quantum that some tribes require to

become an enrolled member? But what percentage is enough? Or are upbringing and knowledge of customs more significant? Some tribes are federally recognized. Others are not. Having been raised on a reservation is a trump card
that settles most challenges. So is speaking an indigenous language. Looking
Indian helps immensely. Being an enrolled member of a federally recognized
tribe is another trump. Without holding at least two of these cards, many Indians find it impossible to speak and be heard. Even Indians themselves are
quick to discount any Indian with whom they disagree as "not real" or "raised
away." And what if you have neither a large proportion of Indian blood nor a
traditional upbringing, but want to identify yourself as Indian? For the moment we will simply have to set this riddle aside, keeping in mind that American Indian is an identity that was imposed on people who thought of themselves as Navajo or Oneida or Quapaw and that it is an identity that is often
contested. We can be certain that people who define themselves as American
Indian or Native American exist in the contemporary American world. Their
numbers are increasing every year. American Indians intermarry at a higher
rate than any other ethnic group, which means that people who call themselves Indians because of heredity will eventually be merged into the general
mass of Americans. However, people who have only a small proportion of Indian blood are much more likely to identify themselves by it than those who
are part Irish or Italian or Russian.

Authenticity, I sense, is a thread that will, no matter how closely we examine it, always return to itself, a closed circle with no end. We can untangle the
history of our own belief in the authentic and come to understand what we have
called authentic and why. But even after we come to this understanding, we cannot sort Indian culture into two piles, the authentic and the inauthentic. No
matter how attached we might be to the notion of the authentic, the circle of
thread leads back only to ourselves and our desire for authenticity.

Another stubborn knot is the curious one in which honor and contempt are tangled together. Is it possible to twist two opposing emotions into one gesture?

The tables in the coffee shop are close together, and as I drink my cappuccino and ponder this, I study the students near me. There is one young couple I find particularly appealing. They are sitting side by side looking at photos in a small album. It is their physical beauty as they bend over the snapshots that attracts me. She has light brown hair and a lovely, open face. He is dark, Asian, and handsome, with a thoughtful expression. The way he leans toward her, one arm over the back of the chair, is graceful and unself-conscious. But as I listen, I realize it's not a tryst, it's a language lesson.

She describes what she and her friends are doing in each photo and he poses questions. "That one? That's TP-ing," she says, exaggerating the unusual word.

He looks completely blank. I'm curious, too.

"TP stands for toilet paper. You know toilet paper, right?" She sounds so encouraging. "Well, you take rolls of toilet paper and you go at night to another house. Then you throw them up in the air so they catch in the branches of the trees. See? When the person comes out in the morning, the trees are all covered with toilet paper. It looks beautiful. But we had to clean it all up."

"When? It's a good question." She speaks carefully and precisely. "You do it to someone when you like them and want to celebrate something they've done."

He nods.

"But . . . you can also do it to someone because you think they're really . . ." She pauses and looks at him apologetically, ". . . well, really stupid."

Her student looks completely baffled.

"It's weird but it can mean two completely opposite things."

Myth and Mascot

The spirit of the Illinois tribe of Indians hovers over the University of Illinois campus—one of our most colorful and treasured traditions. Much of this, indeed, is tradition, with scanty historical source materials underlying it. But we love it just the same. The spirit of the mysterious, the legendary, the mythological, is good for us. We need this dash of "Make Believe," just as we do the results of research and scholarship in scientific and historical backgrounds.

—CLIVE BURFORD, *"We're Loyal to You, Illinois"*

The French semiologist Roland Barthes spent his professional life analyzing how we hold on to certain images and turn them into myth. It was Barthes in the 1950s who first applied semiotics, the study of signs, to popular culture in his book *Mythologies*. Detergents, wrestling, french fries—no subject was too ordinary for his semiotic lens. Myth is, Barthes explains, a language, a form of speech, a particular way of talking about a subject. It isn't the subject that matters. Anything can be raised to the status of myth if described in mythic language. And these descriptions needn't be verbal—a photograph can serve just as well as a story or tale.

Rather than being forgotten, Barthes says, mythic images become ubiquitous. They are "half-amputated, they are deprived of memory, not of existence: they are at once stubborn, silently rooted there, and garrulous, a speech wholly at the service of the concept."

Garrulous the image of an Indian certainly is, for Indians can be found everywhere in advertising and sports. But what concept do these Indians serve? The University of Illinois insists that Chief Illiniwek is not a mascot, but a symbol (a distinction it finds significant) that "symbolizes the spirit of the Fighting Illini." Florida State University says the same thing about the impersonator of Osceola who rides out and plants a flaming lance before football games. A mascot is a good luck charm. The word itself can be traced to French words that bear the taint of witchcraft and superstition. A mascot, usually an animal, is a pet, kept by the team and its fans for good luck and for their own entertainment. When they insist that Chief Illiniwek and Osceola are more than mascots, these schools acknowledge that a mascot may inspire feelings of affection but not respect.

A symbol is more neutral, simply a single powerful image, a mark of visual shorthand that stands for a bundle of beliefs and ideas. The symbol gives physical form to amorphous values: the cross for Christian belief, the American flag not only for our country but also for our feelings about it, our political system, and the American people. The same symbol can be used in different ways: the Star of David worn on a chain by a Jewish person, the Star of David sewn by Nazi order to a prisoner's clothing. In both cases the symbol represents Jewish identity. But in one case, the symbol is chosen freely as a positive indicator. In the other it is coerced, the person is branded with it, and the values attached are all negative. It is also possible that a symbol can mean different things to different people. Picture a white-columned plantation house—is it a gracious lifestyle or an oppressive, inhuman system? Both, of course, depending on who does the looking and which side of the house they know—the front door or the back. The Confederate flag is a contemporary case in point. Some white southerners see it and think of a small but valiant army battling and sometimes winning against a larger, better-equipped force. To them it means not buckling under, having courage and honor in battle, even when you lose. American blacks and most white Americans see the same flag as a standard for slavery and racism. Many realize that its history as a racist symbol goes beyond the Civil War. It was adopted by white vigilante groups during Reconstruction and later was often displayed by the Ku Klux Klan at cross burnings and lynchings. In more recent years it has become a symbol of opposition to civil rights and has been adopted by neo-Nazis and skinheads. The Confederate flag over the South Carolina capitol building, which made the state the target of a nationwide boycott, was raised in 1962, after a national controversy over South Carolina's refusal to integrate its hotels and convention centers. The Confederate flag, in this case, was raised over the state capitol as a standard for segregation.

When most of us look out on the football field and see an Indian chief, what does the symbol bring to mind? Simply and most obviously, fighting spirit and bravery, often attributed to Indian chiefs and needed by every sports team. For many sports fans, these positive qualities are all they see when they watch students dressed as Indians perform. At Illinois, alumni buy soft-focus, backlit, poster-sized portraits of the chief by a photographer who can transform a field of soybeans and a rundown barn into a pastoral paradise. In these posters the football field recedes into a fuzzy abstraction and the "Indian" who stands with arms raised could be anywhere: on the rim of the Grand Canyon, in the Black Hills at dawn, on the ridge after the Battle of Little Bighorn. But even better, he reigns over their own fifty-yard line.

How did he get there? An elaborate and detailed creation myth is recounted over and over to explain his appearance. It has all the components of a heroic quest: an exemplary young man who is interested in Indians from a young age, a journey to the Oglala reservation undertaken at great effort (hitchhiking during the Depression), a meeting with a holy man who gives his blessing to the ritual in the form of a very special suit of clothing.

For Charlene Teters, an artist educated at the University of Illinois and a member of the Spokane tribe, the struggle today is no longer over land, but over Indians' right to reclaim their images. In order to enter one of her large sculp-

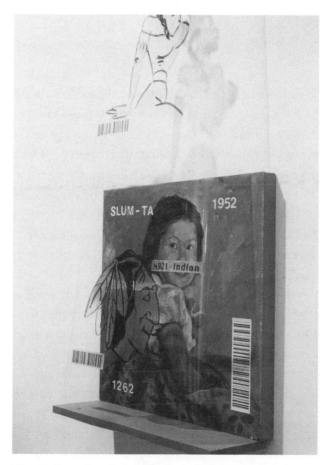

What We Know About Indians by Charlene Teters. Detail of installation. Slum-ta is the artist's Spokane name. Courtesy of the artist.

tural installations, a glowing wooden bar filled with bottles of alcohol named after Indians, visitors walked over a Chief Illiniwek rug. The image was eventually rubbed bare by their feet. (When she put Abraham Lincoln on a rug in another installation, visitors carefully walked around.)

In another Teters piece, names of Indian tribes that no longer exist are printed in raised bas-relief letters, painted white on a white wall, just barely visible. Attached to the wall at regular intervals are toilet paper holders; the toilet paper that hangs down neatly from each holder is printed with the blue and orange Chief Illiniwek insignia. This piece is titled "Wiped Out." In a third piece, "What We Know About Indians," large black and white portraits of members of her family are "blocked" by overlays of brightly colored graphics of Indians designed for advertising, including Chief Wahoo and the logo for the Chicago Blackhawks. Her own portrait as a child is covered by the curvaceous, scantily-clad Pocahontas. This is her visual interpretation of Dorris's "white noise," a constant, continual static that blocks an actual transmission. Clearly, although Illini fans and Charlene Teters have watched the same performance, they have seen different things.

Teters also sees an Indian chief on the field, a clearly recognizable character in appropriate regalia. For her, this image is also a potent symbol, a symbol of leadership that is both political and religious in nature. It angers and upsets her to see this symbol taken out of her belief system and used to represent another group's values—especially when it is a group that has discounted her culture and religion and tried to suppress them for the past three hundred years. In her view, the paint, fringe, and feathers have been appropriated without permission. The symbolic Indian is a prisoner, not an honored guest. When Teters speaks, she often uses the words of Alice Walker to convey this idea. The quote is taken from an essay Walker wrote after viewing a collection of objects that stereotype African Americans. But Teters paraphrases slightly, replacing "sambo" and "placid three hundred pound 'mammy' lamp" with American Indian mascots.

"These caricatures and stereotypes are really intended as prisons of image. Inside each desperately grinning Cleveland Indian and each stoic Redskin Brave or Chief Illiniwek mascot, there is someone we know. If you look hard enough and don't panic you begin to see the eyes and then the hearts of these despised relatives of ours, who have been forced to lock their spirits away from themselves and from us. I see our brothers and sisters, mothers and fathers, captured and forced into images they did not devise, doing hard time for all of us. We can liberate them by understanding this, and free ourselves."

As someone who has lived in an African village and studied African art, I see the performance of Chief Illiniwek as a masking ritual, like those found in some African and Native American societies. Masks are usually incorporated into a multimedia performance of dance and music. The performer, often a young man who is undergoing initiation, is no longer himself once he dons the costume. He is believed to literally become the spirit figure that the mask represents. As this mediator between the human and spirit world, he can tap into powerful supernatural forces.

The face paint and huge feather headdress that Chief Illiniwek wears disguise the young student. We are able to put aside our knowledge that he is a white midwestern college student, a member of a certain fraternity, majoring in a particular subject. While wearing the regalia and dancing, the student not only impersonates but becomes an Indian chief, with the power to command thousands of tribal members to, at the very least, rise and sing. His audience believes that in his regalia, he taps into and makes available to the sports team bravery and stamina, qualities associated with ancestral Indians like the figure he portrays. Not surprisingly, the student who portrays this personage is not allowed to appear in the regalia except during a performance. The students who enact Chief Illiniwek are rarely interviewed or referred to in the local press by name, nor do most people know that Chief Illiniwek is danced at some games by the assistant chief, an understudy. To bestow this kind of attention on the individual performers would dilute the mask's power, for the audience would be reminded that this is theater, not a visit from a remote and powerful personage who graces the stadium with his presence.

Masks are often described as agents of social control. This means that the masks come out at regular intervals to ensure order in the community by instilling fear and engendering respect. They have the authority to humiliate those

Transformation of a student into Chief Illiniwek. His older brother, himself a former chief, applies the paint for the performance. Courtesy of the University of Illinois Archives, Urbana-Champaign.

who have broken the rules or strayed outside the norms. Although athletic young men are usually the masked performers, the decisions about when and where the masks will appear are made by the elder men who organize and control the initiation society.

Masks are also, of course, pleasing as dramatic performance. Artistic skill is lavished on costumes and dance steps. Performers delight their viewers aesthetically at the same time that they present the view of how things were and always should be, according to the group in charge.

Non-Indian Americans, like the students who dance at halftime, have been masquerading as Indians since they disguised themselves with paint and feathers to dump tea in Boston Harbor. Their actions made a statement about who they weren't (loyal English colonists); their disguises showed who they wanted to become. There is no identity as quintessentially, authentically American as an Indian. Scouting, summer camps, and elementary schools all encourage children to imitate Indians, an activity adults believe will help children understand Indian culture and American history, and develop moral character. If you question this pastime, which is viewed as patriotic, many people will confuse your opposition with a dislike for American history, good morals, or even American Indian culture.

Ironically, Indians have also been invoked as a vehicle to express white Americans' critiques of the industrial, materialistic, and destructive tendencies of American society. Environmentalists and New Age spiritualists have worn headbands and dreamcatchers and played Indian as a revolutionary act, stressing freedom and closeness to nature. The same symbol—an Indian chief—has been, over many years, endowed with a variety of disparate and even opposing meanings. This process began before the first Europeans ever set sail from Europe. Even the name Indian arises from European assumptions and wishes rather than from the name of any group of actual people who lived on this continent.

Depictions of American Indians usually fall into two general categories. The good Indian is hospitable to the white invaders, has a handsome physique, unusual stamina, and calm, dignified bearing. He is brave in combat, and devoted to his family and children. He lives in harmony with nature and is aware of all sorts of signs—natural and supernatural—to which other people are oblivious.

The bad Indian is lazy and lecherous, a slippery-fingered thief. He lives in a dirty village where he treats his women like slaves. He is constantly on the warpath to get revenge on his enemies and he cruelly tortures his captives for the pleasure of watching them suffer. He is superstitious, cowardly, and untrustworthy, and when he wins it is through deceit or treachery. Images of the bad Indian were common during hostilities with Indian tribes and also during the period of

Not only were Scouts taught to make Indian handicrafts, they were encouraged to dress up and pretend to be Indians, as this page from the 1943 *Cubbook* shows. The *Cubbook* urges boys to be like Indian men, who are described as self-controlled, quiet, loyal, and "game." Courtesy of the Boy Scouts of America.

Indian removal in the 1830s, when Indian tribes east of the Mississippi were forced to move west. Once there were very few actual Indian people in an area, they were often remembered nostalgically, in images and words, as mythological good Indians.

Both depictions, as described by Robert Berkhofer, Jr., who has written extensively about white perceptions of Indians, share a "curious timelessness." Indians seem to live, in both depictions, outside time and history. No matter how much time passes, Indians are expected to remain aboriginal. When they do change, they have somehow betrayed or forfeited their Indianness. To differentiate between fantasy Indians imagined by whites and real American Indian people, Berkhofer uses "Indian" to represent the fantasy and "Native American" to refer to real people. Athough I understand the need to make the distinction clear to the reader, and the difficulty of doing so, I use the two interchangeably.

To minimize criticism, most teams have retired bad Indian mascots or sanitized their images so that the mascots that remain are mostly good Indians. In fact, even corny mascots are in decline. It's noble or nothing these days. Chief Illiniwek is all nobility and dignity, a wholly good Indian who used to graciously welcome the drum majors of opposing teams until his duties were reduced. He doesn't so much as brandish a fist at enemy teams. But neither does he perish. Resurrected from an imaginary past, he flourishes as a mythic character, a fictional chief of the real Illinois or Illiniwek Indians. Raising his arms, he welcomes the settlers' descendants as the Illiniwek welcomed Marquette when he stepped out of a canoe onto the muddy bank of a river in the center of the New World. The myth Chief Illiniwek acts out is the conquest as we wish it had been—a respectful and gracious meeting. As they watch him, many Indian people see a carefully orchestrated multimedia falsehood. Other Americans are genuinely touched to receive his benediction. The fictional chief gives them the absolution for which they long.

Races of Living Things

Chief Illiniwek is an invention, a fictional character, but he is legitimized by his connection to real Indians, whom he is supposed to recall to our minds. The real Indians in this particular story are the Illinois. They entered the historical record when the French explorer Louis Jolliet and the Jesuit priest who accompanied him, Father Marquette, arrived at one of their villages in 1673. According to Marquette's account in the *Jesuit Relations*, when he and Jolliet went ashore and found "footprints of men by the water-side, and a beaten path entering a beautiful prairie," they followed the path and came to a large Peoria-Illinois village. They gave a cry and then waited to see what would happen. At the sight of the two Frenchmen, the Peoria sent four old men to them.

> Two carried tobacco-pipes well-adorned, and trimmed in many kinds of feathers. They marched slowly, lifting their pipes toward the sun, as if offering them to him to smoke, but yet without uttering a single word. They were a long time coming the little way from the village to us. Having reached us at last, they stopped to consider us attentively. I now took courage, seeing these ceremonies, which are used by them only with friends, and still more on seeing them covered with stuffs [European cloth], which made me to judge them to be allies. I, therefore, spoke to them first, and asked them who they were; they answered that they were Ilinois, and in token of peace, they presented their pipes to smoke.

Marquette and Jolliet were taken to a lodge where another old man stood, arms raised, completely naked, greeting the sun. They smoked with him and were taken to another lodge, where three more old men, also naked and holding pipes, greeted them. After smoking with this group, they were given a slave boy and a tobacco pipe of their own and treated to a feast. The first dish was sagamite, boiled Indian corn mixed with fat. Their host fed them bites himself, as if they were children. Next came fish, and he also placed bites in their mouths. The third course was a large dog, killed for the occasion, but when they learned that the Frenchmen did not eat dog, the dish was removed. The fourth course was bison meat, and again the choicest morsels were fed to them. Before leaving the next day, Marquette promised to return the following year to live with the Illinois.

Marquette goes on to describe the tobacco pipe the French called a calumet; the word was derived from an old French word for a flute:

> There is nothing more mysterious or more respected among them. Less honor is paid to the crowns and scepters of kings than the savages bestow on this. It seems to be the god of peace and war, the arbiter of life and death. It has but to be carried upon one's person, and displayed, to enable one to walk safely through the midst of enemies, who in the hottest of the fight, lay down their arms when it is shown.

Marquette says the calumet dance is "done so well, with slow and measured steps, and to the rhythmic sound of the voices and drums, that it might pass for a very fine opening of a ballet in France." The calumet spread throughout the central United States during these turbulent times; it was used to create alliances and enter into negotiations.

It is not surprising that the guests were immediately invited to a feast; feasts were common among the Illinois; giving them was the means by which a man gained prestige and consolidated his influence. Farmers, gatherers, and hunters, the Illinois grew corn, beans, squash, and pumpkins in the river valleys during the summer. Grapes, plums, persimmons, apples, strawberries, raspberries, mulberries, and many nuts and roots grew wild on the prairies, and were gathered.

Bison had moved to the east side of the Mississippi River sometime around 1600 and Marquette describes huge herds, whose paths "are beaten like our great roads in Europe." They were hunted with bows and arrows even after the Illinois had guns because gunshots frightened and scattered the herds; also, many arrows could be shot in the time it took to reload a musket. The meat was dried over fires; Marquette remarked after eating meat dried four months earlier that it tasted as if it had just been killed.

When Marquette and Jolliet asked the Indians who they were, they said they were Illiniwek. The late Virgil Vogel, a noted historian who spent his career studying American Indian names, has commented in several publications about the term "Illiniwek." He said that most Native groups, when asked who they were, simply answered, "people." It was not a tribal name, nor did it imply a sense of superiority, as Marquette thought. Who are you? We are people. "Illiniwek" simply meant "people." It was corrupted by the French to Illinois.

The Illinois Indians quickly allied themselves with the French for protection from their enemies, especially the Iroquois, whose attacks in the 1650s and 1660s had caused major dislocations of Indian tribes in the Great Lakes area and Ohio Valley. Both the Illinois and the French hoped to benefit economically from the alliance.

The French asked the Indians for only enough land to build trading posts; they were after beaver—not beaver pelts, but the fur-wool, a layer of soft, curly hair next to the skin that was felted to make hats. Missionary priests traveled with the French military, as did coureurs de bois and voyageurs—traders who lived among the Indians, learned their languages, married Indian women, and fathered French-Indian children.

France controlled the northern access to the fur trade through Quebec, and England the southern access through New Amsterdam. The competition between these two European countries profoundly affected the people they called Indians. As beaver populations were depleted, the fur trade moved west. The groups that participated in the trade "re-patterned their culture," as the anthropologist Eric Wolf puts it, around European goods. As cultures changed, so did relationships between Indian groups. The territory that had sufficed for a subsistence economy was too small for hunter-traders. Competition increased—both for hunting grounds and for access to European goods. Warfare between Indian groups grew more intense and more widespread.

Beaver was extinct in New York by 1640, so the British-backed Iroquois used their organization, prowess in guerrilla warfare, and good supply of muskets to conquer or intimidate neighboring groups and expand their territory. The Iroquois moved west, disrupting life for the Hurons, the Ottawas, and eventually the Illinois. These groups also moved west, trying to stay ahead of the Iroquois. Sometimes they regrouped their populations in large fortified villages.

Most of what we know about the Illinois in the colonial period comes from accounts in the *Jesuit Relations* written by French missionaries and explorers who visited and lived among them. Many Jesuit priests wrote about the Illinois (or Aliniouek, Iliniouek, Ilinioues—there are ten spellings in all) over a period of forty years. French missionaries were reformers who wanted to change the very basis of Illinois life, to eradicate belief systems and transpose seasonally nomadic hunter-farmer-gatherers into settled farmers who lived year-round in a single village. Furthermore, the accounts written by the isolated missionary priests who lived with the Illinois were letters written to their superiors; it was important to stress that, despite nearly overwhelming setbacks, their evangelical enterprise was proceeding. Therefore, the most fully developed portrait of an Illinois person in the *Jesuit Relations* is of a determined young woman named Marie Rouensa who defied her father to become a devout Catholic and eventually succeeded in converting her parents. The missionary priests so admired her piety that she was buried beneath the stone floor of the church, a rare honor for a woman or an Indian.

Sauvage de la Nation des Kaskaskias.

This drawing shows a Kaskaskia man in eighteenth-century clothing. It was one of the decorations on a map of the Ohio River exe-
cuted by Joseph Wabin in 1796. The original map, which is quite
large, is lightly colored in pen and ink. Collection of the Bibliothèque Nationale de France. Reprinted by permission.

In the late 1600s there may have been as many as twelve groups who
were part of the Illinois. At least sixteen villages are named in French accounts, but most are mentioned only once. Only five of these village groups—
the Kaskaskia, Peoria, Cahokia, Tamaroa, and Michigamea—survived into the
1830s. The Peoria are the only federally recognized tribe of the Illinois that
remains.

Scholars who have studied the French accounts of how many fires, cabins,
warriors, or souls were in the various villages and tried to add them together

come up with an estimate of ten thousand to twelve thousand Illinois people in 1680. Only sixty years later, by 1740, there were only about 2,500 Illinois Indians left. This dramatic decline was due to exacerbated intertribal warfare, a declining birthrate, epidemics of diseases to which they had no immunity, alcoholism, and the departure of splinter groups. When the Iroquois killed a large number of women and children in 1680, population growth was adversely affected for a long time. Also, when Illinois people converted to Catholicism, monogamy caused the birthrate to decline.

One Illinois subgroup, the Peoria, rejected Catholicism. To maintain a greater independence from the French, they moved west of the Mississippi in the 1770s. This cultural and geographic distance may have enabled the Peoria to survive. Even more than intertribal warfare and disease, the Illinois may have been destroyed by their high level of dependence on the French. They chose to ally themselves with a single European power at a time when that allegiance created numerous enemies for them. This alliance, which initially helped them militarily, economically, and politically, finally rendered them extremely vulnerable. When George Rogers Clark and his soldiers arrived in Illinois during the Revolutionary War, the Illinois served as their scouts. For this, their villages were attacked by pro-British tribes. By 1778 there were only about four hundred Illinois Indians east of the Mississippi.

The Northwest Territory (meaning the area northwest of the Ohio River) was divided in 1800 and Illinois was made part of the Indiana Territory. Up to this time, American settlers had not wanted this land because of a prevailing belief that prairie soil was too poor for agriculture. Good soil, they believed, always had trees on it. Around the turn of the century this perception changed. Between 1801 and 1812, four fifths of the present state of Illinois was opened up to settlement by treaties.

The Kaskaskia, speaking for all the Illinois Indians, signed the Treaty of Vincennes in 1803. They ceded the southern third of what is now the state of

Illinois, giving up eight million acres of land. This treaty, like most made with tribes, gave the Illinois the right to live and hunt on the lands they had ceded.

In 1818, when Illinois became a state, the Treaty of Edwardsville was signed by the chiefs of the Peoria, Kaskaskia, Michigamea, Cahokia, and Tamaroa. This agreement included the Peoria, who received a tract of 640 acres in Missouri Territory, where their village had been located for many years. The Peoria gradually migrated westward toward Kansas.

Arkansas was organized as a territory in 1819 and Missouri became a state in 1821. More and more American settlers were arriving. John Reynolds, who was governor of Illinois in 1830, said about the removal of the Indians,

> Although it may seem hard to force the Indians from their own country to accommodate the white population, yet it is the only wise and humane policy that can be adopted. It is a heart-rending sight to see the poor natives driven from their own country. Their tears and lamentations on leaving Illinois would pierce a heart of stone. We must submit to the decrees of Providence. Nevertheless, it is difficult to find good reasons for the expulsions of the Indians from their own country. But, with or without reason, the Indians must emigrate, leaving Illinois—the finest country on earth, for the peaceable occupation of the white man.

On October 27, 1832, the Illinois Indians signed the Treaty of Castor Hill, agreeing to their removal. They had no choice. The Peoria and Kaskaskia and the united bands of Michigamea, Cahokia, and Tamaroa ceded all their lands in Illinois and Missouri. The United States gave them, in return, 150 sections of land on the Osage or Marais des Cygnes River, including the already existing Peoria village. They were to receive three thousand dollars for ten years, as well as assistance in moving, oxen, cattle, and plows. Only the Peoria and Kaskaskia were present to sign.

The Illinois Indians were moved to northeastern Kansas the following year, near the Leavenworth area. They numbered 132. Government planners had assumed that this land was too remote to interest settlers, but they were wrong. The relocated Illinois were directly in the path of the overland trails to the West. The region was also torn apart by violent conflicts over slavery. And after the end of the Civil War, railroads moved into the area, wanting more land and bringing more American settlers.

The Peoria chief, Baptiste Peoria, tried to hold the group together, but conditions were difficult. Settlers hunted and cut timber on Indian land. The local government also levied taxes, although this was illegal. Alcohol continued to be a problem. The protection they had been promised never materialized. There were also tensions and conflicts between tribes. The Osage, in particular, resented the new arrivals. Baptiste Peoria, who spoke several Illinois dialects, Shawnee, Potawatomi, Delaware, English, and French, negotiated with other tribes and with government officials, both for his own people and for their former enemies, the Miami.

In 1854 the commissioner of Indian affairs negotiated a treaty with the Kaskaskia, Peoria, Wea, and Piankashaw, who decided to unite as the Confederated Peoria. They ceded their land in Kansas in return for 160 acres for each member of the tribe, ten sections to be held in common, and one section for the mission. The rest of their holdings were auctioned off cheaply to speculators, the railroads, and settlers. In 1867 the Confederated Peoria and the Miami agreed to yet another treaty. They were to receive land in the northeastern part of Indian Territory, now Oklahoma. Fifty-five members of the tribe decided to stay in Kansas and relinquished their tribal claims. Baptiste Peoria and 162 men, women, and children signed up to move to Oklahoma. They settled along the Spring and Neosho Rivers, near present-day Miami, Oklahoma, where their descendants still live.

When an anthropologist visited the Confederated Peoria in 1916, in order to make a report to the Illinois Centennial Commission, he concluded that they failed to sufficiently remember their rituals, folklore, language, and dance. Illinois Indian culture, he reported, was extinct.

Some Illiniwek descendants never left Illinois, despite the deportation laws. John and Ela White of Michael, Illinois, have founded the Ancient Lifeways Institute to revive and teach the Tamaroa and Kaskaskia languages and culture. Although there are no living speakers of these languages, the Whites have written their own grammar books, compiling phrases from the three-hundred-year-old dictionaries written by the French missionary priests and from an informant who still spoke some Tamaroa in the 1970s.

John, an anthropologist of Cherokee, Shawnee, and Scots ancestry, married into the tribe. His wife, Ela, is a Kaskaskia/French descendant. They believe, from the oral histories they have collected, that some Kaskaskia, Tamaroa, and Michigamea refused to accept the Treaty of Edwardsville in 1818, moved back to their traditional homeland, "The Land between the Rivers," and simply stayed on. Bill Cappell, the son of the last Tamaroa speaker, revived naming ceremonies and a midwinter ceremony he had learned from his father. Cappell is now too frail to carry on these traditions himself and he has designated John White his successor.

The Whites have no interest in the Chief Illiniwek controversy. Pan-tribal efforts are transitory in their opinion, and they prefer to devote their time to revitalizing the Illinois language and culture and passing it on to another generation. "I have to ask myself what needs to be done to ensure that Indian culture will still be alive two hundred years from now," John says.

John and Ela can be found at powwows, schools, and church picnics, teaching the oral history and language phrases they have gathered. They are closely associated with the Church of the Immaculate Conception at Kaskaskia, the same church (although a more recent building) that Marquette founded. When the diocese threatened to close the Kaskaskia Island church after the flood of 1993, local people united to fight the church hierarchy. The

Peoria, Kaskaskia, Tamaroa, and Michigamea presented an altar cloth and vo-tive wampum belt to the church as a symbol of their commitment to the church's preservation. Many parish members claim both French and Indian ancestry, and many have done the genealogical work to understand the con-nections. Even those parishioners who are not part-Indian see John and Ela White and the small group of people who identify themselves as Illinois In-dian descendants as valuable allies. Both groups are determined to restore and preserve the Kaskaskia Island church.

On the Feast of the Immaculate Conception each December, women who are Illiniwek descendants lay white flowers on the altar and hymns are sung in the Kaskaskia language in a service created by John and Ela White at the request of the church members. At an Easter service, families that wish their babies to re-ceive an Illinois name in a naming ceremony at the church can do so. About one hundred babies have been named.

The decimation of the Illinois Indians is one of the tragic stories of the con-quest of the New World. They welcomed the arrival of the French as a new op-portunity and quickly became important French allies and economic partners in the burgeoning fur trade. The Illinois were on the front line in the struggle be-tween the British and the French for control of the Mississippi River and the lu-crative fur trade. Pitted against British-allied nations like the Iroquois, Miami, and Fox, in one hundred years, they saw their numbers east of the Mississippi decline from around ten thousand to four hundred. The few that remained were not allowed to stay in Illinois; they were forcibly relocated in the 1830s to Kansas and then to Oklahoma. When their culture changed over time, they were de-clared culturally extinct. If their story is tragic, it is also typical.

In 1833, just as the Indians were being forcibly relocated, the poet William Cullen Bryant came to Illinois to visit his settler brother and published his famous poem "The Prairies." In his romantic view, it was the ordained will of God that the Indians must perish.

Thus change the forms of being. Thus arise
Races of living things, glorious in strength,
And perish, as the quickening breath of God
Fills them, or is withdrawn.

And now that the land is empty, the new "civilized" era can begin:

The sound of that advancing multitude
Which soon shall fill these deserts.
From the ground
Comes up the laugh of children, the soft voice
Of maidens, and the sweet and solemn hymn
Of Sabbath worshippers.

This detached view of Indian removal made a political decision appear to be a natural and inevitable occurrence. Reynolds, the governor of Illinois at the time, admitted that he could find no good reason to expel the Indians. But as poets and painters made clear, we didn't need a reason because it hadn't been our idea; we were simply accomplices to "manifest destiny," fortunate recipients of divine intervention. As Barthes reminds us, this is the function of myth, to make the political seem natural.

Thirty-four years later, in 1867, funded by the sale of 480,000 acres of "unappropriated" federal land granted to the state of Illinois by the government, the University of Illinois was founded. The Morrill Act, signed by Abraham Lincoln in 1862, gave any state thirty thousand acres for each representative in Congress. The Morrill Act refused land to states in rebellion and mandated that each educational institution had to teach military tactics. If the state did not have enough unappropriated land within its borders, it received scrip, which it could use to buy other federal lands, sell them for a higher price, and then reinvest the proceeds in bonds. The federal land in which trustees of would-be universities speculated was not, in many cases, vacant; authorities made it available by removing the Indians who lived on it.

The students of other midwestern universities took on the nicknames given to early white settlers: Hawkeyes, Wolverines, and Badgers. These names did not originally refer to animals, and the animal mascots that accompanied these names came much later, in the 1940s or 1950s. University of Illinois students called their lettermen the Tribe of Illini. It is understandable that the Illinois students looked elsewhere for inspiration, for the earliest white settlers in the Illinois Territory were called Suckers.

The first literary societies at Illinois were given Greek names like Adelphic, Philomathean, and Alethenai. But later, as midwestern scholars sought to distinguish themselves from their eastern models, they identified themselves with the original inhabitants of the prairies. The men's junior honorary society became Sachem and its new members were inducted at night by older members wearing Indian blankets and smoking peace pipes. The senior honorary society for men, Ma-wan-da, posted the names of its new inductees on an arrowhead-shaped board attached to the Ma-wan-da elm. Like the Boy Scouts and many summer camps, university students forged a group identity by using Indian words to name their clubs, borrowing Indian rituals such as smoking pipes, meeting at night around campfires, and dressing in Indian-inspired clothing. Upper-class students identified with the pleasures of Indian life as they imagined them—hunting, fishing, and storytelling around the fire—much like a week spent roughing it at Dad's hunting club.

Few Americans questioned their understanding of Indian culture, for everywhere the same images were reflected back at them—chiefs in feather bonnets, tepees, bows and arrows, warriors on horseback, drums and dancing. In photographs, in paintings, in sculpture, and in novels, Indians dressed and acted and talked the same way. No wonder readers and viewers assumed that these depictions were accurate. They saw nothing that contradicted them.

Portrait of two women from a book of "Midway Types" at the World's Colombian Exposition in Chicago in 1893. Courtesy of the Illinois History Survey, University of Illinois, Urbana-Champaign.

Four hundred years after Columbus had "discovered" the New World, the young university sent stone axes and prehistoric pottery from Illinois moundbuilders to be displayed in the exhibit halls at the World Colombian Exposition of 1893. Students who traveled to Chicago to see the fair not only perused artifacts in glass cases; they also saw living exhibits—Seneca, Navajo,

Kwakiutl, Pueblo, and Inuit people, among others, who drummed, danced, and demonstrated handicrafts in their camps inside the grounds. This was the anthropology exhibit, organized by the director of Harvard's Peabody Museum to show the wide range of peoples who had been living on the North American continent when Columbus arrived. Each group's place in the order was determined by the anthropologists' conception of their stage of development, except for the "Eskimaux," who had to be near the lake to demonstrate kayaking. As they walked along and viewed these dioramas populated by living people, thousands of fair visitors were introduced to the new science of anthropology.

In a guidebook called *Midway Types, A Book of Illustrated Lessons About The People of the Midway Plaisance*, this caption appears under a portrait of two mild-looking women wrapped in shawls:

Two Squaws. Any superfluity of sentiment is wasted on the Indian. He prefers scalps to taffy, and fire-water to tracts. He is monotonously hungry to kill somebody, a white man if possible, another Indian if the white man is happily absent. The Indian woman, or squaw, is a shade worse in human deviltry than the male. In the picture above mildness, docility, kindness, loveableness, seem impersonated. Yet the records of massacres, for centuries, show that the squaw is the apotheosis of incarnate fiendishness. These two, "Pretty Face" and "Mary Hairy-Chin," may never have scalped, nor built a fire around a prisoner, or flayed an enemy alive, but that does not signify that they would not do it if they had the chance. Serfs they always are; friends, never; companionable in the inverse ratio of distance. They belong to no ethical societies, dress reform clubs or art cliques; nor are sewing bees or donation parties in their categories of enjoyments. Savages, pure and cunning, they gave to the Midway the shadows of characters that cannot be civilized, and the solemnity of appearances as deceptive as the veiled claws of the tiger.

Another photo of a middle-aged man holding on his lap a pipe, an eagle feather, and a long beaded bag was captioned "A Professional Scalper" and went on:

> Toward the end of the Midway was a little encampment of Sioux Indians. Foreigners must have been surprised when informed that among this band were men who had waged a bitter war against the United States, and who, unpunished, tented upon the most famous arena of peace the world had ever seen. History is not so old, nor memory so weak, as to permit the Custer Massacre in 1876 to be forgotten; yet Chief Rain-in-the-Face, whose picture is above, was a prominent actor in that massacre. His presence secured him an admiring audience, the recollection of his atrocities being no bar to that sentiment of adulation that transforms murderers into heroes.

This reads like advertising copy, a midway barker's spiel in printed form. If white Americans were going to view exhibited Indians, they certainly didn't want them to be ordinary people; they wanted the frisson that came from standing next to bonafide scalpers.

But the Office of Indian Affairs wanted to present a different view of America's Indians. It constructed a two-story schoolhouse. Inside the model school, groups of boarding school students were shipped in to demonstrate the civilized skills they had acquired. As they worked at their forge or sewed clothing, they were living proof of the success of the government's assimilation program. As many as one hundred thousand visitors watched this performance in a single week.

In addition to anthropology's exhibited Indians and the Office of Indian Affairs with their boarding school students, there were the professionals: Buffalo Bill and the Wild West. The fair's organizers refused to allow the Wild West into the fair proper. The Wild West glorified the past; they had their eyes on progress. The Wild West was entertainment; they wanted educational and

The Office of Indian Affairs presented its own Indian exhibit at the Colombian Exposition, a schoolhouse filled with children from boarding schools who demonstrated blacksmithing, sewing, and woodworking. The groups were rotated every two to three weeks. Courtesy of the Illinois History Survey, University of Illinois, Urbana-Champaign.

uplifting exhibits. Undaunted, the show rented a piece of land outside the main gate of the Exposition. The streetcars discharged their passengers in front of Buffalo Bill's show grounds and the Wild West had its best season ever. The performers put on three to four shows a day to sellout crowds, and by the end of the fair two million people had seen the show. Ticketholders were invited to tour the encampment and meet the performers. The most memorable fair experience for many visitors was a walk through the Indian camp of the Wild West. They had no idea this colorful scene was not part of the official World's Colombian Exposition.

At a meeting inside the fair, historians were also considering the meaning of the frontier. It was at the Colombian Exposition that historian Frederick Jackson Turner delivered his famous speech about the frontier. The frontier era was now officially over and Turner claimed that the frontier mentality had molded the American spirit and enabled the growth of American democracy.

As they traversed Chicago's "white city," fairgoers were delighted to find a Chicago cook named Nancy Green in a booth shaped like a giant flour barrel, dressed in old-fashioned clothing and wearing a handkerchief on her head. Green, acting the role of the fictional ex-slave Aunt Jemima, passed out real pancakes and souvenir buttons bearing her catchphrase, "I'se in town, honey!" Fair officials awarded her a medal and Nancy Green continued to play Aunt Jemima at fairs and trade shows until her death thirty years later. People journeyed from all over the country to visit the Colombian Exposition, taking advantage of special trains and reduced fares. When they met Aunt Jemima, they ingested, along with pancakes, the notion that this slave had been happy on the plantation. After a tour of the "professional scalpers" on the midway, the anthropology exhibit, the model schoolhouse, and a performance of Buffalo Bill's Wild West, what would they have learned about Indians?

According to the historians, the frontier had been all-important in developing the sturdy, self-sufficient, democratic American who would lead the way

Sightseers at the Colombian Exposition in Chicago in 1893 visit the Penobscot village, part of the anthropology exhibit. Courtesy of the Illinois History Survey, University of Illinois, Urbana-Champaign.

into the next century. According to the anthropologists, real Indian people and prehistoric pottery could and should be studied in much the same way to better understand the American past. On the midway, no matter how they looked, Indians were and would always remain savage uncivilizable warriors, who, fortunately for the viewer, had recently been defeated by the military. (No wonder they hadn't had an easy time of it.) Visitors were encouraged not to give in to feelings of sympathy.

But to the well-meaning reformers who built the schoolhouse, Indians were neither inherently savage nor backward. It was their way of life that was both. What they needed was to give up their culture and their group identity and become educated Christians like other Americans. In the Wild West arena, Indians and scouts alike were having a great time remembering the old days, which had clearly been the best days.

No wonder Americans were confused after viewing this tangle of contradictory multimedia messages. Indians held a great deal of fascination for most

Americans. But the fascination was filled with ambivalence. According to the midway guide, one mustn't believe one's own eyes. So who knew Indians best? Was it the anthropologists? The missionaries and schoolteachers? Or Buffalo Bill?

The simplest response was to assume that it didn't much matter because Indians would soon be a thing of the past. This idea that Indians were perishing was the only premise to which all the groups could agree. Anthropology became that much more pressing an enterprise since a way of life must be recorded before it was too late. A visit to the Wild West shouldn't be postponed. Get your tickets now! And although the Office of Indian Affairs needed Indians for its institutional raison d'être, its bureaucrats also intended for Indian communities and culture to vanish, leaving only individual assimilated Indian Americans.

This left a marvelous opening. A desirable identity replete with colorful costumes, interesting history, and an exotic vocabulary was up for grabs. Everyone knew what an Indian looked like. Certain images had received the stamp of authenticity through repetition—feather bonnets, tepees, bows and arrows, warriors on horseback, drums and dancing, and leather clothing decorated with beadwork. And since no one really understood Indian values and beliefs, they could be easily adapted to suit almost any need.

To send their sons away for a university education was an innovative act for most American families. Looking for a parallel to this new initiation into adulthood, the university likened its students to young Illini, who, the deans and professors decided, had submitted to years of rigorous training and discipline to become Illini warriors. Like the Boy Scouts and many summer camps, the university borrowed Indian words and Indian rituals to give form and shape to a set of values it wanted its young male students to adopt.

The students liked this image of themselves as modern Indians, living together as a tribe on an isolated corner of the prairie undergoing an initiation into manhood. But where had their antecedents, the original Illini warriors, gone?

Forced removal is not the stuff warrior mythology is made of. The picture of the small band prodded along by soldiers on horseback inspired pity for the refugees and made the Americans seem coldhearted. Surely, good people would have taken pity on them and let them stay. And surely true warriors would not have gone along so passively. They would have fought to the death rather than submit. So during this period, another myth became popular—the tale of Starved Rock. In this "Indian legend," the last Illini died dramatically and bravely by launching themselves, vastly outnumbered, against the warriors of another tribe who were holding them captive on a high sandstone cliff. Knowing they would eventually be overrun, they chose to die fighting.

Starved Rock

It was a cool Sunday in early March when I set off for Starved Rock State Park with my husband, Tom, as travel companion. There was talk of snow that day, which wouldn't have been unusual normally, but it had been a balmy winter and the crocuses were already blooming. As we drove north, the sky changed dramatically again and again. Very low clouds whitewashed the air and we could barely see through the swirling flakes to drive. A few minutes later, we would emerge to clear, bright skies. In the distance, dramatic dark blue lines of clouds marked rain or snowstorms other people were driving through on distant roads.

"Now what exactly is the significance of this place?" Tom asked me. As he drove, I explained that Starved Rock, a 125-foot sandstone promontory on the Illinois River, had been an important landmark in Illinois for both the Indians and the French. A sandstone cliff is an unusual feature in Illinois; in addition, this one marked the location of the last rapids on the Illinois River. For people who traveled in huge dugout canoes that had to be carried around rapids, this was significant. The French called the place simply Le Rocher. The Illinois Indians had a large village on the opposite bank.

Compared to the harsh Canadian winters and the mosquito-infested swamps downriver, the Illinois country seemed like a paradise to the French. Describing the prairies, Marquette wrote that "stags, deer, beaver and otter are common there, geese, swans, turtles, poules d'inde (turkeys), parrots, partridges, and many other birds swarm there, the fishery is very abundant, and the fertility of the soil is extraordinary."

When Marquette arrived in 1673, the Illinois were already trading slaves to the Ottawas for muskets, powder, kettles, knives, and hatchets. The Illinois are often referred to as a confederacy, but this would imply an organized association of tribes under a single leader. This was not the case. In fact, each village was a distinct political unit. In a dictionary written by a French priest, the same Illinois word is given for the French words "tribe" and "village." It was by villages that the Illinois played lacrosse, organized calumet dances, and waged war. Their political structure bewildered the French, who were used to strong, authoritative leaders and hierarchical institutions of power. Among the Illiniwek, the chief had to be mild and nonaggressive. In order to carry out their colonial program, the French created chiefs by handing out large brass medals to leaders amenable to their agenda. This "meddling" in the Illinois political system was quite effective, and leaders who received the medals saw their influence grow.

War chiefs or captains also served as leaders as long as they could persuade warriors to follow them. A captain went on a short fast, and then attempted to convince a group of warriors that his manitou or spirit guide had promised a successful venture. Each man had a bird spirit he turned to in matters of warfare, rarely the hawks or eagles we imagine, but sparrows or thrushes or bluebirds. The Illinois went on raids to get prisoners who could be traded as slaves to other tribes or to avenge the death of a member of the village. They attacked at daybreak and tried to return the same evening. If the raid was successful, the war party was feasted, but if anyone in his charge had been killed, the captain returned covered with mud, carrying his arrows broken, weeping. He was expected to give presents to the dead man's family and to avenge the death by organizing another raid. A prisoner was often given to a family to replace a young man killed in war. These captives could be raised as adopted sons. Prisoners who weren't adopted were usually tortured until they died a slow, painful death.

Success in a military exploit earned a young man the right to be tattooed. A young warrior's back was covered with designs from shoulders to heels. Women were also tattooed on their cheeks, breasts, and arms for deco-ration. Men wore very little clothing, usually only a breechcloth and moc-casins, earrings, and colored feathers on their heads. Women wore skirts made of skins, and after the arrival of the missionaries, leather shirts. A few Illinois men dressed and lived as women. The French called them *berdaches*, although it is not an Illinois word. Later in life they were considered to have acquired spiritual power.

Lacrosse games were an important part of Illinois life, both recreational and ceremonial. There was no limit to the number of players on each side, and once the ball, made from a knot of wood as large as a tennis ball, had been tossed into the air, the game didn't stop. When players were injured, women ran out to pull them off the field. Lacrosse was played between villages and sometimes at funerals.

In the winter of 1680, an army of Iroquois warriors arrived on the Missis-sippi. The Illinois had sent most of their men off on a winter hunt. Most villages decided to flee downriver in their pirogues, large wooden canoes that could hold as many as forty people. The Iroquois killed those who stayed and took hundreds of women and children as captives.

The French explorer La Salle, who came down the river looking for his men just afterward, found the largest Illinois village destroyed and a field of burned bodies. Nevertheless, La Salle went ahead with his plans to build a fort on Le Rocher, across the river from the burned villages. He intended to make the Illi-nois country the center of a vast French empire that would extend from Canada to Louisiana. To this end he made alliances with the Illinois, Miami, Shawnee, and Wea. A French fort on such a strategic site might keep out the dreaded Iro-quois, who if they conquered the area, would turn the lucrative Mississippi fur trade over to the British. The Illinois warriors would serve as La Salle's militia and defend French interests. He left his lieutenant, Henri de Tonti, in charge of Fort

St. Louis. As part of his charter to command the fort, Tonti was to encourage the Illinois to attack the British-supported Iroquois.

Starved Rock had been an important summer village location for the Illinois when the French met them in 1673. After 1680, when the French built their fort there, many Illinois moved their villages to the bank just across from the rock for defense. Other tribes, seeking refuge from the Iroquois, joined them. For a brief period, the village was a bustling town and trade center. The Kaskaskia, a large subgroup of the Illinois, lived there until 1691, when they migrated south to Lake Peoria, and then southward again, into southern Illinois and Missouri. Tonti and the fur traders followed and the fort was gradually abandoned. At some point it burned. By 1720 there was no trace of it left.

This was all fact, researched by historians and substantiated by archaeology, and it was reason enough for me to want to see the place. But Starved Rock was also the location of the best-known legend about the Illinois. According to the legend, the last Illini, trying to escape from their enemies, sought refuge on top of the rock. They awoke one morning to find the ropes they used to haul water cut. Starving, they launched themselves against their enemies and died fighting. In other versions they simply remained stoically on top of the rock and starved to death. None of these accounts said that the story was completely fictional, but none were clear about which parts were which. One version even specified the number of Illini—eleven. Sometimes their enemies were the Iroquois. Sometimes Great Lakes tribes, usually the Potawatomi, who wanted to avenge the murder of Pontiac. It seemed probable that some real incident had inspired the legends, but what had actually happened there? A trip to the place itself would clarify this, I thought, as we drove. I had found in the library a slim, black, old-fashioned volume called *The Last of the Illini* that was published in 1916. It was written in verse that limped and thumped along, so I spared Tom by not reading that aloud as we drove.

(So in time this mighty nation,
Great in spirit and in numbers,
In fame and strength were sadly broken:
In numbers much decreased and lessened,)

I had also found a book of poems published in 1919 by Edgar Lee Masters of *Spoon River Anthology* fame. Masters called his collection *Starved Rock*, after the poem of that name. This one I did read to Tom, all nine stanzas. The legend is recounted in the fourth stanza:

Later the remnant of the Illini
Climbed up this Rock, to die
Of hunger, thirst, or down its sheer ascents
Rushed on the spears of Pottawatomies,
And found the peace
Where thirst and hunger are unknown.

Masters says that the rock's secret is defeat and change. The next to the last verse implicates us too.

This is the land where every generation
Lets down its buckets for the water of Life.
We are the children and the epigone
Of the Illini, the vanished nation.
And this starved scarp of stone
Is now the emblem of our tribulation,
The inverted cup of our insatiable thirst,
The Illini by fate accursed,
This land lost to the Pottawatomies,
They lost the land to us,
Who baffled and idolatrous,

And thirsting, spurred by hope
Kneel upon aching knees,
And with our eager hands draw up the bucketless rope.

As the road curved down toward the Illinois River, I felt excited. Past and present were about to come together; hopefully the boundary between legend and fact would also come clear. But when we came out of the woods onto the bottomland beside the river, we drove onto an enormous asphalt parking lot. Concrete walls lined the bank and the water poured over a dam that crossed the river just at the bottom of an upright yellow cliff that had to be Starved Rock. On the opposite bank where the village had stood, there was a bustle of activity as a barge arrived at the lock. This was not the scene I had expected.

The visitors' center was a trailer, one half for offices, the other half for exhibits. The woman on duty turned on the lights so we could see the displays. In one corner there was an old papier-mâché model of Starved Rock with a small brown stick fort on top. A reconstruction based on probabilities, warned a label. Over the fort hung a stuffed red-tailed hawk with a ratty chipmunk hanging from its talons. The enormous bird overshadowed the little stick structure. It seemed about to drop the chipmunk in an aerial bombardment and crush the tiny buildings.

Taped to one wall were a few newspaper clippings about the legend. These repeated the various versions about warriors who starved on top and others who fought until "the cliffs of the rock were stained red and slippery with the remains."

Taking to the trails, we climbed the winding path up Starved Rock. From the top, we watched a bald eagle wing its way down the river, harassed by a smaller bird. The eagle's white head and white tail shone in the gray light, pristine and gleaming.

A metal historical marker set into the limestone, placed there by the Illinois Colonial Dames of America in 1918, read,

In Memory Of
Louis Joliet and Jacques Marquette
who visited this spot in 1673
Rene Robert Cavelier Sieur de La Salle
who built on this rock in 1682
Fort St. Louis
important French fortress in the Illinois country for 36 years
Henri de Tonty
La Salle's intrepid companion
who died in the fort in 1714

Tonti died of yellow fever in Old Mobile in 1704, not 1714. He'd had a tough life—a grenade in Italy took his right hand, he was stabbed by the Iroquois when he tried to mediate with them, frustrations in Arkansas when he tried to start a colony there, yellow fever. When La Salle died, Tonti had inherited the Illinois fur trade, but it had never made him rich. He had probably traveled through more of North America than any other European. But he hadn't died on Starved Rock. When I ran into historical inaccuracies like this (and it seemed to happen all the time), I was usually annoyed. But for some reason this one didn't bother me. It seemed like a kindness on the part of the Colonial Dames to grant Tonti another ten years of supranatural life to sit on top of Le Rocher and watch the bald eagles fly by. The large bronze marker next to this one was headed "Starved Rock":

Indian tradition tells that about 1765 a band of Illinois Indians was pursued by an overwhelming force of Potawatomi seeking to avenge the death of Chief Pontiac, and took refuge on the summit of this rock which had been the site of Fort St. Louis. The inaccessibility of this natural fortress enabled the Illinois to keep their foes at bay but hunger and thirst united to defeat them, their provisions failed, the enemies cut the cords with which they tried to lift vessels of water from the river. With their vast hunting grounds in a panorama before them they expired of starvation with true Indian fortitude, and thus gave to this lofty citadel the name of Starved Rock.

Returning to the bottom, we followed the trail to one of the eighteen limestone canyons. The narrow canyon with a waterfall at its closed end was bounded by curving limestone walls that rose above us; the gray stone was worn away in graceful rounded lines wherever the water dripped or flowed. Along the walls, the hanging fern fronds and mosses were already bright green, the signs of an early spring. The natural stairs leading into the canyon were filled with water and we had to jump from side to side to climb them. At the foot of one wide stair, where there was only one possible place to step before mounting, a foot-shaped print was carved into the limestone. Had it been made by Illinois Indians? Or by generations of visitors on outings from Chicago? The park had been a popular destination for a hundred years. Of course I imagined La Salle and Tonti walking here, as well as a Kaskaskia man, come to hunt deer to serve Father Marquette, or a woman, come for water. I checked the stream that ran out of the canyon and quickly found a flint chip with a smooth, scooped-out depression that suggested it was human-made.

This moment in the canyon satisfied us and we sought out the trail to the lodge. The Great Room of the lodge was built by the Civilian Conservation Corps in the 1930s and is magnificent. The proportions are gigantic—varnished tree trunks for posts and beams, enormous stone fireplaces. Just inside the entrance, right by the front door, there stood a tall rectangular glass case. Inside was a mannequin, dressed in—what else?—beaded Sioux regalia with a feather bonnet.

"What's this about?" Tom asked me.

I was getting worn out with trying to explain our national obsession with the Plains Indian tribes. I just shook my head and pulled him toward the dining room, where a buffet in the same massive proportions as the architecture was set out.

On the way home, we stopped in the nearby town of Ottawa, where William Boyce, the main character in another legend, lived and is buried.

Apparently, Boyce was in London on business and had difficulty finding an address in the foggy city. A boy came up and showed him the way. But when Boyce offered the boy a shilling, he refused, saying that he was a Scout and had to do a good turn every day. Boyce came back determined to bring Scouting to America.

A brand new Scout museum had just opened in Ottawa and we quickly cruised the cases of merit badges and those decorated rings you thread your bandana through. One case was dedicated to memorabilia from the Camp Fire Girls. Beside it stood a life-sized mannequin dressed in a pseudo-Indian costume. Every Camp Fire Girl made her own costume and invented her own personal symbols. Influenced by Ernest Thompson Seton, the organizers fused Indian play with idealized womanhood. Most organizations that used idealized Indian life as a model to inspire youth aimed their programs at boys. But the Camp Fire Girls invented tribes, songs, and beadwork projects to convince girls that home life was a true and noble calling. The brown felt beanies and green cord boleros in the glass cases stirred my memories of Brownies and Girl Scout camp and I felt a little thrill of nostalgic delight; but even so, the museum was a strangely sterile place.

The docents, seeing our unsatisfied looks, suggested we visit the cemetery. A tiny path of stepping stones leads from Boyce's grave to a bronze statue of a Boy Scout dressed in trademark flaring shorts, neckerchief, and cuffed knee socks. He stands, his weight on one leg, one hand on a hatchet attached to his belt and the other holding a Scout hat respectfully against his chest. This tiny

Scout domain had its own flagpole, but the tattered American flag wrapped around the pole looked like it hadn't been raised or lowered in years.

"So what did we learn?" Tom asked me as we drove home through huge snowflakes that swirled furiously toward our windshield.

"We saw Starved Rock," I said finally. "It's more real now."

"Yes, but I learned more listening to you read in the car on the way there."

"We climbed Le Rocher and stood in the same place they did, looking out." I didn't want him to think he'd driven through the snow with me for nothing. "That meant a lot to me."

"Yes, but you know the significance of the place. What about those other people on top with us? What do they take away?"

I reminded him that there was a placard about barge traffic.

"Barge traffic!" Tom said. He was really enjoying his moment of righteous indignation. It whiled away the miles of boring road. "That place is a disgrace to the state park system. Don't they have an obligation to explain something about Native American history?"

"There was the legend," I reminded him. "And there may be some truth to it."

"Legends, taking refuge with the French. They were turned into mercenaries by the French."

"Well, they did move near the fort for protection."

"What use were the French against the Iroquois?" he asked. "There were only a handful of Frenchmen in the whole Mississippi Valley."

"They had weapons," I replied. "A few guns went a long way then."

"Okay. I accept that. But what about that Sioux outfit in the lodge?"

"What about it?"

"We came for history," said Tom. "We drove two hours to seek it out. But we got the same old things—legends and a Plains Indian outfit in a glass case."

The next day, a Monday, I called Jon Blume, the park superintendent, to sort out the difference between history and legend. Blume's specialty is the military history of the Civil War; he also spent three years in Vietnam. This gave him a feeling for failed French attempts at colonial empire and the impossibility of trying to hold small impregnable places where you're essentially trapped.

"War has very little to do with forts," he told me. "Why would the Illinois Indians want to get up there where there's no food and no water? Once you're up there, you're stuck. It's not that different from what happened at Dien Bien Phu."

He is sure that the French fort existed and that it burned. The archaeologists found, in a burned pit on top of Starved Rock, a fur bale seal, a small piece of lead imprinted with the seal of Louis XIV. "But it's hard for me to believe the fort was as big, with the palisades and all, as the descriptions would have it."

As for the legend of Starved Rock, Blume concedes it's possible that there was a battle in the area. Probably someone, maybe a group of Illinois Indians, was besieged up there. But the motivation usually given—avenging the death of the Ottawa leader Pontiac—makes no sense because of the dates. Pontiac was murdered by an Illinois Indian in southern Illinois in 1769. If his followers came to Starved Rock looking for revenge, they were lost in the very worst way. The Illiniwek had been living in southern Illinois, not far from St. Louis, for over fifty years. Even if every single Illini did travel north, climb the cliff, and perish on top of it in 1769, who signed the treaties in the 1800s? And who was deported from the state in the 1830s?

Blume laughs at the notion that whatever happened on top of Starved Rock was the last stand of the Illinois. "They weren't wiped out!" He's visited reservations where there are descendants of the Illini, intermarried now with other tribes. "You've been up there," he reminds me. "It's not that big. It's very hard for me to believe that all the Illini in the world were on top of that rock."

That Roughneck Indian Game

As they looked forward to the twentieth century, the deans and professors at the University of Illinois encouraged the students' identification with Illini warriors, for they wanted their charges to be sound in mind and body. The notion that an ideal education combined academics and athletics became an important American value. In the 1890s college teams were competing at regional meets that included both track and oratorical events. However, oratory was soon dropped, and track and baseball were eclipsed by the invention of a new collegiate sport around which these values coalesced—football.

Although the past thirty years have been rocky, varsity football at Illinois, can claim a history filled with glorious firsts and famous victories. This is, after all, the home of Red Grange, the Galloping Ghost of the Gridiron, and of Robert Zuppke, the coach they called the "Edison of football," who invented the screen pass and the huddle. He welcomed opponents to his practices and then bewildered them at the game with newly devised and very complicated plays like the "flying trapeze," the "flea-flicker," and the "razzle-dazzle."

Actually, when football was first introduced at Illinois in 1890 by a freshman named Scott Williams, there was little interest. The prominent athletes, who competed in track or played baseball, were scornful about that "roughneck Indian game," an epithet that now seems ironic. Football originated at Harvard and Yale, a combination of soccer and rugby. The game was short and very rough, emphasized kicking, and was played with a nearly round ball. Walter Camp, a player at Yale, codified the rules and is called the father of modern football.

The sport didn't catch on at Illinois until the president of Purdue, speaking at the obligatory chapel held each morning, challenged the team to come to

Lafayette, warning that they would get the worst beating they'd ever had. The Illinois team had so far played only one game and had lost that, but stirred by a challenge, the students raised the money to send the team to Purdue, where they were beaten as promised, 62-0. The first football season ended on Thanksgiving at the county fairgrounds. The Illinois players must have been quick learners because they managed to win against Illinois Wesleyan. When the team members were flagging, one of the students in the stands loosened his tie and joined the play, still wearing his derby hat. In the team photo, each player wears a white canvas uniform that laces up the front like a giant sneaker, and a black fez with a pom-pom attached to the side. Williams described the day as "a gala occasion with the finest carriages of the Twin Cities filled with beribboned ladies and gentlemen." Years later he wrote that "Football's popularity at Illinois dates from that day." Unfortunately he didn't explain the significance of the fez, nor whether they kept them on during the games.

For the first two years the team had no real coach. When team members were unsure about the rules, they wrote to Walter Camp at Yale, who was in the process of working them out. Their opponents were athletic clubs from Chicago and St. Louis. On their first road trip they attempted to play six games in ten days, an overambitious away schedule. The Illinois team was lucky to arrive back on campus able to walk, albeit just barely.

A popular play in 1890 was the "flying wedge," in which players held onto suitcase handles sewed to the pants of a large player in the middle. This moving shield protected the player behind it who carried the ball. Running into a flying wedge produced disastrous, even tragic results. Concerned about the high number of injuries and even some deaths, Teddy Roosevelt convened a meeting at the White House in 1905 and Walter Camp and the other coaches agreed to modify the game slightly to make it safer. One of Roosevelt's sons was playing for Yale that year and he wrote home to Pennsylvania Avenue to say that he had gotten off lightly, with just a broken nose. But even after mass plays like the flying wedge were outlawed, the game remained brutal, designed to test the endurance of middle- and upper-class boys and to prepare them for their roles as leaders. Roosevelt and Camp were both convinced that football should be a physical and moral test of a young man's endurance. How else would America's leading young men, raised in comfortable urban homes, develop the tough fighting spirit they needed to rule American industry and government? Their elders had won their manhood on the frontier fighting Indians or with the Rough Riders. If the training of a football team was organized much like military training and physical brutality was tolerated, then the gridiron could serve as the mock battlefield where young men learned teamwork and sacrifice. "The very language of football—drills, training camps, strategy, and tactics—drew on military life and experience," Elliott Gorn and Warren Goldstein point out in *A Brief History of American Sports*. "And of course the play of the game itself consisted of organized violence and the capture of territory."

It was easy to imagine the football field as a battlefield in the Indian wars in both 1897 and 1898, when Illinois played exhibition games in Chicago against the Carlisle Indians. These Indians were real, although they were in the midst of a long and painful process designed to take the Indianness out of them. At the boarding school in Carlisle, Pennsylvania, run by Richard Henry Pratt, their hair, which often had religious significance, was cut and they were forbidden to speak their native languages or practice their religions. If they were caught doing either they were punished physically or put in solitary confinement. When families did not want to send their children to the school, children were taken by various coercive measures. "Let us by patient effort kill the Indian in him and save the man," Pratt urged Congress. The first time Illinois played Carlisle made football history, as it was one of the first illuminated night games. Since the Illini were ahead at the half, sportswriters attributed the Indians' 23-6 win to that superior stamina Indians were famous for. Carlisle won the second game and no others were scheduled.

Illinois was the first school to have a designated cheerleader, who shouted, "Oskee-wow-wow," a word no one can translate or explain, although its Indian sound must have been part of its appeal. The second verse of the cheer refers to Teddy, not FDR, and the football players it extols have been forgotten now:

Roosevelt may be famous and his name you often hear,
but its heroes on the football field,
Each college man holds dear.
We think with pride of Roberts, Artie Hall and Heavy, too . . .
Oskee wow-wow for the wearers of the Orange and the Blue.

In 1910 a couple of Illinois students had the idea of a "coming back weekend" when former students could return to see their friends, be entertained by student theatricals, and attend a football game. Soon other schools were following the example of the University of Illinois and staging a homecoming weekend for their alumni.

The university hired Robert Zuppke in 1912. He was an energetic young coach who had produced champion high school teams in Oak Park, Illinois. By 1914 "Zuppke's Illini" were national champions. They were conference champions of the Big Nine in 1923 and 1927, and became known as the Fighting Illini after several remarkable upsets against superior teams in the 1920s.

College sports, especially football, were wildly popular in the twenties. Grantland Rice and other sportswriters wrote enthusiastic paeans to sports heroes like Grange and described the big plays in dramatic prose and verse. But fans were being turned away from the games. Harvard, Yale, and Princeton had built stadiums, and Michigan, Kansas, and Ohio State were in the process. So in 1921 a fundraising drive was started to build a massive stadium on the Illinois campus. The stadium would hold seventy thousand people and would be dedicated to the Illini who had not returned from World War I. The students pledged so much of their money to the stadium fund that they staged a "Poverty Day" and dressed in rags to celebrate their penniless state. Carried away, they lifted a streetcar off its tracks, went off with a university fire engine, and tried to push a Ford up the steps of one of the buildings.

A fundraising book was published and mailed to alumni and other potential donors. An oversized volume called *The Story of the Stadium*, it is clothbound in blue. The first page shows an Indian making a speech next to a fire, an enormous full moon rising behind him.

An Indian Tribe Began It Long Ago

Listen to the historian, and learn what manner of man lived where today is Burrill avenue, Green street, and the Boneyard. . . .

The Illini Indian, he was called, and he was a hunter, and a fighter, and more generous in war and in peace than his neighbors, the Shawnees, the Iroquois, the Sioux, the Chippewas, and the Kickapoos.

He was an individualist, and his children, whom he loved, were given freedom to grow as they willed, only they had to be brave and self-denying, and each had to find his own god—his Manitou—to protect and inspire him; for this was the law of the tribe.

Never were people better made than the Illini, said a traveler who observed them. "They are neither large nor small. . . . They have tapering legs which carry their bodies well, with a very haughty step, and as graceful as the best dancer. The visage is fairer than white milk so far as savages of this country can have such. The teeth are the best arranged and the whitest in the world. They are vivacious. . . ."

Although they had religious ceremonies, they were "too well off to be really pious," and to none of their deities did the Illini attribute moral good or evil.

No temples have these ancient Indians left us, and no books. But we have a heritage from them, direct through the pioneers who fought them and learned to know them. It is the Great Heart, the fighting spirit, the spirit of individualism, of teaching our children to be free but brave and to have a God—for these are the laws of our tribe.

See us today living vitally in our heritage. Watch us play football; see us on the cinder track, on the baseball diamond. . . . We are different, somehow, we of the middle west—not particularly better, but different. We are uniquely ourselves.

This is a curious piece of work. The style sounds like that of a storyteller around the campfire, but to make sure we know the account is accurate, the storyteller invokes the historian. We know this on his authority. The first fact we learn about the Illini is that he was more generous in both war and peacetime than Indians of other tribes. The "he" is not the generic male form meaning humanity. Only men are invoked—there is nothing about village life, about farming, or about women, for the myth has no need of any character but a young Illini man. He was a hunter and a fighter, perfect occupations for a mythic hero. He was an individualist (like modern Americans) and as a parent, he was not a rigid, punishing, old-fashioned patriarch, but a loving father who gave his children freedom, just like modern fathers in the America of the twenties. Of course, despite the freedom, they still needed to have strong character, so our Illini father required his children to be brave and self-denying. The Illini were handsome and graceful, never needed dentists, and best of all, not only their teeth, but their faces were whiter than white milk, so race was not an impediment to admiring them.

They were religious, but not overly pious in a rigid, old-fashioned way, so they were probably religious the way our twenties fundraising booklet writers were, in a rather modern way that admitted to a plurality of religions and smiled benignly on a good time. They were not literate and their architecture didn't survive the passage of time. So how did we receive this heritage "direct from them" that the writer calls the Great Heart? In a rather interesting way. We inherit it from the pioneers who fought them and learned to know them. A curious conjuncture takes place at this particular moment. Instead of receiving the heritage of their forebears, the pioneers, the young students receive the Illini heritage, which has somehow been transmitted through the process of battle. This is like saying that contemporary Germans have inherited Jewish values. Or that the hunter's son takes after, not his father, but the deer. This notion of taking on the best qualities of one's prey reminds me of hunting rituals in which the hunter eats the vital organs of the animal he has killed to gain the animal's speed or cunning. It is even like the philosophy behind the cannibalism of some societies, that to eat some vital part of your enemy is to incorporate his strengths and power into your own body.

In the historical record there are no real battles between the Illinois and "pioneers." The French settlers were their allies and although the British were their enemies, Illinois men more frequently battled British-allied tribes because there were so few actual British soldiers. By the time American settlers arrived in Illinois, although those settlers had strong anti-Indian sentiments, there were very few Illinois left.

Of course, this curious slippage of inheritance also puts our young Illini student on the morally right side. Although he is a descendant of the soldier who forced men, women, and children to leave their homes, and of the government officials who made the treaties and reneged on them, he has, through the alchemy of myth, become instead the descendant of those who were here first and had first rights to the land. As a young Illini, he inherits not only those wonderful 1920s values described as the Great Heart—individualism, fighting spirit, children raised to be both free and brave, and belief in God—but also the prairie on which the stadium will stand.

"Our stadium will bring a touch of Greek glory to the prairie," said the president of the university. The fundraising book promised an entire complex around the stadium, including a one-hundred-acre recreation field, tennis and handball courts, a track, and an outdoor Greek amphitheater.

The concept of a massive brick memorial to the war dead was not without meaning in Champaign-Urbana, for World War I had not passed the university by. A bulletin board set up in a corridor of the Administration Building displayed postcards, letters, and photographs from Illini overseas. Many had been sent to Dean Thomas Arkle Clark, the dean of men, in response to the thousands of postcards he mailed out. He wrote many students in the service personal letters and for some even knitted sweaters. He not only kept careful records, but also posted a brief summary of the men wounded, decorated, or dead. Each death was marked with a gold star. When the war ended, over eight thousand Illini men and women were in various branches of the service and over a thousand were overseas. The men of the Illini Battery, who fought in the trenches of France, were lucky. Only one man was lost in the last few days of the fighting, and they were quick to point out that he was "a non-University man." But 183 did not return from St. Mihiel, from Chateau Thierry, from the Verdun. And others perished in the camps when influenza struck. Many more came back disabled or gassed, with permanent consequences for their health.

The 1920 yearbook devotes several pages to the Illini Battery and the ambulance corps formed at Illinois. There are snapshots of trenches, ambulances, and makeshift barracks in old stone buildings. A photo of men around a large gun is captioned, "Ready to send a note to the Germans, to the accompaniment of an oskey-wow-wow." Flying Aces receive flowery praise and close scrapes make dramatic tales of adventure. There are even cocky quips about furloughs in Gay Paree and the score of a baseball game pitched by a champ from the Illinois team. But when the students describe those who died, often next to them, their tone becomes somber. How can you put this into words? How to explain why you are left, when so many from your generation are missing? It seemed to them that this had happened before, to the Illini, and perhaps that parallel provided some comfort.

As the football team acted out the mock battle below, they imagined vanished fighters from both tribes commingling above to cheer them on.

As the old Illini warrior sought his tepee home again,
For a respite from the labor of the chase;
So the younger generations seek their home upon the plain,
With a love that even time cannot efface;
They are come the old time warriors and the young men of today,
From each corner of the nationwide domain;
And their hearts and voices join to pay a tribute to the slain,
To the warrior sons who e'er remain away.

Then loyal sons of Illinois, ye stalwart brave and true;
Unfurl your honored colors twain, the Orange and the Blue;
And as we link our hands today, and lift our voice again;
The spirits of departed braves join in the glad refrain.

("Loyal Sons of Illinois," lyrics by G. V. Buchanan)

When the stadium was completed in 1924 it was dedicated to the Illinois students and alumni killed in World War I. Their names appear on the two hundred columns on the second story. The elaborate plans for a sports complex for all students had been scaled down. The Greek amphitheater was scrapped. The university did end up with a massive outdoor theater, but it was suitable for only one kind of entertainment each year—the six or seven home football games.

Luckily, the dedication game against Michigan was one of the most exciting and unusual ever played. Red Grange scored four touchdowns in the first twelve minutes. The packed stadium went wild. He came back in during the second half and scored a fifth time. What more auspicious christening could a football stadium have?

In the twenties, not only did Illinois have a first-rate football team, an innovative coach, and an impressive brick stadium, it could also boast that at halftime it fielded the best college band in the country. Under the direction of Albert Austin Harding, the Illinois band was the first to spell words on the field and the first to change formations at a prearranged signal in the music instead of using a whistle or gunshot. A reporter from Chicago, baffled, concluded that signals must be sent with mirrors, which the band members carried on their lyres.

Harding liked to tell Zuppke that seventy thousand fans showed up each week to see the band. Zuppke retorted that if that were the case, why did only forty thousand show up to see the band when the team was losing?

A. A. Harding led the football band and the other Illinois bands from 1905 to 1948 and sometimes fielded as many as 380 pieces. John Philip Sousa was so impressed with his friend Aus's concert band that he composed the "University of Illinois March" in 1929. "The trio has a melody of mine that sounds college and will lend itself to a lyrical treatment," Sousa wrote to Harding.

Sousa also willed a great part of his library of band music, more than three thousand titles, to the University of Illinois. On the second floor of the Harding Band Building, the valuable sheets of hand-copied music are stored in file cabinets and cared for by a knowledgeable and friendly archivist. In the small museum, in glass cases, you can see Harding's white baton and the original sheet music for Illinois anthems and fight songs. Inside the glass case, beside the uniforms, sheet music, and carefully labeled framed photographs, and surrounded by drum majors' maces topped with etched silver balls, there is a traditional Oglala chief's regalia once worn by Chief Illiniwek. The buckskin is ragged from use, especially around the neckline. Even through the glass I can feel its weight. It is hard to imagine that someone could wear such a solid thing and yet leap and run in Memorial Stadium. It is easier to imagine a chief who stands talking, who barely lifts an arm in a slow gesture, so weighted down is he by the thick leather. It seems as though, were the hanger removed, the regalia would stand alone, frozen in place.

The glimpses of Grange running and of Sousa and Harding in the stadium, their white batons lifted, will serve, I hope, to explain why the halftime show, the cheerleaders, and homecoming are viewed as important traditions that Illinois had a hand in creating. But none of these evoke anything like the emotional response and fierce controversy created by the appearance of the student who has been dressing up and appearing with the band as a character called Chief Illiniwek since 1926. Fans are deeply attached to his ritual performance, but what they really care about is something they understand unconsciously but are unable to articulate in words—the values described by the anonymous writer of the fundraising booklet as the Great Heart.

Sons of Modern Illini

When the University of Pennsylvania was coming to play Illinois in 1926, its marching band offered to bring a William Penn costume for a halftime skit if Illinois would come up with a character to meet Penn. There was no question how the student who would shake Penn's hand and welcome him to Illinois should dress. Of course he had to be an Indian.

The year before, 1925, was the first time that Zuppke had taken a team east; there was a general feeling that the eastern teams played superior football and that Illinois would be out of its league there in more ways than one. The Penn team was undefeated that year and the Illinois team was young and green. Everything seemed to go wrong: the train carrying the Illinois band was delayed and the field was a sea of mud and snow. Perhaps the miraculous arrival of the band just before kickoff, playing as they marched into the stadium, gave the young Illinois team heart. Although it might seem impossible to pull off a play with multiple passes using a slippery ball, the "flea-flicker" worked like a dream. The Penn team had no idea where the ball had gone until they saw Red Grange holding it in the end zone. Red turned up in the end zone three times that day after long runs through the mud. Although undefeated Penn lost 24-2, and eastern teams lost their perceived superiority, they may have felt it was worth it to be treated to the spectacle of the Galloping Ghost in action. The *Chicago Tribune* headline, in huge black ink, said simply, "ILLINOIS, 24; PENN, 2; GRANGE!"

The next year, when Penn came to Memorial Stadium, the Ghost was gone. He had evaded his tacklers once again after the last Illinois game, turning up not in the end zone, but in the five-year-old National Football League playing for the Chicago Bears. University promotional materials are not quick to point this out, but turning pro before you graduate is also an Illinois tradition. Grange earned $100,000 in his first year of playing for the Chicago Bears and brought legitimacy to the NFL. Before Grange joined up, the Chicago Bears had been playing to crowds of six thousand fans. But thirty-six thousand watched Grange's first game. However, Grange paid a price for his professional success. The man he most admired didn't speak to him for two years: Zup thought that football should be played for love, not money. The manager who brought about Grange's metamorphosis from college star to professional attraction was a movie theater owner from Champaign named C. C. Pyle. He sold the rights to use Grange's name on everything from dolls to ginger ale, and while Red carried the football and earned bruises, Pyle carried off the profits and earned his nickname, "Cash and Carry." It was the beginning of a new era in professional sports.

George Halas, the Chicago Bears player, owner, and coach who had played for Zuppke, came to agree with his old coach that it wasn't a good idea to encourage college players to leave school before their class graduated. Subsequently, they worked out the idea of the draft. The draft provided an orderly system to funnel well-trained players to the professional teams.

For the halftime show on an October Saturday in 1926 the assistant band director recruited Lester Leutwiler, a student who was interested in Indian lore and had made an Indian costume for himself as a Scout project. Leutwiler ran out onto the field and led the band, dancing in front of them as they formed the letters PENN. When the band played Pennsylvania's alma mater song, a drum major came out dressed as William Penn and accepted the catlinite pipe proffered by Leutwiler. After smoking the peace pipe, the two walked off the field arm in arm to (according to university literature) a "deafening ovation." Applause from sixty thousand people is rarely anything less; however, Leutwiler's performance was popular enough with football crowds that he continued to serve as "Chief Illiniwek" until he graduated. It couldn't have hurt that the Illini won again that day without Grange.

The real William Penn would
certainly have recognized Chief Illiniwek as an Indian, for in 1683 he
wrote in a letter to London that the
natives "tread strong and clever, and
mostly walk with a lofty Chin. . . .
Their Postures in the Dance are very
Antick and differing, but all keep
measure. This is done with equal
Earnestness and Labor, but great appearance of Joy."

By 1926 nearly one hundred
years had passed since the last Illinois Indians were forced to relocate
and the conflicts between actual Indians and settlers over real cornfields
had been forgotten. Young Americans were now free to re-invent Indian life as they wanted: Indians
were brave and loved to make war
and they were trained to endure
hardship without complaint. They
rode horses, lived in tepees, and
spent their days hunting and fishing
and their nights orating around the
campfire.

Lester Leutwiler, the first Chief Illiniwek, in
the regalia he made as a Boy Scout project.
From the band page of the Dad's Day foot-
ball program, University of Illinois, 1927.
Courtesy of the University of Illinois Archives,
Urbana-Champaign.

Today, modern paleface Illini have made permanent camp here. Ancient
teepees have been replaced by impressive structures and the old hunting

grounds and battlefields put to new uses. This bit of Illinois prairie, once the testing ground for Indian braves, now serves as a training ground for the sons of modern Illini. It has become a happy hunting ground for the pursuit of knowledge, while the traditions of the native Illini—noted for their bravery and fighting qualities—are echoed in the new regime through the contests in the Memorial Stadium, built for "Fighting Illini" and in commemoration of the heroic sons of Illinois in the World War. (Football program for Dad's Day, 1929)

Where would Illinois students have gotten their ideas about Indians? They had probably read the Zane Grey serials in *Ladies Home Journal* or some other popular novels set in the West. They had certainly seen a touring Wild West show. They might have visited the large Indian encampment outside Chicago in September 1923. Thousands of Chicagoans made the short trip to a forest preserve outside town to watch Indian dances, and students might have been among them. The encampment was held in conjunction with a meeting of the Society of American Indians, a group of prominent American Indian leaders. Despite the excitement over the camp, there was little interest in the society's actual meetings or its agenda for Indian affairs. The treasurer "expressed his regrets that it is only when he exhibits war dances and ancient ceremonies that the public evinces any interest in the Indian."

It's also likely that students had seen reprints of Frederic Remington's paintings and in school they had surely memorized and recited Longfellow's poem "Hiawatha." But if they had actually made Indian crafts or learned Indian outdoor skills, they had most likely done so as Boy Scouts. The Boy Scouts were organized in England in 1908 by Lord Robert Baden-Powell. Had Scouting been started by anyone else, the movement might not have taken off the way it did. But Robert Baden-Powell was the darling of the English public, a hero of the Boer War. As commander of the garrison at a small railroad depot called Mafeking, he held off a superior Boer force for over seven months. Not only did the small town survive the siege, under B-P, as they called him, residents kept up their morale with cricket matches, concert parties, and pony racing. With several war journalists trapped in the town, the British papers heard all about Baden-Powell's ingenuity. The stories were carried through the Boer lines by African runners and the papers printed every detail about his tin can grenades and imaginary minefields. To the British nation, worried that Englishmen no longer had what it took, B-P stood for British Pluck. When an English force finally got to Mafeking to end the siege, the British at home went wild. B-P, given the nickname "the Wolf who never sleeps" by the Zulu, became the youngest general in the British service. In fact, there are no wolves in Africa, so it seems likely that his African nickname really meant something like the "Insomniac Hyena." Nevertheless, Baden-Powell became the "Old Wolf" to generations of Scouts, and their motto, "Be Prepared," echoed their legendary leader's initials.

Interestingly, Baden-Powell's own particular hero was John Smith, the English colonial leader of Jamestown, Virginia, and the young general assured his admirers that he was descended from Smith. In American mythology, John Smith is remembered as the beloved of Pocahontas, a brave and beautiful Indian princess who risked her own life to save Smith from execution.

In America several youth organizations that taught woodcraft and Indian lore already existed. One of the most important was the Sons of Daniel Boone, founded by Daniel Beard, an artist, author of children's books, and outdoorsman. The other was the Woodcraft League of America, or "Seton's Indians," founded by the Canadian naturalist, author, and illustrator Ernest Thompson Seton. When the Boy Scouts spread to America in 1910, both organizations merged with the Scouts and both men became Scout leaders.

The *Handbook for Boys*, said to have been the second most popular book in the United States, contained inspirational Scout rhetoric, as well as informational chapters on bird identification, astronomy, mapmaking, and campcraft written by experts. First published in 1910, it was revised frequently and reprinted every year. An edition from 1914 opens with a letter from Chief Scout Ernest Thompson Seton, in which he describes a boy "wild with the love of the green outdoors." Another thing the boy loved was "the touch of romance" and "when he first found Fenimore Cooper's books he drank them in as one parched might drink at a spring." Scouting, says Seton, can fulfill these longings, make the boy a good athlete, and teach him loyalty, courage, and kindness.

Seton and Beard disagreed about the best role model for American boys. Beard preferred militaristic drills and idealized frontier scouts, while Seton argued for nature study and mythical Indians. As World War I approached, Beard's junior officer model won out. Some Scout leaders refused to give up their focus on Indians and left the organization to form Indian hobbyist clubs. Others formed auxiliary Scout groups that focused on Indian lore such as the Order of the Arrow, which still exists today.

The chapter on "Patriotism and Citizenship" in the 1914 Scout handbook contains a thirty-page history of the United States in which American Indians are never mentioned. In the chapter on "Chivalry," we learn that Scouts trace their inspiration back to King Arthur and his knights, who fought "false knights." Chivalry was next expressed through the Magna Carta, then in the French Revolution. Chivalry was brought to America "when the Pilgrim Fathers founded the American colonies."

> No set of men, however, showed this spirit of chivalry more than our pioneers beyond the Alleghenies. In their work and service they paralleled very closely the knights of the Round Table, but whereas Arthur's knights were dressed in suits of armor, the American pioneers were dressed in buckskin. They did, however, the very same things which ancient chivalry had done, clearing the forests of wild animals, suppressing the outlaws and bullies and thieves of their day, and enforcing a proper respect for women. Like the old knights they often were compelled to do their work amid scenes of great bloodshed, although they loved to live in peace. These American knights

and pioneers were generally termed backwoodsmen and scouts, and were men of distinguished appearance, of athletic build, of high moral character, and frequently, of firm religious convictions.

Frontiersmen, in the Boy Scout version of history, are the direct descendants of the knights of old. They are staunch, honest, brave, polite to women and old people, hospitable, kind, simple in dress and act. "They fought the Indians, not because they wished to, but because it was necessary to protect their wives and children from the raids of the savages."

Younger boys also wanted to be Scouts, so the Cub Scouts were organized. The Cubs had two metaphors. One was the wolf pack, with the cubs following their Old Wolf. Like so many Scout images, this referred back to Baden-Powell. The other metaphor was the Indian tribe. Cub Scouts belonged to the tribe of the Webelos. The Indian, according to the *Wolf Cubbook* of 1943, was self-controlled, quiet, loyal to death, and game. "He did not give up easily—he carried on. He endured pain and even torture without breaking."

Seton, although forced out of the Boy Scouts, continued to be active in other youth organizations like the Camp Fire Girls. His belief that it was healthy for children to play at being Indians was taken up by clubs and summer camps across the country. The Indian lore or Indian hobbyist movement for adults grew out of these clubs and remained closely allied to the Boy Scouts. For Scouts, a merit badge in Indian lore was always an important and popular goal.

Beginning in 1927 the Boy Scout *Handbook for Boys* contained a section with detailed instructions on how to make tepees, tom-toms, bows and arrows, and moccasins. This portion of the book was written by Ralph Hubbard, a biologist and writer who taught Indian dance on his ranch near Boulder, Colorado. Like Seton, Hubbard believed in the value of learning about Indian culture and he served as an intermediary between Indians on the one hand and Boy Scouts and Indian hobbyists on the other.

Hubbard was the son of a remarkable couple, Elbert and Bertha Hubbard. Together they founded Roycroft, an Arts and Crafts village near Buffalo based on the ideas of William Morris. Roycrofters worked alongside their employers to produce hand bound books and mission furniture and had access to a library and free classes, lectures, and concerts. Elbert Hubbard himself had very little formal schooling. His wife and her sisters educated him after dinner each evening and he was so determined to learn that they often sat around the table until midnight. Their student went on to become a successful writer, an immensely popular lecturer, and the publisher of a monthly magazine of down-to-earth commentary called *The Philistine*.

Ralph Hubbard taught Indian dance to Boy Scouts and Indian hobbyists and was revered by both groups. This portrait, taken at the world Scout jamboree outside Copenhagen, Denmark, in 1924 was part of a souvenir album of the jamboree. Courtesy of the Boy Scouts of America.

The Hubbards' mixture of radicalism, Arts and Crafts utopianism, and conservative populism drew a wonderfully eclectic assortment of prominent people to Roycroft, and their children grew up having listened around the hand-built dinner table to Rudyard Kipling, John Muir, Ernest Thompson Seton, Joel Chandler Harris, Stephen Crane, Harriet Beecher Stowe, George Washington Carver, and Eugene Debs, to name just a few. The family was proud of a legend that an early Hubbard had married a Mohawk girl and sent her back to England to finishing school. Another cultural influence was the nearby Seneca reservation. Elbert's father had been the only doctor on the Seneca reservation for many years and his mother had been a schoolteacher there. In addition, many of the people of the town were Seneca or part-Seneca. Elbert's middle son, Ralph, grew up in this world. According to his biographer, Nellie Snyder Yost, what appealed most to Ralph about Seneca culture was the dancing. "I was only hip high to a dustpan when I learned the basic steps of Indian dancing. I loved to watch them dance, and then I'd go home and practice the steps until I had them memorized."

Ralph and his younger siblings left Roycroft abruptly with their mother when she sued for divorce in 1902. Their father remarried in 1904. When Ralph was in high school his father gave him a railroad ticket to visit the battlefield where Custer had made his last stand thirty years before. His Crow guides searched the tall grass of the battlefield and filled their hats with coins, parts of watches, buttons, penknives, eyeglasses, and buckles, which they gave him. Smitten with the West, Ralph homesteaded a claim in Montana and then sold the homestead to buy a ranch outside Boulder, Colorado. Although Elbert was wealthy, he refused to help Ralph pay for college; Elbert had attended Harvard for one semester and concluded that a university education was a waste of time. (Perhaps his wife and her sisters had done such a good job over the dinner table that Harvard was superfluous. If so, he never seems to have said so directly.) Ralph struggled to come up with the money to attend the University of Colorado while everyone around him assumed that the son of Elbert Hubbard did not need financial help.

One day Ralph saw a group of students clustered around a newspaper posted on a wall. It was 1915 and the news story was the sinking of the *Lusitania*. Named in the headlines as the most prominent passenger was Elbert Hubbard. Fiercely opposed to war and never short on ego, Hubbard was traveling to

American Boy Scouts at the world Scout jamboree outside Copenhagen, Denmark, in 1924 dressed for a performance of Indian dances. Their leader, Ralph Hubbard, kneels at the far right. Lester Leutwiler, the first Chief Illiniwek, stands in the second row on the far left. Courtesy of the Boy Scouts of America.

Germany on a self-appointed mission to talk some sense into the Kaiser when the *Lusitania* was sunk by the Germans.

Ralph enlisted in the army and was sent overseas with a medical corps. After the war, as they filled trenches, he was gassed when a bulldozer hit a canister of chlorine gas. He recovered and stayed in France until 1920 identifying American remains for return to the United States.

When Hubbard arrived home from France in 1920 plans were already under way for the first world jamboree of Boy Scouts. Hubbard was tapped to organize American Indian dancing and crafts as part of the American Scouts' presentation. As a member of a prominent family, and as someone Ernest Thompson Seton had known since boyhood, Ralph Hubbard was a natural choice for the Boy Scout leadership. He costumed ninety boys, and their "pony war dances" were one of the highlights of the first international jamboree in London. The group put on two performances a day and went on to perform at the 1920 Olympics in Antwerp. In 1924 and 1929 Ralph Hubbard again went overseas with the Boy Scouts to orchestrate the American Indian dance performances. Meanwhile Hubbard had built a boys' camp and rough resort on his ranch in Colorado. He constructed a large dining room and living room, set up tepees, and acquired a herd of saddle horses. Besides dancing, his summer course offered riding, Indian lore, and natural history. His mother and sister helped out. Hubbard had other helpers at the ranch, too, cowpunchers who taught packing and riding, and Navajo or Pueblo men who taught drumming. The rest of the year he traveled around the country, often with his Indian assistants, teaching at Scout camps and "city jamborees." The programs based on American Indian culture were a huge success at these Scouting events, and the allure of all things Indian was one of Scouting's most powerful tools to recruit young boys.

Hubbard went on to work in the movie industry, making costumes for westerns. He invented his own technique for attaching the eagle feathers in trailing headdresses. Both Indians and Hollywood costumers paid high prices for them. His feather bonnets are also in museum collections. When he watched western movies, Hubbard claimed that he could always recognize his own bonnets in the close-up shots.

During the Depression he organized and led a Civilian Conservation Corps (CCC) group of young Indian men who traveled from reservation to reservation, demonstrating Indian dancing and singing. He was in demand as a teacher for Indian hobbyists, non-Indians who gathered on weekends to dress like Indians and learn their dances. Hubbard also organized and participated in dance performances at the Broadmoor Hotel in Colorado Springs. "Most of the Indians around Colorado Springs were from the Southwest, but all of them could do enough Sioux steps and dances to look good. If any of them didn't have costumes of their own, we would put them into the fine outfits we had and head for the Broadmoor," he recalled.

One night Ralph found himself dancing next to a skilled dancer, a Ute. "Then I asked him how come he was doing Sioux dances, and he told me he had been with a circus that took any Indian dancers it could find." Another night, Ralph found himself next to a Navajo and they became friendly. Ralph asked "where he had learned this kind of dancing, and if he had ever danced with professionals, or show Indians." The Navajo man had worked in Hollywood.

Hubbard lost his ranch during the Depression. Without it, he was no longer able to make a living organizing Indian dance performances and teaching Indian dance. He became a biology teacher who taught his students anatomy by dissecting first a bison and then a steer to see the anatomical differences. He also taught them how to make sinew and to tan the buffalo hide, skills he'd learned from Indian teachers. Hubbard remained active in the Boy Scouts and was awarded the Silver Buffalo Award for his contributions to Scouting.

A collector all his life, he set up museums of Indian handicrafts and the fur trade at Medora, North Dakota, and at Wounded Knee. The Wounded Knee museum burned down during the American Indian Movement occupation in 1973. "That AIM bunch set all Indian progress back fifty years," said Hubbard. He was convinced that all AIM activists were criminals. Clyde Bellecourt, one of the AIM activists who occupied Wounded Knee, remembers the museum clearly when I ask. He says it was filled with beaded shirts and other beautiful objects pawned at the trading post by poor, mostly elderly people. "It was more like a Museum of Exploitation," says Bellecourt, a large man with a round face and long black hair. The museum burned when the village was fired on by the FBI and U.S. marshals, but AIM had removed the items before the fire. "We returned the things to the families if we could find them," Bellecourt answers when asked about the museum's contents. With a smile, he points to a wide silver band inset with coral on his wrist. "Some we wear."

Ralph Hubbard was a boy when his parents took him to Buffalo Bill's Wild West. Cody recognized Elbert Hubbard in the audience. Stopping his horse directly in front of Bertha Hubbard, Cody gave the animal a signal and the horse "went down on one knee, with his other front leg straight out before him, and put his head down to the ground in a beautiful bow to Mother, while Mr. Cody swept the arena sands with that great white sombrero of his that was big as a tub. It was playboy stuff but very spectacular, as all of the Colonel's actions were."

Cody also gave Elbert a photograph, a long portrait of himself and his Indian performers. Most were Oglala or Standing Rock Sioux. Ralph inherited this picture and had it enlarged. By showing it to Indians in Pine Ridge, he was able to identify most of the men. One Indian friend identified his father standing next to Cody, and it turned out that the blanket his father was wearing in the photograph had ended up among Ralph's possessions. The man had fought at Little Bighorn and might have worn his blanket on the battlefield. The photograph given to his father by Buffalo Bill Cody remained an important talisman for Hubbard all his life. This is understandable, for it linked his brilliant and unpredictable father, lost at sea, with Buffalo Bill, Ralph's predecessor, the original organizer of Indian dance performances. His parents had created the world of Roycroft, and its foundry, bindery, and furniture shop were magical places for a child. But that world was lost to him when his family divided, and in his adult life, Ralph replaced the idealism of Roycroft with the mythical Old West and American Indian culture, especially that of the Sioux. Here he found camaraderie and hospitality like he'd known at Roycroft and a similar respect for artisans and beautiful handmade objects. The photograph was a physical link between the two worlds.

If we trace the genealogy of Chief Illiniwek, we find that it leads directly back to Wild West shows, the Indian lore movement, and Scouting. Dan Beard's Recipe for Scouting read as follows:

Take a bowl full of unbounded love for boys, one pint of absolute faith in American institutions, two tea cups of American pioneer blood, one tablespoonful of thrills, one tablespoonful of romance, two heaping tablespoons of adventure, a teaspoonful of Indian traditions, a tea cup of vigor and grit of the Puritans, a tea cup of chivalry of the Cavaliers, a quart of the idealism of Thoreau, John Burroughs and Henry Van Dyke, one heaping cup of sentiment, and the whole seasoned well with patriotism and character and stirred up with the Golden Rule, after which sprinkle well with the Stars and Stripes and SERVE RED HOT!

The man who brought that "teaspoonful of Indian traditions" to the Boy Scouts was not an Indian himself, but the young man raised to revere handmade things and populist ideas at Roycroft. Ralph Hubbard taught thousands of Scouts how to make their own tepees and moccasins, and since he didn't believe they could learn to dance from a book, he traveled the country teaching them what he knew about American Indian dancing. He must have been a natural dancer. He never sought to study any other dance form, but stuck with his first love, American Indian dance, all his life. In some ways this was a positive thing, both for Hubbard and for the many Boy Scouts who profited from his teaching. At a time when no one else bothered to teach American Indian culture to non-Indian children, the Boy Scouts valued certain aspects of it and made them the focus of intensive study. However, it is important to point out that the Boy Scouts preferred a white American as their Indian expert. Indian men were employed only as assistants. Most Americans preferred to have American Indian customs explained to them by other white Americans. These "interpreters" had often studied with Indian informants or lived among Indians. Their depth of understanding and knowledge varied widely. Some were knowledgeable and responsible. Others had only a superficial understanding of the subjects they taught. They filled in the blanks with their own inventions. Many profited from careers as interpreters of Indian culture.

Lester Leutwiler, the first Chief Illiniwek, was one of the many Boy Scouts drawn to the study of Indian lore. The son of a University of Illinois engineering professor, Leutwiler, an Eagle Scout, was chosen to represent Champaign-Urbana in the world Scout jamboree of 1924, held in Denmark. In a large field outside Copenhagen the Scouts tried something new: camping out the way the Indians did when they traveled with Wild West shows. Hubbard says, "that was quite a sight, too, five thousand Scouts from thirty-three nations and many British colonies, all busy taking care of their many camps." It became the model for future jamborees.

The next summer Lester Leutwiler stayed on Hubbard's ranch in Colorado. He spent two months with fifteen or sixteen other boys, "living like Indians," sleeping in tepees, traveling the mountains by horseback, and climbing cliffs to eagle nests to get feathers. This was where he learned the Indian dances he later used with the band. Like many Americans in the Indian Lore movement, Leutwiler took the study of American Indian culture seriously.

After Leutwiler graduated, a student named Webber Borchers took over the Chief Illiniwek role and performed at the home games in 1929 in a homemade costume. Borchers had also learned Indian dancing in the Boy Scouts and in the summer of 1929 he led a Scout troop to the third world jamboree, held in a large park in England. In a memoir deposited in the town archives of Decatur, Illinois, Borchers recounts that he had the boys make up Indian outfits and that he took a tepee, as well as a "calumet peace pipe" that belonged to his family. The Prince of Wales himself came into the tepee and smoked the peace pipe with them.

Borchers campaigned among the fraternities to raise money for a real costume, but times were hard and the fraternities had recently built substantial houses. He "had a lot of bean meals" but didn't raise much cash. So he approached a Champaign clothing merchant, who donated five hundred dollars for a beautifully beaded chief's outfit, and Chief Illiniwek began to travel with the band.

The fourth Chief Illiniwek also learned Indian dancing in the Boy Scouts, and the fifth, John Grable, was another Hubbard protégé. Grable spent three summers on Hubbard's ranch, learning and teaching Indian lore and working as a horse wrangler. For two summers after that, Grable taught handicraft and Indian lore at a Boy Scout camp in Indiana. Grable recounted in a newspaper interview that during the summer of 1937 he and Hubbard were the only two white dancers with two hundred Indian dancers at the Cheyenne Days celebration. This rodeo and fair has been held continuously since 1897 in Cheyenne, Wyoming. Both Indian dancers and cowboys participated in the fairs, precursors of Wild West shows, modern-day rodeos, and competitive performance pow-wows. Halftime and pregame performances like those at Florida State and Illinois are also descendants of frontier festivals. On the prairies of central Illinois, with the state's largest educational institution asserting that Chief Illiniwek is a sacred invocation of the vanished Illinois, and in Tallahassee, where the rider who carries a flaming lance is supposed to represent the Seminole war leader Osceola, it is forgotten or ignored that these performers trace their genealogy not to the Illinois or Seminole tribes but to midway exhibits, Wild West performers, Indian hobbyists, and Boy Scouts.

Folded Leaves

What was college like for a student in the 1920s? Arriving on the train at the University of Illinois, new students might have taken the streetcar straight to the YMCA or YWCA to get lists of accredited boardinghouses. Female students automatically became members of the Women's League organized by the YWCA and were encouraged to attend the league's Wednesday teas. For a fee, students could join the Illinois Union, which gave them access to the union building's facilities and activities. Committees at the union planned dances every weekend, mixers and smokers for the men, torch light parades and pep meetings before games, and twilight sings in the springtime. The progress of the football team, whenever it played an out-of-town game, was reported by telegraph directly to an office in the union.

Students who could afford the extra costs of membership and who were chosen joined social fraternities and sororities. The Greek system was one of the largest in the country. Upperclassmen had special privileges and there was an elaborate system of hats to distinguish the classes. In the spring, the freshmen built a bonfire and burned their green caps. Tradition forbade stepping on the bronze plaque in the floor of Lincoln Hall with the Gettysburg Address imprinted on it. Groups of men passing on campus, whether they knew each other or not, were expected to call out, "Hello Boys!"

Good sportsmanship received a long entry in the student handbook. "At the end of each home football game, whether the team has won or lost, it is the custom of the student body to stand and sing Illinois Loyalty before leaving the field.

"Furthermore, it is a custom that the spectators at all games remain until the final whistle blows out of courtesy to the players, no matter what the score may be."

Rules included no smoking on campus, no cutting corners, no walking on the grass or defacing shrubbery or buildings, no drinking, no betting, no hazing. The YWCA handbook had even stricter "resolutions" for the Women's League.

> Resolved, That strolling on the south campus or in other unfrequented
> places after dark is unwise.
> Resolved, That no member of this League shall knowingly attend a social af-
> fair where there is no chaperon present.
> Resolved, That the practice of patronizing restaurants late in the evening is
> to be condemned except in the University district.
> Resolved, That sentiments be created against cheap vaudeville.

It's not clear to me exactly how the young women were to "create senti-ments against" the particular kind of vaudeville considered cheap. Banjos were the rage on campus in the 1920s. Al Jolson's movie *The Jazz Singer*, in which he appeared in blackface, was popular all over the country and students picked up on the form and imitated it at their talent competitions. The 1920s were an era of migration to urban areas for both blacks and whites and these sudden changes created a nostalgia for all things rural. The blackface acts at talent shows and popular songs about darkies, like the "Illinois Medley" below, taken from a 1926 songbook, were imitations of what was playing at the small local theaters and in the movies.

ILLINOIS MEDLEY

"Don't send my boy to Harvard,"
  A dying mother said;
Don't send my boy to Michigan,
  I'd rather he were dead;

But send my boy to Illinois,
  'Tis better than Cornell;
But rather than Chicago,
  I'd see my boy in ———.

In the evening by the moonlight
  You can hear those banjo's ringing;
In the evening by the moonlight
  You can hear those darkies singing.

Os-kee-wow-wow, Illinois;
  Our eyes are all on you;
Os-kee-wow-wow, Illinois,
  Wave your Orange and your Blue.
    Rah-Rah!

Then cheer that good ole Illini line,
  Spur them on to victory;
Let's give them nine men, cheer all the time,
  We'll show our loyalty.
Then fight, fight, for it's victory or die,
Keep that Orange and Blue waving high,
All you good Illini,
Cheer all the time,
Cheer that Illini line.

(Illini Song Book, published by the Illinois Union, 1926)

While the students at Illinois and other campuses were reveling in the sporty new collegiate culture, attending football games in plus fours and lumpy raccoon coats, joining fraternities and sororities, strumming on banjos, and dancing to touring orchestras, many American Indians, most of whom were still living on reservations, had serious problems. The Dawes Allotment Act, passed in 1887, which converted tribal land into individual homesteads, had resulted in many Indian people being defrauded of their land. Poverty-stricken, with high infant mortality and high levels of tuberculosis and other infectious diseases, many American Indians were barely surviving. The Bureau of Indian Affairs was full of corrupt political appointees, and humanitarian church groups were pressuring the government with their own agendas for Indian education and assimilation. Americans in 1926 agreed that Indian Americans had serious problems and most were willing to concede that the government had contributed to those problems. The disagreements came over what to do about them—or whether to do anything at all. Convinced that Indians had been destined to vanish for a long time anyway, many Americans simply felt that their time had come.

But those were real Indians and their problems were neither romantic nor exciting. Playing Indian was more appealing. Societies, fraternal orders, lodges, and clubs flourished in the twenties, and not only on college campuses. And the more mysterious the rituals and passwords, the better. Thirty million Americans (half the adult population) were active members of secret orders. For these fraternal organizations, which were often both social and service-oriented, nothing added a touch of romance better than invented Indian names, Indian rituals, and Indian clothing. Although real tribes were in serious trouble, white Americans flocked to join play tribes like the Improved Order of Red Men.

Charles Merz, who wrote humorous social commentary for *Harper's Magazine*, poked affectionate fun at Americans of the 1920s whose lives were becoming increasingly standardized and who responded by a longing for glamour and romance and a nostalgia for frontier days. His generation, he pointed out, loved filling stations, which were their version of frontier outposts, lived in misplaced Spanish adobe haciendas or Italian villas, admired newly minted heroes like

Charles Lindbergh, the product of the new "hero-making industry," joined lodges with secret passwords, adored the silver screen, and played golf in plus fours. Merz called golf "a frontier game in the best frontier spirit of America, a game of fording streams, climbing hills for the lay of the land, hacking a new path, if need be, through the underbrush, and pushing on from goal to goal. . . . The Indians are dead. There are no Blackfeet left to conquer. What is modern man to boast about if not his golf scores?"

Merz also turns his pen on the secret societies. "When the password is given and the inner door swings back, it is upon a world as different from the world outside as ingenuity can make it." Merz is tolerant of these desires in a world dominated by "mass production," "carbon copies," and language like "yours received and contents noted." He asks our indulgence if "once a month the Red Men gather at the stake and (Ritual p. 30) the Junior Sagamore cries, 'Warriors, prepare for the execution! Braves, make ready and pile high the fagots!' Man cannot live on bread alone—or on a diet of index files and office routine." According to Merz, that inner door to the secret lodge will "continue to swing as long as life is drab enough for grown men to play Indian."

William Maxwell, the respected American writer who had a long career as a *New Yorker* editor, also evokes the twenties in a lovely and lyrical novel set at the University of Illinois during the academic year 1927–28. *The Folded Leaf* gives us a vivid picture of the campus—the Broad Walk lined with overarching elms, the rooming houses where boys rented "study rooms," the fraternities and sororities and the allure they held for students who lacked the money or the status required.

The book tells the story of two boys who meet in high school in Chicago. Lymie Peters and Spud Latham are complete opposites, and they are also 1920s archetypes: the thin-chested intellectual boy (a future poet or professor) and the handsome towheaded boxer with his physical grace and masculine confidence. Both boys share a sense of loss—thin quiet Lymie for his mother, who is dead, and muscular Spud for the Wisconsin lake town he has been forced to leave, and both are angry at their ineffectual fathers. Somehow the two bond; they complete each other. After high school, they take the train to the university and rent a room in a boardinghouse they call "302," run by an antiques dealer. "302" is a sprawling old wooden house with wide verandas. They share a "study room" and they sleep with all the other renters in an unheated dormitory under the roof. For five dollars a week they eat three meals a day at a boarding club three blocks away. Rounding out their trio is Sally Forbes, a tomboy whose father is a philosophy professor, but who has not inherited her parents' predilection for old books, old prints, and old furniture. Visits to Sally's parents' house give Maxwell a chance to describe the professorial milieu of Urbana. Sally's mother is "at home" on the second Thursday of each month in an ivy-covered stucco bungalow.

> The curtains were drawn, the lamps were lit. In the dining room there were tall lighted candles in silver candlesticks and the table was covered with a lace tablecloth and that in turn by stacks of hand-painted plates, rows of shining silverware, and platters of fancy sandwiches. . . . Everyone there knew everyone else and it was a good deal like progressive whist, or some game like that. You went up to any group you felt like talking to. They opened automatically like an oyster at low tide, and there you were, allowed to pick up the threads of the old conversation or start a new one.

This description of the neighborhood where Professor and Mrs. Forbes live will sound familiar to anyone who has visited Urbana. Dubbed the faculty ghetto, the neighborhood of two-story houses still has an old-fashioned charm, with brick streets, globe street lamps, and spreading street trees. In the mornings, professors bicycle or walk toward the campus, carrying briefcases, and in the evening, the walkers and bikers return in the opposite direction. These days, rather than hosting at-home teas, the women of the neighborhood are likely to be colleagues at the university. My own children have grown up in this neighborhood; experience has taught them that while they might be engineers, lawyers, or concert pianists, most adults are also professors.

Lymie is clearly a failure at sports, delicate and fearful, with bad posture. Spud, on the other hand, seems to be a golden boy, robust and handsome. His shoes are always polished and his pants neatly creased. He is courted by a good fraternity although he hasn't the money to join. Spud is a talented boxer, the next-best thing to a football player, and he works out in the university's gymnasium every afternoon, among acrobats and gymnasts. But the aggressive streak that makes him good is also his downfall. In his first tournament, on his way to capturing the Golden Gloves in Chicago, although he is winning, he can't refrain from hitting his opponent as he is going down. Spud is fouled out and the audience boos him as he stands dazed in the ring.

In one scene in Sally's father's study, Lymie, Sally's father, and another professor admire a Chinese lacquer screen. On one side are inlaid peonies in a vase, on the other a battle scene with charging horsemen, flying arrows, and rolling heads. The other professor turns to Lymie and comments, "The mutual attraction of gentleness and violence, don't you see, Mr. Peters?" It is the book's theme.

Young men of this time were thought to have a certain wildness, which needed to be tamed. One night the college boys build a huge bonfire on a field south of the stadium to celebrate the arrival of spring. When the flames die down, they form into a mob. "Behind their movements there seemed to be some as yet unannounced purpose, some act of violence which would flare up all of a sudden and make the flames turn pale by comparison with it." They head toward downtown Champaign, toward the Orpheum Theater, now a children's science museum. In a park, they pass a student with his date. They beat up the boy, tearing off his shirt and giving him a black eye and a bloody mouth. The girl's skirts they tie over her head. Then, knocking the boy to the ground, they push the girl on top of him, and leave them. Maxwell calls it a "token rape"; it gives the mob confidence to go on. Next they pull a trolley off its overhead wire and rock it from side to side. At this point the dean of men appears: "He was a slight, almost boyish man of sixty-two. His hair and his mustache were snow white. He looked kind, humorous, and fatherly, but the effect on the boys was as if a rattlesnake had materialized right in front of them on the streetcar tracks."

He calls out their names. Chastised, they disperse. The dean is modeled on Thomas Arkle Clark, who was dean of men at Illinois from 1901 to 1931. In fact, Clark, called Tommy Arkle by everyone on campus, invented the notion of a dean of men. He was the dean of all deans of men. He believed it was his responsibility to provide personal guidance for the young men, and once he had taken on a boy as a case, he wrote him letters and dropped in for visits. If a boy needed a job he found him one; if he couldn't pay his rent, Dean Clark interceded with his landlady. If he got into real trouble, Clark kept it out of the papers. He kept records of every Illinois student serving in World War I and wrote personal letters to many of them. For some he even knitted sweaters. When boys were called into his office, he leaned back in his big mahogany chair and asked a double-edged question, something like, "Do they sell liquor in that restaurant you were drinking in last night?" or "Whose car was that you parked in front of 707 Johns Street Tuesday night?"

How did the dean, based on Tommy Arkle, know that the boys were out that night rocking streetcars? His arrival in the fictional scene certainly mirrored fact on the campus, because he knew everything. Did Tommy Arkle have spies? If so, who were they? And if not, how did he do it? These were questions that were frequently asked on the campus during the 1920s, but the question that comes to my mind is how he managed to keep an eye on all those boys and turn out, at the same time, nine books, hundreds of articles, and more than a thousand essays full of advice for them. A former rhetoric professor, he published a weekly column in the student newspaper called "Sunday Eight o'Clock" full of inspiration and advice, and many of his columns were syndicated for national distribution. One book was entitled *Discipline and the Derelict*. Another book explained how to write a proper letter. The students simply couldn't escape Tommy Arkle. When he wasn't coming around the corner in person, stylishly dressed, they were knocking into his prose.

In 1926, the year that Chief Illiniwek first danced at halftime, the biggest debate on campus was whether students should be allowed to have cars. "There is moral danger in the car," Tommy Arkle wrote to parents. He succeeded in banning them. Student editorial writers complained that his apron-strings system was too paternalistic, although they couldn't help but admire its efficiency. When Clark retired, the *Decatur Herald* wrote,

> The question of whether Dean Thomas Arkle Clark, who last year ended a 20 year vigil over the morals of University of Illinois students, actually set a force of spies to watching his charges, or whether the canny little headmaster found out all that stuff himself, is a question which has interested a lot of people, amused more, and which arises naturally out of that other question, all of what stuff?
>
> Before the dean retired from office last fall, he had built up a reputation for being just a little more than omniscient.

At the end of Maxwell's novel, Lymie, shut out of Spud's life, tries to commit suicide with a razor. Before he bleeds to death, he is found by a student coming home from a late night out. When the dean of men calls his father, not only does he tell him what has happened, he also dictates which train he should take from Chicago. When Lymie's father arrives, hurt because Lymie has not left a farewell note for him, he goes into the dean's office. The dean sat behind a heavy walnut desk "under a portrait of himself by a distinguished American painter. The money for this portrait had been raised partly by undergraduate subscription, partly by well-to-do alumni."

Tommy Arkle did have a large portrait of himself behind his desk. It had been installed in 1927, just as Maxwell describes. It is another detail that reminds me how distant a country the 1920s is, for Clark traveled to Cape Cod and stayed a month so that he could sit for the painter thirty-one times for three hours each sitting. It is hard to imagine any working person today devoting that amount of time to having a portrait painted.

The twenties ushered in the modern world that we know. Stunned by the losses of World War I, young people were determined to embrace modernity and to leave the trappings of the nineteenth century behind. They were more likely to have grown up in urban neighborhoods than their parents, and they had more freedom. The older generation, coaches like Zuppke and deans like Tommy Arkle, wanted to raise a generation of young men who would not succumb to the dissipation of urban life. Teddy Roosevelt, an asthmatic, sickly child, had overcome poor health and the temptations of luxury to become a lover of outdoor life, a pioneer, a Rough Rider, a scout, a man with the character required to lead the country. How to impart to the college men of the 1920s fighting spirit like Teddy's, teach them to be both gentlemanly and tough? It is no wonder that the struggle for balance between violence and gentleness became the theme of Maxwell's novel about his college years, for parallel messages about manhood were everywhere in the society of his time.

Athletics was one solution. Programs like the Boy Scouts provided another. Both organizations created motivational figures, men from the past who could be held up as models. Scouting held up the knights of old, the Athenian youth, the frontiersman, the Indian chief, and of course, Baden-Powell himself, the outnumbered soldier under siege who doesn't give up. Athletics at Illinois turned to an imaginary and idealized Indian leader. Chief Illiniwek thrived in this role. Tough and brave, tenacious, this exemplary Indian doesn't go out to seek revenge for the sake of violence or personal glory. He fights to the death—but only to protect his family and the women and children of the tribe. Like the "braves" who never returned from the trenches of World War I, Chief Illiniwek has learned the meaning of duty and sacrifice. He is willing to subsume his individual desires for the benefit of his tribe. The young men who stand and salute him are reminded to do the same.

Maxwell gives the address of the boardinghouse he describes so affectionately in *The Folded Leaf* as 302 South Street. There is no South Street, and I knew that he might have changed the number as well as the street name. But since the boys all called the place "302" and since it had been such an important address in Maxwell's life, I thought it possible that he might have kept the number and changed only the name of the street. So I walked all the 300 blocks, heading past my children's elementary school to the streets at the north end of the neighborhood where there are more student rentals. Maxwell describes the big house as painted white, with fretwork porches that ran around the front and sides. When Lymie and Spud go up to the house, they peer through frosted glass and twist a Victorian doorbell. One of the boys, sleeping on the flat roof of the top porch on a hot night, rolled off and broke an arm.

As I walked, I thought of an argument I'd had with one of my best friends over *The Folded Leaf.* She hated it, which surprised me, but as we talked I came to understand why she felt so strongly. Her family is Polish. In the book Spud refers to some other boys as "bohunks," a word that passed me right by. I had no idea that it was a derogatory term for Polish people, although I certainly recognized "nigger" and "wop" when they appeared in the text.

My reply to her was that it was a book about Illinois in the twenties, a locale in which we do not live. Maxwell's boys speak its language. To have them speak otherwise is to leave us with a romanticized or bowdlerized version of his times. But finally, the book had hurt her feelings, Maxwell had written the painful words, and for that, she rejected both.

One day not long ago I was browsing through an antiques fair with my daughter when we came across a folder of sheet music from the 1930s—"The Ten

Little Niggers," with sambo cartoons on the cover. My daughter drew back with a look of shock on her face. She turned to me in consternation. In her ten years of life she has learned about Martin Luther King and Rosa Parks and she has heard my stories of the segregated South. But the images on the yellowed paper had a power far beyond any of my recounted memories. There must be a way to teach her, without demeaning people, that our society has changed, that grievances were real, that these images and words were once accepted and acceptable.

At each house numbered 302, I was disappointed. Each one was too new, too small, or had no porches. I was still carrying on my end of the argument with my friend. How can you criticize a book for giving us an accurate portrait of another time? It's like ethnocentrism, only having to do with our place in history, rather than our position in the cultural universe. Unfortunately, she wasn't there to answer.

Then, just when it seemed that my walk was a crazy and hopeless quest, I did find a large old house numbered 302, a divided-up, friendly-looking house, with wide porches that sagged and a flat roof on the second floor where it was possible that a boy, sleeping on a hot night, could roll off and suffer only a broken arm. There was no frosted glass door, but the top windows, all of odd, interesting shapes, had divided lead panes along their edges. The paint was peeling and the white picket fence leaned, but 302 West High still held onto a worn, weathered charm. The north side, where Spud and Lymie might have shared a room, now looked out over lawyers' and therapists' offices.

Of course I'll never know if I really did find Maxwell's "302." It may be the wrong house altogether, but whenever I pass it now, I picture the tussling boys and the aggravated landlord with his antiques business and yippy spaniel, helpless to keep order. I imagine Maxwell later, seeing the house in his mind as he writes about Lymie and Spud, trying to make sense of that turning time in his own life, when he left boyhood behind.

The Wild West

For most Americans, to be Indian is to be Sioux. The final wars between the U.S. army and the Great Sioux Nation took place after photography had been invented, and images of the fighting Sioux were published in popular newspapers and dime novels. After their defeat, Sioux men toured with Wild West shows to reenact their battles with the U.S. cavalry. A combination circus, rodeo, and traveling outdoor theater, Wild West shows were enormously popular from the 1880s through the 1920s. The originator of the Wild West show and the person always connected with it is William Frederick Cody, known as Buffalo Bill. Buffalo Bill always pointed out that he had really lived the life he depicted. He claimed to have ridden for the Pony Express at fourteen and to have been a dispatch rider for the Union army when he was fifteen. He got his nickname working for the Union Pacific Railroad. He killed over four thousand head of buffalo in eight months to feed the railroad construction crews. In the Indian wars, he served the army as a scout, dispatch rider, and guide and was a veteran of sixteen Indian fights.

Buffalo Bill refused to call his show a circus. Nor did he like "Wild West show," for both suggested the imaginary theatrical world. He sometimes allowed Wild West Exhibition, but most often when Buffalo Bill and his performers came to town, they were simply the Wild West. He combined a genius for showmanship with a reputation for authenticity. The audience, sitting on bleachers under a tent, were convinced they were watching the history of western expansion.

Buffalo Bill's Wild West, like modern sports events, began with "The Star-Spangled Banner" played by the troupe's own band. Then there was the grand entrance of all the performers, not just cowboys and Indians, but the "Rough

Cover of the program for Buffalo Bill's Wild West at the World's Colombian Exposition in 1893. Although it is reproduced here in black and white, the original cover was printed in color. The program included excerpts of letters attacking Buffalo Bill's treatment of Indians and his defense. Courtesy of the Chicago Historical Society.

Riders of the World." As many as four hundred riders came cantering in. Last of all, Buffalo Bill himself rode into the arena, dressed in beautiful fringed buckskin. Audiences adored him. Tall, mustachioed, with long gray hair flowing from under his trademark Stetson hat, he always played to the top rows of the bleachers.

Five to seven separate acts followed. The riding and roping tricks were called "cowboy fun." They developed out of contests at Fourth of July celebrations in western towns and eventually evolved into the modern rodeo. A performance of Indian dancing often separated events. Then there were short theatrical pieces—an attack on a settler's cabin, for example, or an attack by "marauding Indians" on a wagon train. All attacks were repulsed by Buffalo Bill, the frontier hero, who galloped in with his scouts in the nick of time.

Sharpshooting was another popular act. Annie Oakley was the best marksman ever to tour in a Wild West show; she was also the audience favorite. Smiling shyly, she put a bullet through a dime tossed in the air, split the thin edge of a playing card, and shot off the burning tip of her husband's cigarette at thirty paces. She could sight into a mirror with her back turned and shatter every one of the hundred glass balls thrown into the air.

More theatrical reenactments followed: a buffalo hunt, a Pony Express ride. There were also horse races and demonstrations of horsemanship. The show always included a scenario about the Deadwood mail stage traveling from Deadwood to Cheyenne and being attacked by hostile Sioux. Buffalo Bill always rode up just in time to save the stage. The grand finale was often Custer's Last Stand. To add to the drama, the performers who came to town had been participants in the real-life battles they now acted out. The actors were historical figures and vice versa. The stagecoach they attacked was the very one, riddled with bullet holes, that once ran on the Deadwood line.

Just as exciting as the actual performance was the Indian encampment. Imagine a large group of Sioux setting up their tepees outside a midwestern town in 1907. No wonder the boys flocked to the fairgrounds. Part of being a Wild West show performer was accepting that strangers wandered through your camp, stared at you as you ate, and even looked inside your tepee.

Wild West shows began as the wild frontier life that they depicted was ending. There were no more limitless expanses of land for the taking, no more bands of nomadic Indians. Buffalo Bill took American nostalgia for the frontier experience and played it for all it was worth. Traveling through America with one circus or another, or on his own, he spread in his wake the image of the West as a romantic place. Cowboys, who had been hired men tied down to boring jobs with livestock, were transformed into kings of the wild frontier. Indians, reduced to the common denominator of warlike men on horseback in Plains attire, were the other half of an equation that added up to the romantic sum of how Americans, particularly American men, wanted to see themselves.

For Indians who were nostalgic about the old days on the Plains, life as a Wild West performer had tangible benefits. Reservation life was difficult and Indians who did not accept forced assimilation were penalized. In the arena of the Wild West show, Indian dancing was encouraged, and riding and shooting skills were valued. And being a principal in a Wild West show was one way to gain the ears and eyes of the public. When they traveled with Buffalo Bill, Indian leaders met with princes and heads of state and gave interviews. Newspaper readers were treated to the rare experience of an Indian point of view. In addition, when these men returned to the reservation, their wages allowed them to make large shows of generosity, which consolidated their influence.

Sitting Bull toured twice, the second time with Buffalo Bill. A poster showed the two men clasping hands and advertised, "Former Foes, Now Friends." The famous chief never took part in reenacting battles. He rode in the parades that preceded the performances and greeted visitors at his tepee. At a performance in Philadelphia, a young Lakota man on leave from Carlisle Indian School was in the audience. Later he recounted that Sitting Bull gave a serious speech about the need for Indian children to receive an education. The "translation," however, was an account of the Little Bighorn, turned into an Indian ambush, complete with many lurid and bloody details about the slaying of Custer.

Wild West shows kept up a grueling schedule, playing one-night stands in small towns all over the country and longer engagements in major cities. As an example, Wild West shows came regularly to the two towns of Champaign and

Urbana. A retired bank president reminisced in a 1960 newspaper article that "the best thing about being a kid in the early 1900's was going to the circus. Buffalo Bill always had the best one.

"They'd come into town and set up in the southwest part of Champaign. Of course, every kid in town went. We wouldn't dream of missing a chance to see cowboys fresh off the range and what we thought were real wild Injuns. Bill's wild west show bore no resemblance to the tame dog and pony shows that you see in these parts now."

The retired banker had an uncle who lived in Tombstone, Arizona, and "the high point of my childhood was one unforgettable day when my uncle from the wild and wooly west brought Buffalo Bill to our house for dinner. To hear them tell it, they alone conquered the West, personally chasing Sitting Bull out of business as well as finishing the buffalo. Of course, I sat there wide-eyed and for years believed that if it hadn't been for those two the country never would have been civilized."

Most of the time he and his friends did what most kids did back then— swam at the swimming hole and ice-skated on the park pond. "But nothing could compare with those rare days when Buffalo Bill and his wild west show came to town."

For a week before the show's arrival, there were large ads in the newspaper that promised, among other attractions, "one hundred full-blooded Indians." Shop owners were pleased at the prospect of farmers coming to town; the mayor worried that there wouldn't be a quorum at the city council meeting that night; extra police were on duty to handle the pickpockets. When the Wild West came to town for the first time on May 30, 1896, there was a free parade through the town followed by two performances under a tent that seated twenty thousand people. Every advance ticket for the two shows was sold and the druggist who handled the ticket sales said he had never seen such interest for any show. Although it was the first time the show had come to town, it wasn't the first Wild

Buffalo Bill and the show Indians, like most traveling circuses, often paraded through town to generate interest in the upcoming show. This postcard shows them on a European tour. Collection of the author.

West for many. "Champaign people know all about this aggregation. They saw it in Chicago, during the progress of the World's Fair, and it was considered one of the prime attractions of the fair."

Fifteen thousand people crowded the streets that day to watch the "unusual rumble of feet, the prancing of fiery steeds, the waving of beautiful plumes of all colors, the rustle of feathers, brandishing of tomahawks, swinging of lariats and the bristling of swords, the glitter of gay uniforms of all nations." The cavalcade "swept by so easily and majesticly [*sic*] that when it was all gone, when the last little pony from the far western plains had trotted by, people who had been standing in the streets for nearly three hours, waiting for it, rubbed their eyes and walked away to get something to eat, wondering if they had just awakened from a dream, in which they had seen bad Indians, and the like."

The paper went on to note that "Col. Cody has had his day as a character for patriotism only, and he is now out for the dollars, and is picking them up rapidly, while he is furnishing the people amusements that delight, please, and instruct." Admission was fifty cents; children under nine paid a quarter. It poured rain during the show and the tent held, but the audience had to leave the grounds through ankle-deep mud, ruining their clothes and losing their shoes.

When Buffalo Bill passed through town in 1907, an article pointed out the show's "double mission" as "pleasurable excitement" and the "acme of in-struction." No matter how many times one has attended, the writer contends, one will always find something new "that fixes itself indelibly on the mind and memory." And for youth, "it presents a school where there is nothing to criticize."

The show that came through in 1909 was an especially large one, Pawnee Bill and Buffalo Bill's shows having united into a touring city of eight hundred performers and crew members. The ads promised a new attraction: football on horseback. While in Champaign the show Indians went on "one of their peri-odical strikes." The paper reports them as "leaving the fairgrounds in a bad humor and coming down town where they were rounded up by a number of the cowboys, who threatened them with Pawnee Bill's punishment if they refused to return." The article continues, "Outbreaks of this kind are common with the warriors, who feel occasionally that they should have more freedom than is given them or that they have been mistreated because some of their childish whims are not approved by those in charge." Unfortunately, the article tells us no more; the performers returned to the fairgrounds for the afternoon and evening shows.

Most Wild West show performers were recruited from Sioux reservations, often Pine Ridge, and so America's picture of an Indian became synonymous with the picture of a feather-bonneted Sioux warrior. Having seen a Wild West show with their own eyes, most Americans in the early part of the twentieth century were sure that other Indians, who didn't look like the beaded, war-bonneted Sioux performers, were less than genuine. Others who dressed and acted differently were either not pure-blooded Indians or had abandoned their Indian ways. Humanitarians and missionaries opposed allowing Indians to participate in Wild West shows because the shows disseminated a backward image of Indians. Other people, including the performers themselves, insisted that it was their right to choose their own employment and they chose the entertainment business with Buffalo Bill or other traveling circuses. Opposing groups argued not only about American Indians themselves, but about what image of the Indian would be presented. Visiting every corner of the country as they did and even going abroad, Wild West shows had a powerful and lasting effect on our perceptions about Indians.

Their influence did not die out when the big shows ended around the time of World War I. Many circuses still included a Wild West act in the 1920s. Even more important, the theatrical scenarios from Wild West shows were filmed. The attack on the stagecoach, inspired by Buffalo Bill's Deadwood stagecoach, became a staple of the western. How much easier (and more profitable) to send a roll of movie film around the country than a troupe of actors and horses. When television became popular in the 1960s, the western scenarios were revived and made into television serials. Although my parents discouraged television, on Saturday nights I settled down to watch westerns like *Gunsmoke* and *Have Gun Will Travel* with my father. I remember the exciting scenes of Indians galloping alongside a moving stagecoach while passengers swayed in terror inside and the driver tried to control the horses and shoot at the same time. The boys in my neighborhood all played cowboys and Indians, pumping their cork guns as they ran. Or else they lined up plastic models of little bowlegged men, some with rifles, others with bows and arrows. I had no idea that rough tough cowboys and marauding feather-bonneted Indians, a conjoined entity we took for granted, came to us as a gift from Buffalo Bill's Wild West and the touring American circus.

Fittingly, the Indian chief created by the University of Illinois band wears Sioux regalia and a feather bonnet like a Wild West performer. So do most other mascots. If they didn't, they wouldn't seem truly Indian to us. Is Chief Illiniwek authentic? His clothing is authentic twentieth-century Oglala and he certainly has William Penn's "lofty chin." But as modern anthropology reminds us, authenticity is a relational construct. Something can be authentic only in relation to something else, which is not. White explorers, missionaries, anthropologists, artists, and photographers have all played a part in defining what is truly "Indian" about Indians. Even a soldier like Custer was sure that he knew real Indians when he saw them. Only four days before Little Bighorn he wrote to his wife, "I have some Crow scouts with me, as they are familiar with the country. They are magnificent-looking men, so much handsomer and more Indian-like than any we have ever seen."

"Authenticity was everything to Daddy," the daughter of the second Chief Illiniwek is quoted as saying. With five hundred dollars in his pocket donated by a local merchant, this student, Webber Borchers, headed to South Dakota to visit the Sioux. Borchers went on to have a controversial career in the Illinois House. In 1975 he was convicted on charges of misusing state funds. The conviction was overturned by the Illinois Supreme Court and he was reelected to the House for one more term. An outspoken conservative who relished making colorful and inflammatory remarks, he claimed to have used state funds to infiltrate radical student groups in 1969 and 1970. Never hesitant to take credit for the Chief Illiniwek tradition, Webber Borchers recounted the story frequently:

> In the summer of 1930 I went, at my own expense, to the Pine Ridge Reservation in South Dakota. I hitch-hiked out, called on an Indian agent and explained my mission. He and an Indian trader called in an older Sioux Indian woman. She and two younger women made the suit. I stayed there nearly a

month. The suit was not finished when it became necessary for me to return home for the fall term.

The regalia was not ready for the first few games, but was ready in time for me to wear in the Army-Illinois game in Yankee Stadium, New York, November 8, 1930.

Not only did he purchase the beaded leather pants and shirt, but to make sure that he looked truly "Indian," Borchers bought an eagle feather bonnet to wear. Frank Fools Crow, a well-known Oglala holy man who dictated his memoirs, said,

That same year, 1916, Black Elk (his uncle) gave me my first eagle feather headdress. It was a beautiful head bonnet, and it had thirty or more tail feathers in it. The headdress was made especially for me as a reward for my success in relay horse races at the Cheyenne Frontier Days, at Colorado Springs, at Salt Lake City, at Chicago, and at Cedar Rapids, Iowa. I came in first in all of these, and so was given the bonnet.

During the depression, and sometime after 1930, I sold it for one hundred and fifty dollars, which was a lot of money in those days. I have many times regretted its sale.

Although it can't be proven, it may have been the feather bonnet of Fools Crow that Borchers and succeeding chiefs wore until it was replaced in 1967. In his homemade costume, Borchers had performed only at home games, but once he acquired an elaborately beaded Oglala outfit and feather headdress, the band began to take Chief Illiniwek to every football game. Band members weren't allowed to bring luggage, so Borchers wore the regalia everywhere he went. New Yorkers took him for a real Indian chief, which pleased him; he considered himself a blood brother of the Oglala after his month in Pine Ridge.

The *Alumni News* noted the occasion. "Illiniwek was all decked out in his new eagle feather outfit, and later obliged with a whooping war dance up and down the field." The "new regalia" was "made by the Sioux Indians, and so far as the real thing is concerned is the catamount's whiskers."

Although it has been left out of the official university version, when Borchers told the story, he always noted that the old woman who sewed the outfit had been a girl at the time of the Battle of Little Bighorn. He claimed that it had been her job to go out on the battlefield and mutilate the faces of the dead "palefaces."

If a football team is going to be symbolically linked to an Indian tribe, there is no doubt in any football fan's mind which tribe it should be. The Oglala are famous for their victories against the U.S. cavalry and claim among their war chiefs Red Cloud, who was never defeated by the U.S. army. In the (tongue-in-cheek) words of Vine Deloria, Jr., who is Standing Rock Sioux himself, "The Oglala were, and perhaps still are, the meanest group of Indians ever assembled. They would take after a cavalry troop just to see if their bow strings were taut enough."

Borchers said he chose to go out to Sioux country because the regalia was picturesque and because he admired Red Cloud and Crazy Horse as warriors and cavalry officers. A member of the ROTC cavalry, Borchers trained a pinto pony so that he could ride it bareback into the stadium, stop on the beat of the drum, and slide off to begin his dance. In various accounts he either tosses a lariat around the goalpost or throws a lance over it. The first game things went well, but the second time it rained and Zuppke was furious at the damage the pony did to the field. He forbade any more mounted hijinks, forestalling Borchers's attempts to impersonate both Wild West performers and mounted Sioux warriors.

When we hear the story about the old woman who made the costume, we see her hands, nimbly threading the tiny glass beads on a needle and attaching them in elaborate patterns, and we remember the young girl who used these same hands to deftly wield a scalping knife. Returning to Illinois with the Oglala clothing and headdress, Borchers succeeded in creating a powerful association between a football team in Illinois and the most-eulogized event in white-Indian history, the defeat of Custer at the Battle of Little Bighorn. The football team could only stand to benefit.

Chills to the Spine, Tears to the Eyes

The thirties were not great years for Illinois football. Attendance went down. Zuppke thought the rules needed an "appendectomy"—the removal of the extra point, for which he blamed his team's losses. Zup loved the challenge of teaching a runner to play football or molding an ordinary player into a good one, but he refused to go out of his way to recruit high school stars. In the years after Grange left Illinois, he hadn't needed to. Every young player wanted to run on the field where the Ghost had scored. But by the late thirties Zuppke's refusal to recruit was forcing Illinois football into decline. Zuppke, who always said, "Only a dead man leaves the field," resigned in 1941. In his retirement Zuppke continued what had always been a serious hobby—oil painting. To those who saw no connection between art and athletics, Zuppke gave an eloquent little dissertation on rhythm and movement—essential in both—and pointed out that good painters, just like good football players, needed to demonstrate vigor and endurance.

Ed Kalb had been a clarinet player, but when he was recruited by the concert orchestra he switched to oboe for the chance to come to the university and play for Harding. It was 1933 and tuition was thirty-five dollars a semester, but Ed paid seventy since he used musical instruments. Music ran in the family. His father played trombone and his mother was a pianist who played sheet music in the "dimery"—the old Kresge variety store.

When football season began his freshman year, the first game was Boy Scout Day and Scouts got in free. Ed put on his Scout uniform and attended. When he saw Bill Newton dancing with the band as Chief Illiniwek, he decided then and there that he would perform as the chief himself someday.

Ed Kalb as Chief Illiniwek IV, 1935-1938. Courtesy of the University of Illinois Archives, Urbana-Champaign.

That spring, Newton was leaving, and the band held a tryout. "Newton's kid brother wanted to be chief." Ed chuckles, a deep throaty chuckle, at the memory. But at the end of the tryout, the assistant band director announced that Ed had the job. There was no interview. He was an Eagle Scout, a requirement in those days, although he doesn't remember anyone asking. He became the fourth Chief Illiniwek and served from 1935 to 1938.

"I learned my Indian dancing from the Indians in Scouting. This was during the Depression. Roosevelt tried to buy us out of the Depression. He would send the Indians. There would be three, government wards, they were called. Roosevelt would send the Indians around to Boy Scout camps—two old men who were craftsmen and one young man—a dancer. I learned weaving and stonecutting and silvercraft, all that in Scout camp."

Ed has a strong, deep voice. It's a little gruff. At first he talks about the old days with a kind of distance, but as we keep on talking, it seems as if he moves closer to those times, and his voice fills with enthusiasm. "Indians dancing told a story. These two old characters that taught crafts by day, they would interpret the dancer around the campfire. The two old characters would tell the story of the dance." Ed pauses to laugh. "Thinking about the Boy Scout camp and those old Indians—it really takes me back. At night, the old guys would tell the story of the dancer and the young guy would dance. And I guess we had three or four summers of that. It wasn't the same Indians every time. The Hopi, the Zuni, the Navajo. There was a fourth tribe I forget. They taught us the Ghost Dance, the Sun Dance." He turns to me with enthusiasm. "I remember the Hoop Dance— the Hopi Hoop Dance. The Hopi had a hoop measured just so it would fit over the shoulders. They would dance and flick that hoop over their head!" Ed gestures with his arms to show what he means, but gives up at bending over to demonstrate how they slipped the hoops over their legs. "For years I tried to do that. I couldn't do it now."

"I started when I was twelve. All summer we lived in cabins with screens on the upper half and bunk beds. I spent at least four summers doing that."

After Ed was picked as chief, he and the football captain made a tour of the state. The physical plant built a tepee on a pickup truck and they drove it to every large town, Chicago included, handing out the poster with the game schedule. As far as Ed knows, that was the first time anyone had ever done that. It was his only duty as Chief Illiniwek other than dancing at halftime.

I ask Ed how it felt to be Chief Illiniwek in the 1930s. "Were you the honored symbol of the University? Did people hold you in awe and reverence?" Ed laughs. "No! I remember at Ohio State some drunk wanted a feather out of my headdress. I took off the headdress and rolled it up. He was falling down drunk." Ed's deep voice turns emphatic. "I was part of the marching band. Period."

Ed doesn't care for the way the chief's dance has evolved. "He behaves like a ballet dancer and I don't go to the football games because I don't approve of the chief." Ed won't buy products with Chief Illiniwek on them, either. "The heck with Indian dancing, that's their attitude now."

What about students who feel they respect Indians? I ask.

"I would question their knowledge of the chief, of Indian culture, period," Ed replies in his deep, serious voice. He worked at the State Museum in Springfield for many years. He drove the museummobile and taught schoolchildren about Indian culture in Illinois. "They didn't know anything about Indians. I didn't either when I started. I thought I did. But," he said, laughing, "I soon learned. The dioramas taught me."

Maybe students had other rituals then, I suggest. Maybe the University was smaller and more personal so the students didn't need one symbol to unify them.

Ed shakes his head. "The university was big then, in the thirties. We all had our own groups." As a musician, he hung out at Smith Music Hall and worked his way through school waxing pianos in the practice rooms. There were sixty pianos. "Heck of a lot of wax," says Ed laconically. He also worked as a driver for the director of the music school. "And then I copied music for Harding at five cents a page. It took me about half an hour to do a page. Boy, I hadn't thought of that in years!"

One difference in Ed's day, before television, was the excitement generated by the live performance of the university band. "People used to come to the game to see the band. Harding would always direct one concert number. I think half of the people came just for that."

Like all the other chiefs, Ed wrote his name on the back of the headdress in

India ink. But he remembers that as he performed the intricate steps he had learned in the summers from the old Indians, the headgear was always in his way. Not surprising, according to Ed. "Indian chiefs don't dance," he told me in his gruff, matter-of-fact voice. "The underlings do."

After Zuppke retired, his successor never had a chance to turn the football program around. New teams showed up as adversaries: the Great Lakes Naval Training Station, the Iowa Seahawks. By 1942 the Roll of Honor in the football program listed twenty-eight Illini killed in action. There were three navy training schools on campus. The women's residence halls were turned over to the officers and the ballroom of the Illini Union became a mess hall. Fraternities and sororities declared a no-flower dance season and wore corsages and boutonnieres of war stamps pinned to their lapels instead.

Football games weren't luxuries, however. MacArthur himself had said otherwise: "Men who engage in fighting games such as football develop a combative spirit, the kind of spirit needed by all of our men in the fighting forces." A Chesterfield cigarette ad from a 1942 football program showed a football player in a brown leather helmet directly in front of an air force pilot in a nearly identical helmet. Below them, framed in a decorative border, was this quote from MacArthur: "On the fields of friendly strife are sown the seeds which, in other years on other fields, will bear the fruits of victory." A Spalding ad showed a team of football players with the caption, "Next year they play Tokyo."

The 1943 team was pieced together from seventeen-year-olds, 4-Fs, and the naval engineering students who were in training on campus. The band had "Princess Illiniwek," played by Idelle Stith, a coed from Oklahoma who had spent much of her childhood on the Osage reservation where her father was an attorney. According to the football program, she was an "authentic honorary Osage princess." Later chiefs were not impressed with her credentials: they removed her name from the list on the back of the war bonnet; nor did it appear in the list of former chiefs in the football program until feminism arrived in the seventies.

During the war, Indians disappeared altogether and patriotic imagery—eagles, flags, tanks, and soldiers—dominated the football programs. Every advertiser tried to show how its product helped the war effort. Kellogg proudly announced that its Kel-Bowl-Pac, the box of cereal you cut open and pour milk into, was used by the army in the field. In a long shot, Oscar Mayer, an Illinois trustee, pointed out that the continuous yellow band around his wieners looked a lot like a cartridge belt.

After the war, the university was full of veterans. Football flourished. Illinois went to the Rose Bowl as the underdog to play powerful UCLA on January 1, 1947, and won against all odds. Now that the war was over, the theme for the Tournament of Roses parade was an old favorite: "Our Golden West." One of the flower-covered floats reproduced *The End of the Trail* in flower petals. This sculpture by James Earle Fraser, who also designed the buffalo–Indian head nickel, depicts a drooping Indian man seated on his equally drooping horse, dragging a lance. Originally made in the 1890s, a monumental reproduction of *The End of the Trail* was displayed at the Panama-Pacific Exposition of 1915 in San Francisco. Reproduced on calendars and as ashtrays, bookends, and even parade floats covered with flower petals, this image has been influential in creating and expressing the stereotype of the Indian who is doomed to extinction. Unable to hunt or make war any more, he has given up. He is the last of his tribe. Fraser hoped to install a monumental cast of the sculpture on a cliff overlooking the Pacific Ocean, a visual assertion that American Indians had been pushed right off the edge of the map into watery oblivion. But he could never raise the funding for the project.

Presented at every turn with this image of the defeated warrior, alone and dejected, many Americans had no idea that communities of Indians still existed and were wrestling with complex questions about education, assimilation, alcoholism, communal versus private land ownership, and corruption and paternalism in the Bureau of Indian Affairs.

When Illinois went to the Rose Bowl again in 1952, it was to battle the Stanford Indians. "I hope your football team is not as good as your band," Governor Earl Warren said when he welcomed the marching band to California. A. A. Harding himself came out of retirement to go along. The band members practiced barefoot on cold muddy fields to keep their shoes clean and at halftime produced an elaborate show that began with an innovative moving train formation.

"Dreams of the Future" was the parade theme that year and the winning float, "Every Girl's Dream of the Future," featured a bride who poked out like a cake decoration from a sweeping floral hoop skirt. Illinois fans went to Chicago and rented hotel rooms with televisions so they could see their team play in the first college football game to be nationally televised. A family and a house with a television might be the dream of the future, but in 1952 many students still wanted to see the action live. Any student who could produce the stub of a Rose Bowl ticket was granted an extension of Christmas vacation. Illinois won 40-7.

On their return, the band stopped at the Grand Canyon. Photographs show them on the South Rim in the ILLINI formation. The Chief Illiniwek that year, Bill Hug, faces the canyon, his arms raised in a grand gesture. The *Alumni News* reports that "Hopi Chief Porter Temiche, himself a famed Indian ceremonial dancer, escorted Hug across the hotel's courtyard to Hopi House where Hug was made a real Indian chief in a Hopi ceremony." In photos they smoke a pipe and try on each other's headdresses. "This meant that I was now a member of the Hopi tribe and he was a member of the Illini," Hug explained at the time. The most striking photograph of all shows Hug, his legs split wide, seemingly suspended in midair. Temiche watches with his mouth open. It was Hug's idea to add the acrobatics—two stag leaps and the split leap—to the routine. "I almost hate to admit it," he says wryly when I call to ask him about it now. He's aware that the dance has been criticized in recent years for its lack of authenticity. "I didn't see it as a spiritual or religious dance. It was in a football stadium. As a performer, I was thinking of the people in the top bleachers."

And the dancing itself? "It was a celebration," Hug says. "It had nothing to do with American Indians. I had never, until recently, seen it as anything but a great honor. It never even occurred to me that anyone would object."

A perusal of the football programs, with their ads and interviews and profiles, gives a reader a popular history of America in this century. Sincerely sober during wartime, sincerely hankering for glory in peacetime, and sincerely believing in fair play. The country portrayed by the boosters is a hopeful, upbeat place.

Indian imagery has been part of the programs ever since the students began to call themselves Illini. In 1926 tiny Indians decorated the bottoms of the pages of the football programs, saying things like "Ugh! Ketchum Hawks!" and "Heap Big Medicine." In 1932 the referee's hand signals were demonstrated by an assortment of horridly drawn Indians. The caption says, "The little Illiniweks pictured above are not doing a war dance, but merely presenting to you the most common hand signals used by the referees. Our apologies to the referee!" Obviously, there was no need to apologize to the Illiniwek. They were a vanished race. Chief Illiniwek was listed as a member of the marching band and sometimes the band page carried an inset photograph of him, but he was not the band's best-known feature in those years. At the 1948 homecoming, A. A. Harding was honored and at halftime the band spelled out AAH. The history of the band in the program did not mention Chief Illiniwek. In the fifties, long-nosed caricatures of Indians and photographs of the Chief became more prevalent in the programs. The band had new formations: UGH, Three Little Indians, HOW, and tepees. Opposing teams also used the Indian to represent Illinois, of course, and these depictions were often derogatory.

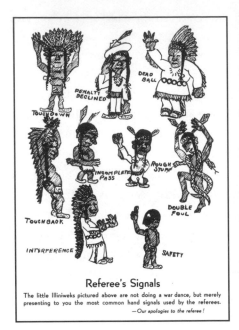

Referee's Signals

The little Illiniweks pictured above are not doing a war dance, but merely presenting to you the most common hand signals used by the referees.

—Our apologies to the referee!

Indian-theme teams generate a wake of caricatured Indian images like these two examples of Indians as buffoons from football programs in 1932 (upper left) and 1957 (upper right) and the advertisement from 1956 (lower right). Courtesy of the University of Illinois Archives, Urbana-Champaign.

The Illinettes, dressed in "mod Indian" attire in 1970. Indian-theme bands and flag squads accompany most college and professional football teams with Indian names. Courtesy of the University of Illinois Archives, Urbana-Champaign.

After an up and down decade in the sixties (a Rose Bowl win and severe penalties from the NCAA over a slush fund), the seventies began with a fresh start for football and halftime—a new coach for the team and women for the first time ever in the marching band. According to one reporter, the "female invasion had no visible effect" because "so many male members of the band have shoulder-length hair that it was next to impossible to pick out the girls." A flag corps and herald trumpet corps, both all-female, also made their debut. Their costumes were described as "mod Indian." This meant head feathers, fringed shirts and boots, and bright orange hot pants. They were greeted with "loud cheers from the appreciative crowd." Those of us old enough to remember know that this probably meant catcalls and wolf whistles.

In 1972 faculty achievements were showcased in the football program. These included the appearance on the best-seller list of *Bury My Heart at Wounded*

Knee by a University of Illinois librarian, Dee Brown, a popular history that made many white Americans realize for the first time that some "battles" had actually been massacres perpetrated by the U.S. Army. Readers bought millions of copies of this compelling account of the last wars with the Plains Indians. They read about Crazy Horse and Red Cloud with sympathy and outrage, but once again, their interest remained focused on the past and did not carry over to modern Indian people.

The back-to-nature movement was an important part of the 1970s. Americans now routinely considered how their actions made an impact on the "environment," as they called the natural world. Even that made it into the programs when the Marching Illini created a halftime act that featured flowers, a pollution factory, a bright sun, and the word YOU. Idealized Indians were favorite role models for students who wanted to live lightly on the earth. With the rise of the American Indian Movement, American Indian students and activists brought the issue of sports mascots to campuses. Clyde Bellecourt, one of the founders of AIM, spoke at Illinois in 1975. That year's yearbook devotes two pages to his visit with the headline, "A Challenge to the Chief." A former Chief Illiniwek replied, "Other university mascots are just caricatures but Illiniwek portrays the Indians as they would want to be portrayed."

During this period, the Dartmouth Indians became the Dartmouth Big Green. There were protests at Cleveland against Chief Wahoo, Oklahoma State retired its "Little Red" mascot, and Syracuse dropped its Saltine Warrior. The Stanford Indians became the Stanford Cardinal (singular) with no significant loss of alumni support.

Stanford's change, from the Indians to the Cardinal and the retirement of their mascot, Prince Lightfoot, seems to have been accomplished smoothly in the seventies. John White, who now devotes his energy to keeping the Illinois Indian languages alive, was a graduate student at Stanford at the time, and resident advisor for a new undergraduate Native American studies program. About twenty students on scholarships lived in Tecumseh House together. As the students talked about what it meant to be Indian at an elite institution like Stanford, the subject of the sports logo and mascot quickly came up. The group decided to invite the man who played the role of Prince Lightfoot to the house. He was not a student, but an Indian man in his forties, John remembers, and came from a tribe that lived on the northern California coast near the mouth of the Klamath River. During sports events, he came out dressed as a Plains Indian and did a sort of "fantasy dance," as John puts it.

When they sat down in the living room with him, the students became quiet and deferential. Although they talked a long time, none challenged him directly. Finally, a student who was Sioux asked him, "Why don't you wear clothing from your tribe and do a dance that your people do?"

The man looked surprised and drew himself up. "I come from a very old family," he said. "My family calls the salmon. I would never degrade my family and my people that way."

After he left, they looked at each other in surprise. *Did you hear what I heard? Did he actually say that?* they asked each other. They began to write letters to the student paper and to the deans and had a meeting with a high-level administrator who was sympathetic. John left before the actual change occurred about two years later. He suspects that the administration was sympathetic because it had just made a large investment in the undergraduate Native American studies program and was committed to its success.

None of these changes stopped the fiftieth anniversary of Chief Illiniwek in 1976 from being celebrated with reunions of former chiefs and a large photo of Chief Illiniwek on the inside back cover of every football program. Webber Borchers's account of hitchhiking to Pine Ridge was reprinted over and over like a mantra. The Marching Illini had a new director, Gary Smith. The band had deteriorated, he says, and had a reputation as the organization to join if you were looking for weekend trips and big parties. The football crowds interrupted the band's halftime program, shouting, "Chief! Chief!"

According to Smith, he instituted strict discipline and within a few years began to attract serious musicians back to the band. Smith asked the university administration about Chief Illiniwek, and receiving assurances that the chief came under his jurisdiction, he created new policies about what the student who played the role could and could not do. In recent years Chief Illiniwek had visited schools and spoken about American Indian culture; he had also opened shopping malls, danced at alumni weddings, visited children in hospitals, and been photographed with politicians. Legend has it that local farmers, desperate for rain, called to ask the chief to dance in their cornfields. Smith put an end to most of these activities. He limited the chief's appearance to football games and men's and women's basketball games. He allowed the chief to go to schools and talk about his role as Chief Illiniwek, but he forbade him to wear the costume. He could carry it along with him and show it, but he could not "be" Chief Illiniwek except for those five minutes of dancing. Despite Smith's edicts, the chief still posed for oil paintings, turned up as a backdrop for the local weather forecast, and went to alumni events. Smith claims that highly placed campus administrators simply bypassed him and sent the chief where they would. Despite improvements in the band, band members still felt that the halftime show was just a warmup for the chief and that the band existed to provide the music for his performance. And although they didn't start until just before he came on, the football crowd still yelled impatiently for the chief.

The best thing that ever happened to his band, according to Smith, was being invited, through the auspices of an alumnus, to play at a Detroit Tigers game. Smith told the alumnus that he wouldn't bring Chief Illiniwek with him since nobody in Detroit knew about him, but this alumnus said that if they didn't bring the chief, they could forget the Silverdome. He was convinced that

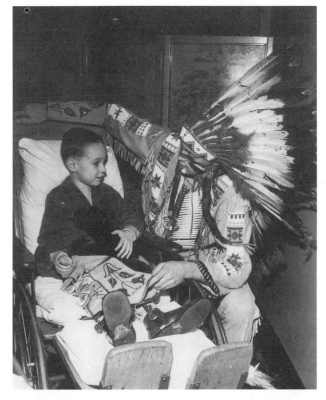

**A Chief Illiniwek in the 1950s visiting children in a polio ward.
Courtesy of the University of Illinois Archives, Urbana-Champaign.**

Chief Illiniwek would be the high point of the performance. The band did a Star Wars program, complete with rockets, which got a huge ovation. But when the music for the "Three-in-One" started up and the chief came dancing out, the crowd got up and left for the concession stands. The Illinois alum admitted to Smith that he was shocked by this; he had thought there was something inherently stirring about the costumed student's acrobatic dancing.

Unlike the students of the 1970s, who were anti-tradition, the students of the 1980s were ready to dress in their team colors and cheer. At Illinois the campus was awash in orange and blue and fans yelled oskee-wow-wow until they were hoarse when their team went to the Rose Bowl in 1984. For some people, unnerved after a decade when you couldn't tell the male trombonists from the female, bringing back a little dose of that Teddy Roosevelt manly virtue Chief Illiniwek embodied seemed like an important restorative.

The chief's clothing was falling apart by 1982 and Smith was wondering about the whole notion of the chief. Smith decided to go out to Sioux country himself. He went to Pine Ridge and spent several days with a ninety-three-year-old holy man named Frank Fools Crow, the superintendent of the Indian Affairs Agency, Anthony Whirlwind Horse, and the elected chief of the Oglala, Joe American Horse. Smith showed them videos of halftime at Illinois. "They said they had no objection to Chief Illiniwek's performance—what they disliked were caricatured Indian mascots," Smith repeats. Once he had their approval, Smith brought up the subject of a new buckskin outfit. To make one would take several years, they told him. However, Whirlwind Horse confided to Smith that Fools Crow had two chief's outfits already made. His house had recently burned to the ground and the old man was destitute. Would Smith be willing to buy one of his?

Fools Crow was a remarkable old man. He was born shortly after the massacre at Wounded Knee and raised nine miles from where it took place. His parents hid him so that he could not be kidnapped and taken to boarding school as were other Indians of his generation. By the time the agent found him, he was eighteen and too old to be coerced to go. Raised as a traditional Oglala, he was trained by his famous uncle Black Elk and other holy men to perform healing ceremonies. Knife Chief, Frank's grandfather, was wounded and miraculously cured by a healer on the battlefield of Little Bighorn. His father had been given the name Crazy Crow to encourage him to seek revenge for a brother killed by Crow Indians, but his father was a gentle man more drawn to healing than warfare. Although it was not intended to be passed down, the name was translated from Lakota into English as Fools Crow and became a surname in the American sense. The son was then named Frank to distinguish him from his father. In his memoir, told to the California writer Thomas Mails, Fools Crow recounts his vision quests, the miraculous healings he has performed, and the story of his two happy marriages. It is a fascinating story.

Gary Smith had been profoundly moved by his meeting with Fools Crow and gladly agreed to look at the outfits. They went to Fools Crow's modest house and were warmly received. One of the two outfits was decorated with blue and orange beads. It seemed like fate. The headdress was made of eagle feathers. Although Smith was unaware of the restrictions, the three men explained that only Native Americans could own eagle feathers because of the eagle's status as an endangered species. The Native Americans could give feathers away from their allotment, but they could not sell them. They reached an agreement that if Smith could raise the $3,500 to buy the clothing, they would give him the feather headdress. The tail of this bonnet was short, but Smith offered to send some of the feathers from the old bonnet and Fools Crow agreed to attach them. They urged Smith to return at the end of May to pick up the regalia and to attend a three-day powwow as their guest. Smith returned to campus determined to buy the regalia and to invite Fools Crow to Illinois to formally present it. His excitement is evident in a memo he wrote after his return, addressed to "Everyone in the World," in which he calls the outfit "priceless" and Fools Crow a "real medicine man," and says urgently that the band needs the money "right now or we will lose the deal." Smith also wrote to both Fools Crow and Whirlwind Horse. It is clear from these letters that his few days in Pine Ridge touched Smith deeply. He admired both men and felt particularly privileged to spend time with Fools Crow.

A local businessman/alumnus came forward and offered the price of the regalia. Two other alums offered to fly their private plane to South Dakota to pick up the three guests for a ceremony at the first home game.

In late May, Smith drove back in his van, taking his two sons along, to attend a powwow and visit with Fools Crow. He brought eagle feathers from the old bonnet so that the tail on the new bonnet could be lengthened. By the end of his visit, Fools Crow trusted Smith enough to speak in English to him under his breath, a fact Smith recounts proudly.

When Fools Crow, Whirlwind Horse, and Joe American Horse arrived in Champaign-Urbana the day before the football game, there was still no train on the eagle feather bonnet. Fools Crow told Smith that he no longer had the feathers; they had been stolen from his truck. At the pregame ceremony, Fools Crow, who had emphysema, had a coughing attack at the microphone. The crowd took his hacking for a Sioux incantation and cheered. Webber Borchers began scooping up dirt and pricking his fingers for an impromptu ceremony with his blood brothers, and before Smith could move them off the field, the teams came running on and the official blew his whistle for play to begin. Smith shrugs and laughs as he tells the story. He genuinely intended the ceremony to honor Fools Crow. But the Oglala holy man's presence also legitimized the transfer of the regalia from Indian hands to those of the marching band.

Fools Crow died in 1989, believed to be ninety-nine years old, and was buried in South Dakota. Seven hundred people attended his funeral. Ten years after they presented the clothing, in response to questions from reporters, Whirlwind Horse said that Fools Crow had found the dance "comical" but that they had said nothing so as not to insult their hosts. Gary Smith obviously takes this change of heart personally and feels betrayed. Native Americans also feel betrayed by the incident, as they hold Fools Crow's memory in high esteem. He stood by AIM when they occupied Wounded Knee and even traveled to New York to seek support from the United Nations. Between the old world of traditional religion and chiefs and the younger Indian activists, Fools Crow provided an important bridge, his life spanning the years from one Wounded Knee to another.

American Indians remind themselves that he was penniless. Tim Giago, a well-known Oglala journalist and the former publisher of the newspaper *Indian Country Today*, the largest Indian-owned newspaper in the country, grew up on land that adjoined Fools Crow's. His father and Fools Crow rode horses together as boys and were lifelong friends.

Giago recalls stopping in a restaurant once when his family was traveling. "We don't serve Indians," the waitress informed them. His father simply bowed his head and left. Giago still remembers the double fury he felt, at the restaurant and at his father. "I wanted him to stand up for himself, say something. But he was from another era." He sighs. "Fools Crow, too. They were products of their time."

After Fools Crow's death the university returned his feather bonnet to his family since it had no permit to possess the eagle feathers. Chief Illiniwek continues to use an older war bonnet made by an alumnus who makes Indian regalia for a hobby. This headdress contains only turkey feathers.

In order to keep up in the world of college football in the 1980s, every athletic program needed a corporate logo, a distinctive design to trademark so it could cash in on the new craze for merchandise imprinted with team insignias. At Illinois, Chief Illiniwek, dressed in new handmade regalia, was promoted. No longer just a halftime act, he was now a university-wide symbol printed not only on clothing, but on stationery, wallets, earrings made from orange Ping-Pong balls, mugs, Christmas ornaments, watches (with a floating chief second hand), diaper covers, stadium seat pads, baby bottles, toilet paper, urinal screens, rugs, and afghans.

The design that was printed on all these objects was created in 1981. It shows a war bonnet as a perfect circle of feathers. In the center of the sunburst feathers there is a highly stylized and very anonymous face. This logo is clearly the trademark of a professional athletic corporation. It was designed by freelance designer Jack Davis, who has worked with the athletic association since the 1970s. Davis, a dapper man with a ready laugh, says that before he designed the chief logo, the athletic association had no single image. One team would use a chief's head in profile, another would use the stadium, another had an arrow motif. He offered to come up with a single athletic logo, "something good-looking and really slick."

Merchandising was just taking off then and the advantage of a unique image designed by Davis was that it could be trademarked. He charged the university a small fee and donated the rest as a gift-in-kind to the athletic program. "If I had just one penny for every time they've used that design," he jokes good-naturedly. He continues to be amazed and gratified by the response. "I probably shouldn't say this, but in this town, it was like I had designed the cross."

Up to this point, University of Illinois products displayed the same standardized Indian graphics, the same generic chief's head and dancing brave, as every other school that had an Indian mascot. These designs had been created by the companies that produced the notebooks, wastebaskets, and sweatshirts for the collegiate market. But in order to use the round chief logo, companies pay licensing fees and their products must be approved.

Identifying with your favorite team by wearing its logo is an important part of contemporary American fashion and identity. And clothes aren't the only big sellers. Sales of licensed products have risen steadily in the past decade as the variety of objects has expanded. The university makes about $500,000 each year in royalties from licensed University of Illinois products, including those depicting Chief Illiniwek. University officials in charge of licensing feel sure that sales would go down if Chief Illiniwek were retired because the Indian motif is a popular one. However, they have not conducted any marketing surveys. They are tired of being maligned about Chief Illiniwek toilet paper and are quick to point out that none has been licensed for years. When I asked about the silk boxer shorts with the chief logo on them that were for sale in 1996-97 in the university bookstore, the athletic program told me they must be unlicensed. However, a tag attached to the shorts was marked "Officially Licensed Collegiate Product." Shortly after I asked this question, the boxers were moved to a markdown rack. They remained in this retail purgatory for some time and then vanished completely.

In the movies of the 1970s and 1980s, the heroic pioneer family attacked by savage Indians was often replaced by the embattled Indian trying to save his family from brutal soldiers. Perhaps Illini fans who watched these alternative versions of the frontier viewed Chief Illiniwek even more sympathetically. But it wouldn't do to have an icon for whom fans felt pity, nor one about whom they felt guilt. The sentiments the athletic program and marching band wished to inspire were awe and reverence. So Chief Illiniwek became more remote and more mysterious, and like all icons kept hidden away in secret, more powerful and potent when displayed.

The alumni publication often interviews graduates, especially athletes, about why they return to homecoming. Alumni from the 1930s, 1940s and 1950s rarely mention Chief Illiniwek in their statements. They talk about seeing friends, revisiting favorite places, or a particular game they remember. My neighbor Frank, who graduated in 1933 and who hangs out an orange and blue flag on the Saturday of every home game, told me, "I don't think we had a Chief Illiniwek when I was a student." Webber Borchers must have turned over in his grave at being so easily forgotten. But graduates from the 1980s nearly always talk about "the chills up my spine" or the "tears that come to my eyes" when Chief Illiniwek emerges from his hiding place in the band. Their responses are eerily standardized.

I wonder why the reaction has grown so much stronger when the music and dance ritual have changed little since the 1930s. Perhaps we, who are more media-dependent, have become more attuned to visual symbols than those Illinois fans who traveled to Chicago to watch their team play on television. Certainly we accept the notion of wearing our affiliations printed on our clothing. If Harding and Zuppke returned from the twenties and walked across the campus today, they might think that printed T-shirts had taken the place of sandwich boards and that students were being paid to advertise sportswear. But more than anything else, I suspect that Chief Illiniwek's rise in the 1980s to iconic status can be attributed to the new emphasis on making athletics profitable by selling licensed merchandise. As the athletic program promoted the mascot's importance, fans wanted to own their own personal version of the icon to take home or to wear.

In the 1980s Chief Illiniwek became a sports marketing success story, the symbol of a profitable union between entertainment, consumerism, sports, higher education, and the mythology of what it means to be American. In the American symbolic code, Indians—especially pre-reservation Plains Indians—often represent nostalgia for a past that seems to have been wilder and more exciting. Illinois football has never regained the momentum it had in the legend-making days of Grange and Zuppke. Ever since criticism arose in the late 1980s, Illinois fans have insisted that Chief Illiniwek honors the Illinois Indians. But perhaps it is the golden era of Illinois football, the wild and wonderful twenties, when the fans at the newly built stadium felt that they were at the center of something glorious, that Chief Illiniwek really commemorates.

The Speakers Have It All Wrong

In 1988 the art department at the University of Illinois recruited three students from the School of American Indian Arts in Santa Fe. After a couple of weeks on campus one of them, Marcus Amerman, wrote a letter to the student newspaper, the *Daily Illini*. The letter explained his objections to Chief Illiniwek in the context of the "near genocide of my people" and the continuing campaign to humiliate them. These were novel ideas for most students and they set a philosophy major named Robert Honig to thinking. What really made Honig uncomfortable were the letters written in response. They said things like, "The Indians don't know what they're talking about. This isn't offensive to them."

Honig, who was Jewish, knew he would be offended if his people were dismissed like that. He succeeded in bringing the question to the pages of the *Daily Illini* and started an organization of faculty and students to oppose the chief. Marcus Amerman, the Indian student who had written the letter, was taunted, mocked, and threatened by other students in the dormitory where he lived. Two weeks after writing the letter to the editor, he got drunk and scrawled graffiti all over a painting studio. When he had repainted the studio white, as asked, he left the university without a word to anyone.

The other two American Indian graduate students were advised to lie low and get their degrees. Charlene Teters says she intended to do just that, but the reactions of her two children, fifteen and eighteen, changed her mind. Teters, who is Spokane and grew up on the Spokane reservation in Washington state, had worked hard to instill pride in her children about their heritage. As the first person in her family to go to college, she was thrilled to have the opportunity to get a graduate degree from a first-rate university; she wasn't about to turn it down because of a sports mascot.

The Fighting Illini were heading to the Final Four that year and excitement on campus was running high, so when her children wanted to go to a basketball game, Teters agreed. She saw how they slid down in their seats in embarrassment when the chief came out to dance. In a filmed interview, she breaks down as she recalls watching her son's attempt to laugh it off. "You laugh," she says in a choked voice, "when you're the butt of the joke and you don't want anyone to know that you're hurting." In a place where the image of an Indian chief was stamped on every university product, used to promote many community events, and often caricatured, Teters worried about her children's self-esteem. One bar near campus had a neon sign of a drunken Indian who fell down and got up again and again. After carefully teaching her children that paint and feathers were articles of spiritual devotion, she found herself in a place where these things were used as entertainment by a community that knew nothing about American Indian culture.

Teters decided that for the sake of her two children she must speak out. She had no idea what to do, but she felt that she must respond in some way, if only as a gesture for her children. She made a sign that said, "American Indians Are Human Beings Not Mascots!" and stood outside a basketball game. She expected to be ignored. She did not expect to be spat upon or to have empty beer cans thrown at her. When the local papers covered the story, she received threatening phone calls and saw cars drive slowly past her house at night. One night when the phone rang, she heard a raspy voice on the other end. "This is Vernon Bellecourt from the American Indian Movement," the voice said. "What can I do to help you?" Someone had forwarded the articles about her to AIM in Minneapolis.

In November 1989 Senator Paul Simon attended a powwow and signed a petition Charlene Teters had written calling for the removal of Chief Illiniwek.

Many of his constituents, downstate football fans and Chicago alumni, were enraged. Within days, two state representatives countered with a House resolution to keep the chief. This nonlegislative statement of position died in committee.

The next Saturday Simon was scheduled to accept a 4-H award at a midfield ceremony during halftime, but he moved the award ceremony to the university's performing arts center, saying he didn't want to detract from halftime. An airplane flew over Memorial Stadium trailing a sign that said, "Keep the Chief, Dump Simon."

In the 1980s Chief Illiniwek was described in football programs as "the most colorful and memorable tradition in college football." It was pointed out that he's not a mascot but a character who "symbolizes the spirit" of the Fighting Illini. After 1989, instead of being "colorful and memorable," Chief Illiniwek is always described as "dramatic and dignified." In response to criticism, the university stressed its mascot's dignity, which placed him beyond reproach. In fact, he was no longer a mascot at all; he had been promoted to the more dignified-sounding status of a symbol.

In October 1990 the university trustees voted on whether or not the university should continue to use Chief Illiniwek. A former chief said that the chief was a dignified symbol, one of pride, reverence, and respect for all Native Americans. Gloria Jackson Bacon, the only African American board member, pleaded, "The chief cannot continue to exist or we will never come to grips with the concept of coming together. We have a magnificent opportunity to begin to deal with the things that plague our society, and the chief is as good a point as any to start." Jesse Jackson, who attended the university in 1960, sent a letter asking the board to "use its moral authority to select a new symbol." Charlene Teters asked board members not to continue the history of insensitivity. She ended by crying out, "We are not mascots. We are human beings." After her speech, the board voted 7-1-1 to keep the Chief. Bacon voted against and one trustee abstained, saying, "I feel it's possible that we just don't understand how Native

Americans feel." The chancellor of the Champaign-Urbana campus announced that Chief Illiniwek would remain as the official symbol of the university. However, cheerleaders, Marching Illini, and Block I members would have to give up their "warpaint" and Chief Illiniwek could no longer paint his chin with the Roman letter *I*, which of course was not authentic. Chief Illiniwek, the chancellor insisted, was both a positive and an authentic representation of Native American culture.

The university removed the dancing chief from the band's jurisdiction, where he had been since 1926. Now he is under the supervision of the athletic association, with oversight provided by the chancellor's office. The representations of the chief that were sold by private businesses were monitored, and most of the caricatures of Indians gradually disappeared. But Chief Illiniwek continued to reign over halftime.

In the past, Chief Illiniwek had embodied school spirit and identity, unified the fans, and made halftime more dramatic. But in response to criticism of the mascot, a new idea emerged on campus. Sudents insisted that Chief Illiniwek was their way to honor Native Americans. He didn't honor just any American Indians, but the Illiniwek, who had, the students thought, completely vanished. They thought this would settle any opposition.

The chief's role was reduced, but the accolades to him increased. In the football program for 1992, the section introducing the marching band begins, "Performing with Chief Illiniwek, the Marching Illini . . ." Albert Austin Harding and John Philip Sousa must have turned over in their graves, simultaneously, in three-quarter time, without a prearranged signal or gunshot.

In 1993 the University of Illinois hired as assistant dean of students a clinical psychologist named Dennis Tibbetts, who was Ojibwa and Shoshone. Tibbetts's area of expertise was counseling athletes. The administration asked his views on the chief and, learning that he opposed the mascot, suggested that he wouldn't be comfortable in the athletic association. However, they were looking for someone to initiate a program on diversity and group relations. A new chancellor was coming to the university and Tibbetts was impressed with the statements he had made about creating a more diverse and inclusive community. Tibbetts took the job.

Tibbetts, who is a soft-spoken middle-aged man, admits now that he didn't realize until he moved to Champaign-Urbana how entrenched the chief was. At the reception he attended for new faculty, he gave the new chancellor a poem he had written called "Minstrel Show." Written as a letter to his grandfather Redsky, it is composed of alternating verses about the halftime show and Ojibwa traditions. One verse reads,

> They tell me they honor us Grandfather
> by remembering our fierceness in battle.
> Powerful image makers, more powerful
> than cavalry bullets and soldiers' bayonets.

Tibbetts began to talk to administrators about retiring the chief. He attended a meeting between Latino students and the chancellor and was pleased with the chancellor's receptivity. But when he asked for a similar meeting to discuss Native American students' concerns, he arrived to find not just administrators, but lawyers and security guards. "I think they believe their own rhetoric," he quips in his quiet voice. "They think Indian men are dangerous warriors." When he couldn't find any support in the administration for retiring the chief, Tibbetts talked to the Illinois Human Rights Commission. But the commission was unresponsive and said that it would be two years before it could even address the issue. "Illinois alumni probably," Tibbetts says wryly.

Next he contacted the U.S. Department of Education's Office of Civil Rights. When the Office of Civil Rights heard that the university had a written policy making the chief its mascot, it conceded that there might be grounds for a complaint. Subsequently, Native Americans—graduate students, faculty members, and Tibbetts, who was a staff member—filed complaints. They charged that the university policy of Chief Illiniwek was discriminatory to one minority group. The Office of Civil Rights conducted interviews on campus. A group of Illinois congressmen met with the OCR and suggested that the issue was better dealt with within the state. Ultimately, the complaint was dismissed for insufficient evidence of a violation. However, in a letter, the Office of Civil Rights urged the university to take "proactive steps" to prevent the controversy from "leading to a hostile environment that impairs the educational opportunities available to Native Americans on campus."

Meanwhile, the chancellor instituted a long-range strategic planning process. One of the committees was mandated to study the promotion of a "more inclusive community." In October 1994 this faculty group suggested, as one of twelve recommendations, that the university do away with Chief Illiniwek. The committee felt that the presence of the chief undermined attempts at inclusiveness and called into question the university's sincerity on the issue. It also noted the divisiveness and tension created by the chief's presence and the "intolerant speech and behavior" his use encourages. Committee members said they were convinced when they met with "very thoughtful and articulate members of the Native American community." A doctoral candidate in psychology, Joe Gone, who is Gros Ventre, explained how stereotyped Indians like Chief Illiniwek prevent other Americans from seeing Indians as real individuals who live in the same contemporary world they do. Chief Illiniwek freezes American Indians in the past, focuses on their supposedly warlike nature, and collapses all Indian cultures into Plains Indians. Most damaging, the ritual promulgates the concept that the dominant white culture understands how to honor and commemorate American Indians better than they do themselves.

Although this was only one suggestion by one of ten committees, it was the one that got the attention of the local press. There was a large response because it was the first time an official university body, albeit one in a preliminary advisory role, had suggested retiring the chief. Members of the committee received anonymous threatening phone calls at their homes.

The trustees didn't see a need to revisit the issue. "The Chief personifies the highest dignity of the Native American culture. To me that increases our diversity," said one. Another trustee, Judith Reese, thought she recognized names of faculty on the committee who were from minority groups themselves. "We've known for a long time that there have been some faculty members who have been opposed to the Chief. They tend to be from Third World countries or the recognized minority groups, so that's not surprising. If they put people on the task force who already had a bent in that direction, then that report is not surprising."

The daily newspaper of the two towns asked, "What will UI profs want to ban next?" A letter to the editor warned that alumni contribute substantially to the university and alumni want the chief. "If the committee isn't moved by the Chief, then the committee doesn't understand the tradition," another reader asserted. Only one alumnus wrote a letter to say that he was embarrassed by the comments of his fellow alums. He had always enjoyed the chief but had done so without understanding. "In reality, we borrowed an image and those that we borrowed it from, want it back!" Despite all the hoopla, when the final report was submitted, there was no mention of the chief nor of any initiative to encourage Native American enrollment, although other minority groups were mentioned.

Meanwhile, a local television station sent a news anchor to interview the Peoria. Her special report on "The Real Illini" aired on the local news on three consecutive nights. The three Peoria men who appear in the segment, one of whom is Chief Don Giles, said that they had no objection to Chief Illiniwek. In fact, what bothered them were the protesters who claimed to speak for all

American Indians. What the reporter told or showed them was never made clear. They also said that until the television crew arrived to ask their opinion, they had never heard of or seen Chief Illiniwek.

Local Native Americans made a videotape and sent it to the Peoria chief. They explained that having to live in the same town as Chief Illiniwek was demeaning and requested that Giles come to Champaign-Urbana and check things out before taking a position. Joe Gone also published a letter to Giles in an American Indian publication. This put Giles in an awkward position in the Indian community. He apologized to the group of local Native Americans over the phone for getting involved in something he didn't understand.

A Republican candidate for state representative, Rick Winkel, trying to take the local seat from an incumbent Democrat, jumped into the fray. "I'm the pro-chief candidate in this campaign," he announced. The incumbent, Laurel Prussing, said she thought the university community should make its own decision. Winkel managed to oust her in a close race; his win was attributed to his successful efforts to register and turn out conservative students.

One of the first bills Winkel sponsored in the Illinois House was a bill to make Chief Illiniwek the university's official symbol. A group of anti-chief demonstrators, including Native Americans, went to Springfield to protest, but they were not allowed to speak. They gathered on the lawn outside the state capitol around a bronze statue of Pierre Menard, the state's first lieutenant governor. Menard, dressed in a double-breasted coat, stands over an Indian man who kneels, bare-breasted. The two men's eyes meet in a look of pathos—the one looking down, the other up. According to a brochure about the capitol, the statue's iconography is intended to imply that Menard was a particularly "gentle and gracious man."

On May 15, 1995, the bill to make Chief Illiniwek the official symbol of the University of Illinois was discussed by a committee of the Illinois Senate. This time, when Native American organizations petitioned to speak, the committee agreed. The Native American spokespeople held a press conference on the second floor of the state capitol. To enter the press room, they passed under a forty-foot-high mural called *Treaty with the Indians*, painted by a German artist directly onto the wall and then framed with an immense gilt frame. George Rogers Clark, who captured Illinois for the Americans during the Revolution by showing up and persuading the French settlers to join the American cause, stands in a circle of light. All the Indians turn toward him, and his white shirt and pale blue uniform fairly glow against a pastoral landscape of trees and sky. At the left, winding toward the horizon, is the Mississippi River.

The Indians in the painting are difficult to make out. The foreground where they sit looking toward Clark is shadowy. In the dark lower left corner, oddly out of place, are two tepees. In front of these tepees stands Chief Illiniwek's truest Illinois ancestor, an artist's creation. Like his fictional descendant he wears a Plains Indian feather bonnet that trails down his back.

At the press conference, an Oneida elder said a prayer and those who stood were blessed with smoke, both back and front. After the prayer, a spokesperson for the American Indian Council of Illinois stated forcefully that the majority of Indian people in Illinois strongly oppose Chief Illiniwek. The next speaker was Tony Rodriguez, a student who is Mescalero Apache and Tarahumara.

"What exactly do you find racist about the chief?" a reporter asked.

"The same thing as someone in blackface, or a dancing Jew, or Catholic."

"Do you find the Minnesota Vikings offensive?"

"I don't know any Vikings," Tony returned.

"What about Swedish Americans?"

"Well if they find it offensive, I'd support them."

"But what about the Peoria Indians who were contacted by the TV station? Aren't they the rightful descendants of the Illinois Indians? And if they say they don't have a problem with it?"

·   ·   ·

The meeting of the senate committee took place in a room that used to serve as the state supreme court's quarters. It was lavishly decorated with ornately sculpted plaster flourishes. In the center of the ceiling was a large mural of the Goddess of Justice. The goddess was a dark-haired woman in classical garb who reclined among draperies. In one hand she held the Ten Commandments and in the other, a long, gold-handled sword. Her bare foot rested on a cornucopia of gold coins that spilled out over an old map. She had two assistants, both naked cherubim; one held the American flag and the other, a large volume of what I took to be laws. During the hour in which we waited for the senators to arrive at the meeting, there was time to reflect on this painting and what it might augur. The map with the gold coins piled on top seemed particularly significant.

Enough senators for a quorum finally arrived and the opponents of the bill were asked to choose several speakers. Each member of the audience was invited to fill out a record of their attendance. The slips of paper came in pads already marked either proponent or opponent. Although the large room was filled, not a single proponent of the bill filled out one of these slips.

Dennis Tibbetts looked discouraged. He said he was tired of talking to people who didn't listen. He had resigned as assistant dean of students and was moving back to Michigan. Ironically, the diversity program he had come to Illinois to run had finally been funded, after being stalled for two years, and his colleagues were annoyed with him for leaving.

Dennis did speak, however, going first, and talking about the psychological effects of a race-based mascot, not only on Indian students, but on other minorities, and finally on white students. He quoted from a letter members of the psychology department had written that stated that in their professional opinion the chief was damaging psychologically. He also invoked the image of the senators' own children. "How would you feel," he asked quietly, almost in a monotone, "if you sent your child to the university, a child that holds a special place in your family, and that child felt that who they are was being mocked?"

A spokeswoman for the American Indian Economic Development Association in Chicago, which represents urban Indians, urged lawmakers not to spend time on football mascots when the state budget and welfare reform were also on the agenda that day. She gauged correctly that wasting time on a trivial issue was a sensitive point with the lawmakers. She also spoke as a representative of the American Indian Council of Illinois, a group that represents the approximately thirty thousand American Indians who presently reside in Illinois. "We oppose any manifestation of Chief Illiniwek," she said forcefully, and pushed for the formation of a task force involving university representatives, representatives of the state legislature, and Native Americans.

Tony Rodriguez spoke next. He made sure to mention his service in the Marine Corps. Tony cited his research into the laws of the other forty-nine states, none of which have a statute on their books dealing with a mascot.

When Tony finished, a grandmotherly-looking senator was recognized. I assumed that the words of Dennis Tibbetts had touched her. But Senator Adeline Geo-Karis announced loudly that she has been to football games and the speakers have it all wrong, because Chief Illiniwek is there to honor the Indians. And if anyone wants to make a mascot out of her birthright, which is Greek, she'd be proud to see it. She invoked the Peoria. "Now they think it's an honor," she said in an outraged voice.

Senator Earlean Collins, a Democrat from Chicago, asked Senator Weaver, the other sponsor of the bill, if he knew of any other human mascot that represents a cultural group.

"I haven't researched that," he said.

"I wonder how I would feel if they portrayed an African American swinging from a tree at halftime," she speculated aloud, and then supported the idea of a task force.

"The Peoria Indians feel it's an honor for Chief Illiniwek to portray them," he replied.

"Why are they not here today to testify? It bothers me that there are no pro speakers here today," she answered.

The Senate minority leader, also a black Democrat from Chicago, spoke up against the chief, casting his vote against sending the bill on before he left for another meeting.

Another senator found it odd that the university, which has fulltime lobbyists, had not signed in at the hearing, nor come forward to speak. "If this bill is passed," he asked Weaver, "wouldn't every high school and college in the state ask the legislature to codify their mascot?"

"First, let me say, this is not a mascot. This is a symbol."

The audience snickered.

"Well, every school has a symbol. Will we have to codify all of them?"

Someone had sent a message to the university lobbyist, and shortly after that he appeared. The lobbyist was in an awkward position. The last thing the university administration really wanted was for this bill to pass. It set a dangerous precedent for the legislature to decide internal university policy. On the other hand, the university wanted to maintain its pro-chief stance. No wonder he had stayed clear of the hearing room that day.

For the next few minutes the lobbyist spoke and said absolutely nothing. "The university is a place of dialogue" was one of his frequently repeated lines. "We welcome discussion and of course we support Chief Illiniwek, but we do not have an official position on this particular bill, but we feel discussion is important and we certainly welcome it . . . the University of Illinois is a place of dialogue . . ."

When he finally stopped, the sharp energy that had filled the room had been dissipated. Everyone sighed tiredly.

Someone asked about other universities with Indian mascots. Tony replied that Marquette, Dartmouth, and Stanford had all had Indian mascots at one time, but have retired them.

"Is there any objection to professional sports teams like the Chicago Blackhawks?"

Tony explained that there was a movement to persuade these teams to change, but he made a distinction between the rights of individuals in business and the state university, which receives state and federal money. Tony was asked whether, if there were a referendum by the students and alumni to uphold the chief, would the Native Americans abide by that?

"No, sir, we would not," Tony replied.

One senator pointed out that when the Europeans came here, there weren't many women so they had to marry Indians [?!] and that we are all part Indian but don't know it. Another complained querulously that when he served on a committee to plan a celebration for the quincentennial of Columbus's arrival, the Indians opposed all the plans. Yet another used the logic that since Native Americans didn't object to the Blackhawks or the Redskins, that made it all right. Another senator said he had seen worse stereotypes of Indians on casinos on reservations.

The bill passed the committee and moved into the Senate, where it was overwhelmingly passed. However, the bill designed to protect the chief by legislation was vetoed by the governor.

The last salvo of the debate for the academic year 1994–95 was fired by two African American students who wrote and put on a play called *They Landed at Plymouth*. Raw and angry, the play confronted white viewers with a rare look into how the campus appears to minority students. One of the characters was a parody of Chief Illiniwek, who wore orange crepe paper fringe and came out at intervals to stagger drunkenly around the stage. His appearance was startling because Chief Illiniwek is almost never parodied on campus, even by his detractors, who are careful not to mock Native American culture. The directors' notes decry the "programming" given to minority students in the American educational system, which makes it hard for the small groups of minority students to act in unity.

> This struggle can be summarized in the University of Illinois' usage of Chief Illiniwek as a mascot/symbol/token/moneymaker. For many people of color, the Chief serves as a symbol of all of the things this school is doing wrong. The question we pose is this: If you take away the Chief, what recognition do we have of the people who used to occupy this land before any of us were here? Folks, we been had. This country ain't a melting pot. It's a microwave.

The university downplays Chief Illiniwek as much as possible these days. The outworn costumes are no longer showcased in the Student Union as they used to be. He appears only for football, men's basketball, and women's basketball and volleyball games. He no longer accepts invitations to speak about Indian culture to schools, to open shopping centers, to pose with politicians or dance at alumni parties. Auditions for new chiefs are held discreetly and applicants are carefully screened since the tryouts were infiltrated in 1994 by anti-chief protesters.

This is a story that Joe Miller, an academic advisor in the political science department, tells me with quiet relish. Joe is a member of Vietnam Veterans Against the War and his e-mail bears the VVAW slogan, "Remember the dead and fight like hell for the living." Joe speaks carefully and slowly in a quiet voice. He became involved in local protests against the Gulf War, and these connections led him into the movement against the chief. This was natural for him, according to Joe, since the Vietnam Vets Against the War have been longtime allies of AIM. Joe's friends and colleagues in the VVAW organization in Chicago trained the local anti-chief activists to provide security for their group while they demonstrate. The security provides a living fence between the demonstrators and the football fans outside the stadium. As he stood there, Joe was yelled at, cursed, jostled, and spit on, although perhaps the spitting was not intentional, he clarifies, just the result of excited people coming very close to curse in his face.

On the night of the tryouts, Joe remembers, he was outside the gates of the stadium with twenty or thirty other anti-chief protesters. They had a bullhorn and signs. They could see into the stadium. Out of the eight or twelve students trying out, four, who had gone through all the workshops to learn the dance steps, were anti-chief activists.

"I guess they drew lots to see who would go first and just by chance, the first to go is ours. He comes out to the music and does a sort of pseudo-Catholic Mass. Each guy had worked this out himself, what to do if he got this far. The people in the stands see this and they don't know what the hell is going on." Joe chuckles quietly at the memory. "But they have to let him finish because you're allowed to do your own thing. That's what they were told. We're figuring we're going to be there all night. The music starts up and the next one is ours also. What does this kid do? Oh, I remember, he does a striptease. And as he takes off his clothes, he's got anti-chief slogans painted on his body. And after him, they're going nuts in the stands. We couldn't hear them because they were too far away, but we could see them shaking their heads. They just didn't know what to do. And right then we started the chant, 'They're all ours! They're ALL ours.' We just shouted it out. We could see them and they could see us and the dancers were in between.

"The next guy did a doggie thing, barking and crawling on all fours and lifting up his leg. And then the fourth one comes out. He's ours, too. By that time we were just ecstatic. They had all made it."

An even more public protest was performed by the homecoming king and queen at the 1997 homecoming game. As they were introduced on the football field, they raised their arms and opened their coats to display anti-chief T-shirts.

There was an angry buzz in the alumni magazine and the student newspaper. Pro-chief students complained that the king and queen had ruined the happy moment by dragging politics into it. The following year there was a homecoming court, but no king or queen.

Many University of Illinois sweatshirts are now designed with the official seal rather than the chief logo. The university is delicately introducing a new logo, too—a classic, very educational-looking Doric column. Now that the "modern paleface Illini" has proven so problematic, maybe a return to the "Greek glory on the prairie" theme is in order.

The chief no longer travels to away games. Three Big Ten schools, Wisconsin, Minnesota, and Iowa, have forbidden him to set even one of his dancing bare feet on their football fields or gym floors. The student who played Chief Illiniwek for 1998, Scott Brackenridge, tells me it doesn't bother him. "It's appropriate that you only see him on our own home turf." And so he remains in Champaign-Urbana, where he still reigns over Memorial Stadium and Assembly Hall.

The university claims that a long tradition, good intentions, and responsible stewardship of the image have proved their worth to retain it. With a little more imagination, the university might argue that Chief Illiniwek is not a representation of Native American culture at all, but an icon of popular culture created by off-Hollywood, and that as a fictional character in musical gridiron theater, he belongs to whoever dreamed him up. To retire him without departing from this theatrical tradition, one campus minister and longtime activist recommends that the band stage a halftime show in which blue-coated cavalry ride in and shoot him.

In Whose Honor?

Jay Rosenstein remembers perfectly his first football game at the University of Illinois. He had just come down from Chicago for college, and was in his words "a huge sports fan." He can't forget because it was a football fan's worst nightmare, a 0-0 tie between Illinois and Northwestern, "who had a terrible team in those days."

"I must have seen the chief, I had season football and basketball tickets. But to me things like the chief, band, cheerleaders, pom-pom girls . . ." He shrugs. "Maybe I went to get a soda at halftime." He graduated in electrical engineering in 1982 and moved back to Chicago.

A couple of years later, he moved back down to Champaign-Urbana. One day he found himself at the YMCA. A panel of three or four Native Americans was speaking about the chief. Charlene Teters was among them. "To this day I'm not sure why I went. Maybe I went there to eat lunch. . . . I don't remember thinking beforehand, 'that's interesting' or 'that's important.'" Jay smiles at his own bafflement. "It must have been one of those moments in your life—a defining moment. For whatever reason, I was there."

She was probably the first Native person he'd ever heard speak in his life. "I actually remember thinking, 'oh . . . so that's what an Indian person looks like.' I was probably twenty-nine years old. I wasn't a child. I just had no clue.

"I remember sitting there and thinking, hmm, something's wrong here. I've got two sides of this story and they completely disagree with each other. There's absolutely no common ground. That is a white kid dressed up and dancing around—I see that. Now what do I think about it?

"I started to pay a lot more attention to the articles in the newspapers and think about it on my own. Hearing Charlene talk about these degrading cartoon images, and there were a lot of them then, in ads, in newspapers . . . seeing them, I remembered cartoons of Jews I'd seen in films about Nazi Germany. I looked at those Indian cartoons and recognized how Jews were portrayed and what resulted. That kind of imagery can be so powerful that it can turn a country into wanting to kill people. Once I saw that and it was clear in my head, there was no turning back."

Jay participated in a protest at a homecoming game in 1991 or 1992. "Our plan was to hold these masks in front of our faces to point out how stereotyping changes you from an individual to a stereotype. We were warned before the march—people are gonna be drunk, they may attack you, whatever—so I was on edge. They even said that we should watch out above our heads, people might throw things down on us. There were these two huge black guys in the march, they looked like football players. So when we got in line, I got right next to them." Jay laughs. "I thought if anything happens, I'm ducking behind these guys, nobody's going to screw around with them.

"When people talk about respect and honor, you have to stand there and see what happens to know that's a bunch of crap. People make excuses—they're just fans, they've been drinking—but that doesn't matter. The fact is, if you're an Indian person and you go out there, you have to be subjected to this incredible abuse—people scream at you, they swear at you, nothing physical happened when I was there—but it's relentless.

"One guy, an Illini fan with his son who's maybe seven, they walk by us standing there silently. He's holding his son's hand and this guy, this father, starts screaming at us at the top of his lungs, 'Fuck you! Fuck you! Fuck you!'"

Jay decided not to show that in the documentary he made. "I had some really nasty stuff that I left out." He feared it would undermine the credibility of the piece. "I'm still not sure if I couldn't have done that part better."

Around this time Jay took a class in documentary film. The class was going to make a group documentary and the students all pitched ideas. Jay pitched Chief Illiniwek, "but it was turned down flat." Over and over people told him that there was no story, or that everything had already been said in the newspaper articles that continued to appear at a steady rate.

Jay saw himself as the person who could bring Charlene's message to the community. "If only people knew this, they'd get rid of it. They just need to know." Jay laughs ruefully. "That's how naive I was politically."

Jay worked for three and a half years on the film in his spare time. Meanwhile he held down a job at the National Center for Supercomputing Applications. Although he had taken a class and done some small projects, it was his first real documentary film. He was sure activists would be interested, and he thought the local television stations might air it. But he couldn't help wondering whether he would manage to come up with something that people would actually want to watch.

When it was halfway done, he heard about a new Native American film festival in Santa Fe and although the piece wasn't finished, he submitted it. "I sent it in because I needed some feedback. I was really questioning—is this any good?" The festival agreed to show it as a work-in-progress and invited Jay to come for the screening. "I was terrified. The audience was primarily Native American and I thought, what if these people hate it?" But not only did the audience give him a huge ovation, many people came up to express their gratitude for what he'd done. "I came back with a real sense of commitment to the piece. After that I got the editing done fairly quickly. I just had a commitment I hadn't had before."

All along, there was one showing Jay wanted more than any other. This was the public television program *POV* (Point of View), which airs films by independent filmmakers. They take submissions once a year and you can submit only once. There was one loophole. You could submit a work-in-progress. If *POV* didn't take it, you could submit the finished work again the next year. Since the film still wasn't quite finished and the deadline was approaching, Jay decided to submit as a work-in-progress. Two months later, *POV* called. Would he be willing to shorten the film and make some editorial changes?

Jay agreed with the program's producers that *In Whose Honor?* was too long and said that he'd consider any changes they suggested. Eventually the producers called back and said they wanted it in the series.

The film shows Charlene Teters as she protests, at first alone with a poster-board sign in front of Assembly Hall, later with other activists. It follows her to Minneapolis and to Washington, D.C., to protest against the Washington Redskins. It is hard to imagine a more sympathetic character for our times than Charlene—attractive, with high cheekbones and long black hair, straightforward, artistic, articulate, determined, and unafraid to be emotional, especially about the effects of stereotyping on children. Some women have complained to Jay that Charlene is too weepy a warrior. They criticize him for including so many scenes of her in tears. But Charlene is tearful by nature, so it's an accurate portrayal.

The documentary also shows short interviews with University of Illinois trustees and members of the alumni association. The board of trustees, the group that has the power to retire the dancing mascot, adamantly supports him. The attitude of their chairperson, Susan Gravenhorst—her absolute confidence in her own point of view and her patronizing tone of voice—has brought new members into the anti-chief movement whenever the documentary has been shown. "Maybe those people that oppose Chief Illiniwek haven't seen him," is one remark she tends to repeat. "Maybe they should come to a football game." She always wears either a blue or an orange suit with a scarf of the opposite color.

Through *In Whose Honor?* many people have heard the Native American side of the issue. And for the first time, the university felt the heat of negative national publicity. Charlene Teters was featured in October 1997 as a "Person of the Week" on the ABC news with Peter Jennings. And some alumni, after seeing their university portrayed twice on national television in an unflattering light, wrote to ask that the chief be retired. Although many alumni remain staunchly pro-chief, the Alumni Association claims, officially at least, that it is neutral on the debate.

Jay says that one of his motivations for making *In Whose Honor?* was that "Ninety-nine percent of the American people have a blank slate about this. A dancing Indian? Who cares? I wanted to switch that consciousness switch on in people's heads. To have people think for the first time—yes, they are dressing up like a living group of people, and this Cleveland Indians logo—yes, I guess it is a cartoon of a person. So much of that stuff is cultural wallpaper. You don't even see what it is."

One activist says that by making the film, Jay turned the clock forward a decade on this issue. The film was instrumental in convincing Los Angeles educators to call for an end to American Indian mascots in their schools. The national attention also gave Illinois faculty permission to take the issue seriously. In the spring semester of 1998, eight years after the chancellor had called Chief Illiniwek authentic, the anthropology department published a long letter to the trustees explaining why the chief is an educational issue that undermines their teaching and research. The history department endorsed the letter. Professionals at the campus counseling center, who do not have academic tenure, signed a joint letter as individuals asking that the chief be retired for educational and professional reasons. Other departments and campus units added their voices. And seven hundred faculty members signed a resolution demanding his retirement.

Eight years after the trustees' vote, the faculty decided to vote on the matter themselves. In March 1998 the Faculty-Student Senate considered a resolution to retire the chief, drafted by a commitee on equality. In a rare show of interest in this body's deliberations, the balconies of the old auditorium were filled with students. Several faculty members protested that this was not an academic issue and should be dismissed. But masterminding the resolution were two longtime women professors, one from English and one from music. One after another they nimbly leapt up to the aisle microphone and explained that indeed it was. Once that question was settled in their favor, the chairperson of the Equality Committee, Heidi Von Gunden, the faculty representative from music, turned on an overhead projector. The first overhead was a multicolored graph that charted alumni giving at Stanford. "The year of the change was 1972. There was no significant change in the number of donors, the numbers of gifts, or in total revenues. If I may have figure 2 please?"

This table showed the comments of development directors at other institutions who had changed American Indian mascots. She read them off briskly. "Dartmouth. Not a cause for losing funds. Stanford. No impact on fundraising. Oklahoma. No effect whatsoever. Syracuse. Did not affect donations. Montclair State. There wasn't any effect. Eastern Michigan. Absolutely no effect. Bradley. No effect. Arkansas State. No effect. University of Tennessee at Chattanooga. No effect. Miami of Ohio. No decline in gifts. In fact they experienced a record year in terms of both annual and total giving." She repeated the remarks of several development directors that those who objected to the change were rarely big donors.

A whisper of surprise went through the audience. A devastating loss of funds from alumni had been predicted so many times during the past decade that most people had come to believe it was inevitable. In the nearly ten years that I had listened to both sides debate, this was the first time I had heard anyone offer a single fact on the subject.

"I move that be it resolved that the university administration and board of trustees retire Chief Illiniwek immediately and discontinue licensing Native American Indian symbols as representations of the university." Only members of the university community could understand the courage it took to read those words.

Three speakers had been brought in by the committee. They were Charlene Teters, an American Indian student named Bill Winnieshiek, and an anthropologist, Brenda Farnell, who does linguistic research among Native Americans and who, although she did not yet have tenure, had been the catalyst behind the anthropology department's letter. Each had three minutes.

"When I came here," Charlene Teters said, "I came with a great deal of hope. I was very honored to be here among all of you. But what I found here destroyed my dreams. My dreams quickly turned to nightmares. What I found was Home of the Drinking Illini and the Miss Illini Squaw Contest." She expressed concern about how "these symbols undermine our young people's self-esteem" and about university graduates who go on to positions of power in government, and "make decisions based on this misinformation." She ended by saying, "This is not about honoring Indian people, it is about acting honorably. An educational institution is no place for these race-based images. As I said many years ago, it's important to understand we are human beings, not mascots."

Bill Winnieshiek spoke next. "The chief of the Ho-Chunk nation, as is the case with other tribes, is to function as the spiritual leader. The chief of the Ho-Chunk nation is my great-uncle Ben Winnieshiek. The headdress he wears is earned. It was not bought nor would he sell it for any price. The eagle feathers in his headdress represent brave deeds he has performed or they represent services he has performed for our community." He went on to speak about the meaning of facial paint and how the designs are specific to each clan. Winnieshiek recounted how he had written a letter to the board of trustees to express his concerns about the mascot. One trustee, Thomas Lamont, wrote back that perhaps Winnieshiek would be better served at another school.

The last speaker was anthropologist Brenda Farnell. In her crisp British accent, she pointed out how the chief "sends a covert message to students that inaccurate information is acceptable and especially so if it supports your belief system. The sentimental attachment many students hold for the chief frequently overrides critical reflection and creates an anti-intellectual climate dismissive of critical thinking and reasoned argument. . . . Attachment to the chief creates an ideological commitment with all its attendant emotional fervor. . . . As an educational institution shouldn't we be working to counter this disturbing trend instead of covertly supporting it?"

Four students were given the chance to speak. The first put his remarks in the form of a poem dedicated to the board of trustees, entitled "Change Is Gonna Come."

The second student, a young woman, argued in a ringing voice that "we should not retire Chief Illiniwek and the Illini culture but take some necessary steps to improve the representation." She continued to speak about the pride students, alumni, and members of the Illinois community feel because Chief Illiniwek is not a typical mascot but a "dignified symbol that sets this university apart and sets Native Americans apart—in a positive light—putting the Native Americans on a pedestal." She spoke out for a Native American studies program to combat prejudice with education but felt that "these changes will only be successful if the chief continues to exist."

The third student said, "it is not the intention of the performance and the symbol of Chief Illiniwek to provide a history lesson. Rather Chief Illiniwek is a dignified representation of ideals all of us aspire to achieve. . . . To destroy a tradition cherished by hundreds of thousands of Illinois students and alumni will not solve academic problems. Destroying this tradition will not create a Native American studies program, create scholarships for Native Americans, help students to remember the heritage of Illinois or amend the crimes anthropologists have committed against Native Americans by desecrating grave sites." Except for the jab at the anthropology department, now seen as foes, his speech invoked the familiar rhetoric of the pro-chief students—pride, a bond that unites generations, the spirit of the Illini. It received the loudest applause from the pro-chief students in the gallery.

The last student to speak was Debbie Reese, a Pueblo graduate student who spoke as a member of the Native American Students Organization. In the last three weeks alone, she said, the group had received over thirty requests from teachers and librarians asking members to speak about Native American culture. Many of these educators specifically said that although they realize he is inaccurate, Chief Illiniwek is all they know about Native Americans.

Faculty members lined the aisles for a chance to make a short statement. "As Americans, we all inherit a past, most of it glorious, some of it troubling," said a gray-haired mathematician thoughtfully. "I've often visited Germany and speaking to younger people there, they all feel great pain when they consider the recent past. Not one university in Germany would contemplate having a rabbi as a mascot. They would consider it obscene. Now our past, the past we all inherit, is not as horrific as that, but it is troubling. As our nation matures, I think we need to see that past in its true light and not have symbols like Chief Illiniwek."

Several people felt that the chief was a positive and honorable symbol, but they preferred to see him retired to stop the endless wrangling. A cultural anthropologist remarked that the chief failed as a symbol because he divided groups rather than uniting them. The director of women's studies said that her staff felt keenly the parallel because women had also suffered from having been stereotyped and put on pedestals. "We're not opposed to school spirit," she pointed out, "only its embodiment in a racist mascot."

"I've talked to a lot of people and outside of academia no one really sees this as a racist mascot," replied one of the students. "If we retire him, we're erasing history."

The final vote was ninety-seven to twenty-nine in favor of the resolution. About half of the twenty-nine who wanted to keep the mascot were students.

Board of trustee member Tom Lamont, who had suggested that the Ho-Chunk student find a different school, replied to the faculty by saying, "This won't change anything." He pointed out in the daily newspaper that faculty would not appreciate trustees interfering with sabbaticals and tenure. In the same vein, trustees did not expect faculty to take formal votes on issues that are board policy. Many faculty members did not appreciate the implied threat.

Shortly after this meeting, the board of trustees told the student newspaper that the chief issue was closed. The anti-chief groups would have to submit new information before the board would consider the matter again. Apparently, the faculty's opposition to the mascot was not new enough information to warrant the dialogue the Native American students had requested. "It's just disappointing and unfortunate to see that they [the faculty] cannot appreciate that the Chief is such an important part of campus tradition," lamented trustee Susan Gravenhorst.

The pro-chief students remain convinced that they are a beleaguered silent majority. Some of them have responded by forming an organization called Students for Chief Illiniwek; they intend to take an approach that is "anti-racism and pro–Native American." Outside the stadium they do a brisk business in orange T-shirts with the slogan, "It's Our Turn."

When I inquired whose turn it had been up to now, there was a long pause. "Nobody's," one student finally offered, shrugging. Other pro-chief students and community members have created an educational foundation centered around the mascot. They want to use him as a "gateway" to educate students about Native Americans. In recent comments, both groups say they share the concerns of the anti-chief movement about caricatures like Chief Wahoo of the Cleveland Indians. They continue to make a distinction between a caricature and a fictitious but positive character. Their most recent T-shirt slogan is, "It's an Illini thing. You wouldn't understand."

The anti-chief students are encouraged by their recent victories. They vow that the chief won't dance in the twenty-first century. To show their support for the Illinois movement, activists from the nationwide movement against racial mascots converged on the University of Illinois in April 1998 for two days of talks and workshops. Vernon Bellecourt and Charlene Teters, of the National Coalition on Racism in Sports and the Media, Barbara Munson from HONOR of Wisconsin (Honor Our Neighbors Origins and Rights) and the Wisconsin Indian Education Association, Kenneth Stern of the American Jewish Committee, Floyd Red Crow Westerman, a Native American actor who was in *Dances with Wolves*, among other films, and Seminole activist Michael Haney, who was one of the first to come to Illinois to support Charlene Teters, all spoke. The meeting began with a prayer from Clyde Bellecourt, AIM cofounder. And Billy Mills, an Oglala Olympic gold medalist, gave the opening address and called Charlene Teters one of his heroes.

Michael Haney said about returning to Champaign-Urbana, "This used to be an ugly place—T-shirts everywhere. They've sanitized it somewhat but they haven't gotten rid of it. It's like pulling a knife out of your back and stopping halfway."

Kenneth Stern spoke about how he evaluates incidents of racism as he travels around the country. It's not so much the KKK or other racist groups he looks at. He knows what they are up to. But what do institutions in the community do in response to a racist incident? That's what matters. "As long as one group is being targeted, we are all potential targets," he reminded the audience.

The next day Charlene Teters and Vernon Bellecourt went on to Cleveland to protest at the Cleveland Indians' opening game. They were arrested for burning an effigy of the Cleveland mascot, Chief Wahoo, outside the stadium.

The following week, only four of nine trustees were present to listen to public comments about retiring the chief. Debbie Reese asked the trustees to consider the welfare of the youngest citizens of Illinois. Bill Winnieshiek, the Ho-Chunk senior, referred to the mascot as Mr. Illiniwek, "because the title of chief is earned. You can't become a chief by dressing in buckskin or spending a week on a reservation." He announced that Native American students had decided to postpone the annual powwow until the chief was retired, and invited the trustees to join him in a roundtable discussion. Stephen Kaufman, a feisty cell biologist with a New York accent, asked the trustees to respond to the faculty senate's resolution. The students who have worked in the anti-chief movement promised that this issue would not go away. One reminded the trustees, "We may graduate, but we'll be alumni forever." The trustees replied to none of these comments. They declined to meet with community leaders, Native American students, or faculty.

Ever since I learned about dean of men Tommy Arkle Clark, I had intended to go on a search to find his portrait. Someone told me he was in the library, but the portraits there were of the university founders and dated to an earlier era; they were dark shadowy oils whose subjects were barely discernible in the dim library foyer.

When I came into the room where the board of trustees was meeting around polished wooden desks, I looked up to the wall, and there he was. Tommy Arkle. He looked natty in white linen, one hand casually draped outside his pocket, trademark rings on his fingers, his shock of white hair setting off the white suit. The painting looked like his times—modern, compared to the earlier portraits. The background was composed of abstract zones of bright blue.

A senior in anthropology was telling the trustees that, contrary to popular belief, there had been a Native American studies program going on at their university for the last ten years, but they hadn't listened. It had provided a valuable lesson in how our culture stereotypes Native Americans. The trustees looked down stonily at their desks. I looked up at Tommy Arkle. They're thinking of banning cars again on campus. Tommy Arkle would be pleased. But he wouldn't understand the reasons—that there are just too many of them to park. Tommy Arkle watched over the students when they invented Chief Illiniwek. He knew their every move. I wondered if his painting might someday soon look down on the chief's demise.

Signaling

Carlos Montezuma in a portrait sent from the Western Shoshone Agency, where he was working as a doctor, to Adelphic, a literary society at the University of Illinois of which he had been president. Courtesy of the University of Illinois Archives, Urbana-Champaign.

Although the best-known Indian at the University of Illinois is the fictional Chief Illiniwek, the university can claim one illustrious Indian alumnus, Carlos Montezuma. He graduated in 1884 and went on to become a doctor, a prolific writer, and an important advocate for American Indians.

Montezuma was a member of the Yavapai tribe. At the age of six, he and his two sisters were kidnapped by Pima Indians. His mother was forbidden to leave the reservation to look for her children, and when she disobeyed, she was killed by an army scout. The Pimas sold the boy to a traveling Italian photographer for thirty dollars. The photographer renamed him Carlos Montezuma and did his best, despite his meager means, to give the child a good education.

After his adoptive father's death, Carlos ended up in Urbana, Illinois, in the care of a Baptist minister. After doing preparatory work, he entered the University of Illinois, graduating with a degree in chemistry. He went on to study medicine, earning his M.D. from the Chicago Medical College in 1889. He worked on several western reservations as a doctor for the Office of Indian Affairs, but frequently clashed with the Indian agents over their policies. Then he was offered the post of resident physician at Carlisle Boarding School in Pennsylvania. Montezuma stayed there three years. Carlisle was run by Richard Henry Pratt, who was staunchly committed to advancing the conditions of Indians by assimilating them as children into white Christian culture. His methods were often harsh and he was rigid and inflexible in his views, but Pratt became a lifelong friend and mentor to Carlos Montezuma. Montezuma was one of Pratt's success stories. Montezuma seems to have accepted a personal mission to prove to white Americans just how much an Indian could accomplish if educated and given a chance.

In 1911 he and other educated American Indians founded the Society of American Indians. While groups of whites that advocated for reforms in Indian policy already existed, this group was probably the first multitribal, national organization of American Indians.

Beginning in 1916 he published a monthly called *Wassaja*, which was his Yavapai name. It meant "Signaling" or "Beckoning." Fiercely opposed to the Bureau of Indian Affairs, he agitated all his life for its abolition. "It claims that it knows better what to do for the Indians than the Indians themselves," he wrote. In *Wassaja* he lobbied continually for citizenship and self-determination for Indian people. The University of Illinois yearbook for 1899 contains an essay by Montezuma in which he urges that Indian children receive the same public school education as their peers. He says he is tempted to load the American Indian children onto boats, ship them around Cape Horn, and bring them into America as immigrants. Then they could be assured of a public education.

Since he had been taken from his home at the age of six, he had little experience of tribal life and favored total assimilation for Indians. But after many years of practicing medicine in Chicago, Montezuma returned to Arizona and was reunited with Yavapai relatives. His experiences with them on the Fort McDowell reservation gave him a more complex understanding of other Indian lives. Although he had previously viewed reservations as prisons, in the following years he devoted himself to defending Yavapai rights to land and water, and largely because of his efforts the Yavapai succeeded in holding on to the Fort McDowell reservation. He also worked as an advocate for the neighboring Pima tribe that had kidnapped him.

The Bureau of Indian Affairs policy forbade dancing, so Montezuma used his influence to obtain special permission for dances when he visited the reservation. This was a significant reversal; until then he had seen little value in tribal culture.

He had invited the Society of American Indians to hold their annual meeting for 1923 in Chicago, but when time came to begin planning, he was critically ill. Aware that he was dying of tuberculosis, he returned to Fort McDowell and spent his last year living in a brush shelter on the reservation. He is buried there. All American Indians were finally granted the citizenship he fought for in 1924, one year after his death.

Montezuma died in 1923, so he never saw Chief Illiniwek. But in *Wassaja* in 1921, the same year that the Bureau of Indian Affairs again outlawed Indian religion, dance, and ritual on reservations, he left words that beckon to us still:

> It seems that the world will never get rid of fakers. For good or ill, there have been and are, a great many people using the Indians as their mascot. They pose as real Indians, when they are not in reality Indians.
>
> An Indian conversing with one of them knows that they are not Indians, and walks off disgusted, while the great majority of the people look on

at the feathers, the long false hair, and their Indian paraphernalia, and believe they are Indians.

These imposters are generally in business of some sort that requires Indianism, such as imitating the songs and dances of bygone days. . . .

From the foregoing description of the Indian impostors, the question is, do they do any good to the Indian race? They may do some good to other people, but they do more harm than good to the Indian people. . . . Any one who poses as an Indian does not help the Indians.

The Spoils of Victory

I'm in Paris, France, for an entire school year, with my husband and two children. People ask me what I am writing about. It's a book about mascots, I say. American Indian mascots.

They regard me blankly.

I begin with the football team of the university where I teach writing. (Classes in creative writing require an explanation themselves, but I leave that for another time.) So, football.

My listeners are all nods. Yes, football.

American football.

Ah oui, futbol americain. D'accord.

Well, at every game there's a halftime.

They're still with me, but I have to somehow translate, transform really, the midpoint of a soccer match into the spectacle of Big Ten football at Memorial Stadium. I have never seen the equivalent in France. Lacking an analogy, I launch into a description. There is a band. They wear uniforms and they march and play at the same time. As they do this, they form and reform into words and shapes on the field. Girls wave flags to create designs in the air. This is halftime.

They look confused.

It's an outdoor musical performance, I say. In the stadium. Anyway, I continue, now an Indian comes out and begins to dance.

Oh, an Indian. They perk up momentarily and look at me with new interest. Maybe I am part Indian. The Disney movie *Pocahontas* has just opened in Paris. There are Pocahontas dolls and plastic raccoons for sale in the store windows. A children's television program features Indian dancers and singers and for the occasion the hostess dons a buckskin dress with thigh-high fringe and a very Parisian décolletage.

He's not a real Indian, I say. He's a student dressed as an Indian.

I glance at my audience, my French friends. Their eyes have glazed over. They've stopped listening.

I begin to doubt myself. Why am I writing about an imaginary Indian who dances during the intermission of an athletic event? What does he matter? He is just an image. Here in Paris, where I pass the graves of Simone de Beauvoir, Sartre, and Baudelaire on the way to meet my children at school, a college boy dressed as a fictional Indian dancing at halftime doesn't seem like a subject worth writing a whole book about. It's obvious that my French listeners agree.

With one exception. This is our oldest friend in Paris, Claude, an anthropologist. Claude and I have spent many hours walking through his neighborhood or sitting over tea in his apartment. Now he walks more slowly and we are more likely to sit around his table for tea and cake than to pace the Jardin des Plantes as we talk. When I get to the end of my account and the Indian has danced, Claude's eyes flash.

"Of course," he says. "People have always done this. When one people conquers another, religion is one of the spoils. So are whatever other elements of the culture appeal to the conquerors. Think of the Romans. When they conquered the Greeks, they took their gods, renamed them, and began to worship them. This is part of warfare. He's a trophy, your Indian."

Paris is adamantly Parisian, and while I am there, I do everything possible to blend in. I do not become Parisian, but I modify the way I dress, walk, speak to people in public, and eat. I do not like to stand out so I leave my wildly patterned prints at home and wear every navy blue item I own. I whisper on public transportation and I try to master the art of leaning forward and brushing friends' cheeks in a pretend kiss. I train myself not to smile at strangers on the street.

When I return home to Champaign-Urbana, I am struck immediately by its cultural variety. On the campus paths, in the coffee shop, there is, compared to what I felt in Paris, a great deal less pressure to conform. There isn't just one right way to dress, to eat, to greet someone. There are myriad ways to be American, even in a prairie university town.

Once I return home to the incessant arguments, I remember why it seemed important to write about Chief Illiniwek. After a long hiatus, I begin again, trying once more to understand. He is just an image. But in our world, at the present time, images matter a great deal.

Coloring Books

My mother never believed in coloring books. She banned them from our house, although there were always piles of blank manila paper, the thick yellow kind, and crayons. Even without coloring books, when we drew, we called it coloring. It was something I always loved to do. When I went to school, a disconcerting thing happened. No one recognized the images I colored with the classroom crayons. When I drew a large purple iris with sharp spear leaves like the ones in my mother's garden, they asked me what it was. Next to it, I drew a group of jonquils, trying hard to make their orange ribbed cups stand out from the yellow petals behind. They fell over slightly, the way the ones in our yard did after a rain. Around the flowers I drew the crumbly brown leaves my mother spread over the surface of her flower beds.

They looked at it in disbelief. That's a garden? Oh, you want to draw a garden? A garden looks like this. And they drew many green sticks in flat rows. Coming straight out of the green sticks were taller green sticks. On top of each of these there was a strange flower I had never seen, a bit like a daisy but with rounder petals. Its leaves stuck out from its thin stick stem and I wondered how it stood up. The green sticks were grass, I knew. But grass was something we carefully weeded out of our flower beds.

My attempts to draw our small house with the concrete steps in the front were also unrecognizable to them. Their houses were always large two-story boxes with perfectly symmetrical windows and doors. Smoke always rose in a curling line out of a large chimney. This seemed odd to me. I had seen two-story houses, but there were very few of them in the new subdivision around the school where we all lived. And although we did have a fireplace, fires were a special treat in Memphis. We had them only once or twice a year on the very coldest nights. My house did have a chimney, yet when I looked at the house from the front yard the chimney could barely be seen.

Being a child who liked to blend in, I learned this drawing code and used it. Wagons were red rectangular boxes with two wheels and a line that slanted diagonally upward for a handle. Suns were yellow circles surrounded by an outer circle of yellow stick lines. Clouds were small things with protruding rounded knobs. A bird was a V in the sky. Now the other children and the teacher knew what was in my drawings. There were no more iris and jonquils and cannas and weeping willow trees. There were just trees and flowers. My house now looked like all the others. But everyone knew instantly what I had drawn. These drawings were much easier to make than the other drawings, with which I had struggled, trying to force the front steps to stick out, or the wooden fence to stay behind the flower bed. And everyone liked these drawings much better.

When my family goes on vacation we often play a guessing game like charades in which you communicate a word to your team by making a drawing. One night when I turn over my card, my word is "Indian." I don't need to think. I know what I will draw—a man wearing pointed feathers that stick up around his head. I don't even consider drawing a woman or a man dressed any other way. I trace the lines quickly. I have hardly finished the second feather when my team shouts, "Indian!"

What Do I Know about Indians?

Where, I ask myself, did the Indians in my imagination come from? My only exposure to real American Indians in childhood came at a place called Chucalissa, on the Mississippi River just outside Memphis. My mother and her friend Ruth were great ones for throwing me and Ruth's son Little Jack into the back seat and driving to the country for an outing. If the destination was also educational, my mother was doubly pleased. Chucalissa, an archaeological site and restored village, satisfied on all counts. The four of us began each visit in the museum, examining the dioramas of Choctaw life and looking at the bits of pottery. Then, invariably, in an empty darkened room, the only viewers on the metal folding chairs, we watched the film. It began with a rising and falling song unlike any other music I knew. The volume was always turned up loud even though we were the only ones listening. After a brief history of the cultures of the lower Mississippi Valley, the film ended with a demonstration of hunting with a blowpipe. The Choctaw man who narrated the film had a strong voice that rose and fell like the music.

From the darkened museum we passed into a long earthen tunnel where animal bones, cinders, and house posts were indicated on the dirt strata of the walls. The tunnel led to a large room, cool and shadowy even on a summer day, with a musty smell of damp earth. Standing behind a rail we looked out upon twenty or thirty skeletons, all in hard-packed graves cut into the orange dirt. Numbers next to the skeletons referred to a key, which told their approximate age and their sex, and sometimes even speculations that the archaeologists had made based on the condition of their bones. Even now I can remember the smell of being underneath the orange earth. Like any place that you return to again and again as a child, this chamber became familiar, a kind of sanctuary.

Emerging into the bright sunshine, we walked a large circle of rebuilt houses and climbed the steps of a pyramid-shaped mound. From the top we could look down on the Mississippi River. Outside one of the houses, we would come upon a Choctaw family dressed in brightly colored appliqué clothes working quietly at intricate beadwork. Their crafts were spread out in front of them—blue or red beadwork necklaces that dangled little girls or pairs of moccasins. Bamboo blowpipes and darts tipped with cotton. It was never very hard to talk my mother into a quarter for a beadwork brooch. It fastened onto my blouse with a brass safety pin that had been neatly sewed to its felt back. Sometimes when we went to Chucalissa, college students were excavating. When this happened, my mother's eyes gleamed. This was truly educational—archaeologists at work.

After our tour of the Indian village, we picnicked along the river. Of all the various woods we tramped through with our mothers, Little Jack and I preferred this one because it had the thickest grapevines, scratchy bark ropes that descended from the treetops and angled oddly left and right to create swings for our pleasure. But except for the archaeologists and the Choctaw family, I don't remember ever seeing anyone else at Chucalissa. Perhaps other people came on the weekends. Our outings were weekday affairs and always ended in time for my mother and Ruth to be back at home with dinner cooked when the fathers arrived from work.

An Indian village, I learned, was a special place, worth driving an hour to reach, interesting enough to visit again and again. But Chucalissa was clearly a deserted place peopled by a single family when there were houses for twenty. Its most arresting feature was the large room of unearthed skeletons who lay neatly numbered in their hard-packed open graves like objects on red earthen shelves. As for the Choctaw family, I never understood whether Chucalissa was their home, their place of work, or simply a piece of earth they could not abandon. And I never came close to putting this question into words.

What I knew about Indians: *Indians walk quietly, not even the dead leaves rustle when they pass, no twigs crackle.* I spent hours in the woods near our house trying. *They go long hours walking like that, eating only nuts and berries.* My favorite possession was a little leather pouch that attached to my belt. Filling it with pecans I slipped out of the house and spent all afternoon under the trees. *Indians take back things after they give them to you. If you play in the sun too long you will look like one. If you yell too much and jump around, you are acting like one.*

Again and again the bulldozers arrived and the vacant wooded lots where I spent afternoons walking like an Indian were turned into paved subdivisions. Memphis was a Sun Belt boomtown, constantly expanding. Memphians liked streetlights and sidewalks and cul-de-sacs (which they called coves) dotted with new houses. Only Indians, I thought, understood about trees. When workers from the city arrived in our backyard to cut down six massive elm trees in order to turn a creek into a cement flood-control ditch, I became an ardent pantheist, although I didn't know the word. I threw my heart in with the Indians. I read under the trees that remained, and my favorite books were about pioneer girls who were captured by Indians. I dreamed of being kidnapped and learning to tan deerskin and make pots with curved round bottoms like those in the glass cases at Chucalissa. But of course I had been born too late for any hope of that. The next best thing was Girl Scout camp, where for two weeks each summer we whittled soapstone and peach pits, built furniture out of branches and rope, formed our canoes into floating stars, and sang at night by huge bonfires.

When I was in high school and just waking up to the larger world around me, Dee Brown's *Bury My Heart at Wounded Knee* was published. I was shocked when I read it, for it was 1970, the era of Vietnam, and it made our government's policy there seem not like an aberrant mistake but rather another step in a long history of bloodshed. For the first time, in that book, I heard Indian voices and saw the faces of the Indians who spoke. In my mind these words and images were mixed up with Vietnam and with what we called "ecology," which became the environmental movement. My friends and I papered our walls with sepia-colored posters of the lined, weathered faces of Indian chiefs. Their sober expressions seemed to reflect our own feelings about the current state of affairs in America. Written across the posters were eloquent phrases about reverence for the land. For my birthday, someone gave me a copy of *Seven Arrows*, by Hyemeyohsts Storm. It was a book like none other I'd ever seen and I pored over its mysterious passages. I could no more understand them than I could pronounce the author's first name.

In college I talked my way into an advanced course on southwestern Indians taught by Ruth Bunzel, who came to our school to teach for one semester after her retirement from Columbia. A small white-haired woman of seventy-five when I knew her, Bunzel had done fieldwork among the Zuni when she was young. Along with Margaret Mead and Ruth Benedict, she had been a student of Franz Boas, an important figure in the development of American anthropology. Boas and his students steered American anthropology away from the premise that cultures evolved, gradually moving up a hierarchy that had savagery at the bottom and Western civilization at the top. They refused to use anthropology to justify racism scientifically.

I was the only freshman in the class. Her reading list was pages and pages long; most of the entries were books. It seemed to us that we had never worked so hard for any teacher and yet Bunzel rapped her cane on the floor and told us we were the laziest students she had ever taught. When I did come out of the library for a breath of air, I muttered snatches of Papago singing ceremonies or Hopi creation myths. I learned that you could find out a great deal about Indian culture from books. Even more, the discovery of culture and the realization that each one was structured differently from any other, a puzzle that could be decoded and examined, a complicated pattern that could be held up and compared to other patterns, excited me tremendously.

One of my friends had a boyfriend named Lance, a tall, handsome non-student with a long brown ponytail. He had been living in the West on Indian reservations and he pitched his tepee in the woods near the campus. When I wasn't studying I would sit with them, passing a catlinite pipe filled with kinnick-kinnick, a mixture of willow bark and other herbs that he ordered through the mail from a brown-on-brown brochure. Whether he was Indian or just another seventies kid looking for an alternative to suburbia I don't know. That he might actually be Indian never occurred to me at the time. He was too young. I thought of Indians as old men like the informants in the ethnographies, always looking backward, valued because they remembered the old days when their people lived "traditionally" and therefore authentically. From the pages of those books, from some nostalgic blank space between the lines, you could hear a soft rustle rising. It was regret made audible, the sound of the informants and ethnographers sighing in unison over every symptom of change.

That summer I worked at the Florida State Museum on archaeological digs, just like the students I had seen at Chucalissa. I learned to identify Florida Indian pottery styles and to differentiate a worked tool from an ordinary rock. Our crew excavated oyster middens and dug exploratory trenches. Archaeology, at least for a student, was mostly manual labor.

Sometimes farmers came in holding an arrowhead or part of a pot they'd unearthed in their fields. Gerry, our local folklorist, spent hours with them, explaining in plain talk the significance of what they'd found, encouraging them to come back when they found something else. Gerry had grown up around Gainesville. He held no degrees, but knew Florida archaeology from the intimate perspective of a shovel handle. Gerry knew more about the one-hundred-mile radius he lived in, its geography and history and folklore, than anyone I'd ever met. He was generous with his knowledge and eternally curious; he welcomed a backwoods story he hadn't heard and a new theory about flint knapping with equal enthusiasm. From his moonshine running days, Gerry knew every back road in north Florida and a drive with him on the sandy roads always included stops at unmarked archaeological sites. He was a volunteer warden on patrol for pothunters.

When the museum had no other job for me, I sat on a high wooden stool in a basement room and numbered pottery shards that had been found on the surface of an excavation. These shards, although they could not be reassembled, were always given acquisition numbers. Dipping an old-fashioned pen nib in India ink, I wrote a long series of letters and numbers on the curved inside surface of each broken piece. As I worked, I chanted to myself the names of the different pottery styles: Santa Rosa Stamped, St. John's Linear Check, Fort Walton Incised.

At the museum I learned you could make a living and structure your life around the study of Indian artifacts—pottery, flint knapping, stone tools, leather, beadwork, basketry. It was fascinating stuff, this unraveling of physical clues, and I appreciated the specific and detailed way the museum staff talked about the land and the waves of occupants who had lived on it. But the pottery shards and flint tools were classified into periods; very little was known about the daily lives of the people who had made them. Every item that we handled in the museum was ancient and valuable; these objects were carefully labeled and filed in drawer-sized trays in rooms whose humidity was regulated. We technicians were there to care for the artifacts because the people who had owned them had vanished long ago.

Archaeology seemed barren to me after the rich oral histories and elaborate rituals recounted in the ethnographies. And despite the museum staff's familiarity with the Paleolithic Indians of Florida, in the months I worked there, I never did meet, see, or hear about a modern-day Indian person. This was north Florida and real Indians, I figured, lived out west, although there were some in the Everglades. An anthropology student I knew left for Brazil so that she could live with a tribe that still hunted in the forests. My internship at the museum ended and my life took me in other directions. Like most Americans, I continued to assume that Indians belonged to the far away and long ago.

This is why, when I moved to a town in Illinois where a fictional Indian chief was an important icon, I never thought about appropriation or stereotyping. I never thought about racism. My son, too young to have been exposed to many imaginary Indians, understood perfectly when he made the analogy of another boy impersonating him on the playground to embarrass him. Even his choice of friends was telling, for he named the oldest boy on our block, the one who had the power to invite the younger boys to join the neighborhood games. In fact, this boy was kind to the younger boys. But my son understood that his voice would be the deciding one.

Children hate "copycats," and adults often have trouble understanding why they object so strongly. Imitation is flattery, we tell them. He wouldn't imitate you if he didn't admire you. Often powerless themselves, children are astute about what "copycatting" really is. Admiration yes, but not respectful admiration; instead it is muddied and twisted with the desire to control, to own the most beautiful and creative aspects of someone else. Even if they can't put into words what has been stolen, children know they have been robbed. They understand that copycats appropriate the power of the people they mimic.

The Wistful Reservoir

When I used to drive through North Carolina, there was a Cherokee Indian village and at the entrance, there was always a bonneted Indian. One time I asked him, "Why are you wearing Plains Indian dress?" And he grinned and said, "Because that's what the tourists want."

—DEE BROWN

Accuracy and authenticity have often been invoked as criteria to evaluate images of American Indians. Critics invoked accuracy when they discussed the early American painter George Catlin's portraits. Although they couldn't visit the Indians themselves to make an independent evaluation, the critics decided the artwork must be accurate. After all, he drew himself in one portrait sketching an Indian chief. And why would he travel so far and endure such uncomfortable conditions to paint Indians inaccurately?

In 1839 photography was invented. Matthew Brady, thinking that Americans would want to see the Civil War firsthand, as only photography could show it, assembled a corps of photographers and mobile developing equipment. He thought there was a fortune to be made in prints of important battles. However, when he tried it, he was faced with the tragic reality of new military advances and armies that moved too quickly to stay fixed on a photographic plate. What Brady and his corps were able to capture was the devastation that remained after the battle. His photos of the dead and wounded did not find many buyers and Brady was nearly ruined financially. His glass plates were sold to build greenhouses. After the Civil War, his corps of trained photographers was looking for work and many of them went along on government surveys of the American West. No one questioned the accuracy of these images, for they were, after all, photographs.

John Wesley Powell led an expedition to the Rocky Mountains in 1867 and collected botanical and mineral specimens and Indian vocabularies. Powell, a one-armed veteran of Shiloh with boundless curiosity, founded the Bureau of American Ethnology of the Smithsonian Institution. He was a firm believer in the idea that societies passed through stages of social evolution. The transition from a tribal society to an industrial one was a matter of evolutionary progress. It might require hundreds of years for tribes to evolve into civilized societies like ours, but it was inevitable that eventually they would. By studying tribal cultures, Powell and his followers, the pioneer American anthropologists, believed that they could reconstruct the evolutionary history of our own society.

The newly formed Illinois Industrial University, which became the University of Illinois, contributed to Powell's expedition and received botanical and animal specimens in return. Powell was made a professor of natural history at Illinois and given a salary of six hundred dollars to support his second expedition. Powell never taught at Urbana-Champaign and he resigned his position in 1869. But the bearded, one-armed explorer did come to the new campus to meet with the trustees and to report on the specimens he had collected for them. Perhaps he brought photographs of his expedition and passed a stereoscope around the table so that the trustees could see the wonders of the West for themselves.

Printed on cards, these stereoscopic photographs of rocky canyons and Indians were sold in sets and viewed in eastern parlors. Powell had costumes made for the Ute and Paiute people who sat for the camera, including feather bonnets. Powell must have felt that the costumes he commissioned were authentic, for when he was finished with them, he donated them to the Smithsonian for its collections. Of all the photographs of the West viewed through stereoscopes, the portraits of Indians—both savage warriors and bare-breasted princesses—excited the most interest.

Most of us feel we know how Indians looked and lived because we have seen reprints of Edward Curtis photographs. Between 1900 and 1930 Curtis filled twenty volumes with photographs of American Indians. Sepia-tinted faces lined with wrinkles. Eyes that seem to gaze into a mythic past or a darkening future. There is something so beautiful, so melancholy, and so convincing about the tints of that sepia. His photos are certainly works of art, for Curtis was a master of dramatic composition with light and shadow, but as ethnographic documents, they leave a lot to be desired.

As the Native American writer Vine Deloria, Jr., put it, "Since the photographs did not in the slightest degree speak to the reality of the American Indian, either past or present, they became the perfect format for expression of the wistful reservoir of emotions that lay behind the general perception of Indians."

Deloria writes this in the foreword to a book on Curtis by Christopher Lyman. According to Lyman, Curtis had a very clear idea about how real Indians should dress and act. It was impossible to find Indians who had not been in contact with white culture, so Curtis cropped his portraits and retouched his negatives. Suspenders and hats, wagons and parasols were removed. If tepees were sewn from feed sacks, he erased the labels from the plates with a stylus. If his subjects lacked embroidered leather shirts and feather bonnets, he supplied them, and he also carried wigs in case the Indians had cut the long black braids he knew they should have. To make their camps look more romantic and their hunts more dramatic, he retouched irrigation ditches into ponds and day into night. To an image of women cooking over a fire, he added a scratched-in pot and called it a shot of potters firing. Chiefs of different tribes wear the same feather headdress and mothers of different tribes hold the same cradleboard; what they have in common is the experience of being posed, photographed, and paid by Curtis.

Contemporary photographers realized that he was photographing something that did not exist, but most of them, like Curtis, believed that it had existed at one time, and that he was therefore simply documenting, as best he could, what was in the process of vanishing. According to a 1903 review in the *Seattle Times*,

> He dug up tribal customs. He unearthed the fantastic costumes of a bygone time. He won confidences, dispelling distrust. He took the present lowness of today and enshrined it in the romance of the past . . . he changed the degenerated Indian of today into the fancy-free king of a yesterday that has long since been forgotten in the calendar of time. He has picked up a bundle of broken straws and erected a palace of accuracy and fact.

But a more thoughtful ethnographic photographer criticized Curtis, comparing his portraits of Indian men in feathered war bonnets to photos of young women in their bridal gowns; both reduced a life to only one of its many facets.

One well-known Curtis photograph is a portrait of one of his interpreters. This man was also photographed by someone else in the woolen suit jacket he usually wore. But that photograph is rarely reproduced. In the familiar Curtis portrait, he wears a feather bonnet to hide his short hair and a bead breastplate over his bare chest.

Curtis very consciously devoted his life to a monumental task. He was determined to provide lasting images for our collective memory, and in that he succeeded. Our memory has been shaped by his images. When the activities of Indians did not fit in with Curtis's ideas of Indian nobility, as when Hopi snake dancers took an emetic and vomited, his shutter remained closed. We have remembered what he so artfully staged and photographed and forgotten what he never saw, never knew, or never deemed worth saving.

Dancing

The passage of time, the changing of the seasons, a new status in a person's life—birth, death, graduation from school, or return from war—any of these can be marked by appropriate dance and music in an American Indian community. Dance can be religious or social, and is often both at the same time. Dancing expresses and consolidates a sense of belonging.

Charlotte Heth, an authority on Native American dance, says that "Indian dance is not particularly acrobatic. It is in fact somewhat restrained, with the dancers staying close to the earth, for practical as well as philosophical reasons. Dancers usually take small steps—because of space, the number of participants, or the need to conserve their strength in order to dance for long periods of time (sometimes all day or night)." She also points out that there are few solos, but many ensemble forms.

Dancing is one activity that non-Indian people recognize as distinctly Indian. What do American Indians do when they are not attacking wagon trains with bows and arrows? They play drums and dance, usually around a fire, and they always dance before they go on the warpath. We prefer it if they do these dances gaily costumed and painted. We prefer it if they dance with wild abandon.

Non-Indian Americans have been ambivalent about Indians dancing. Although spectators flocked to watch Pueblo festivals, and although Wild West shows featured Indian dancers and were popular all over the country, the government and church groups feared the deeper significance of dancing and ceremony in American Indian life. The power of dance to unite tribes and create cohesion made the government uneasy. And missionaries were frustrated by the tenacity with which Indians held on to their religious beliefs. So church reformers and government agents did everything possible to suppress dancing as a ritual that had deeper meaning and to reinvent Indian dancing as a superficial entertainment that they controlled.

The Civilization Act of 1819 called for the active destruction of Native religions. Missionary efforts on reservations were subsidized and supported from the 1870s onward. Church groups did not acknowledge that Indian people had a real religion, of course. But they did have dancing, whose meaning these observers failed to comprehend. Dancing frequently became the target of forced assimilation policies, something to be suppressed as quickly as possible, at any cost. In the nineteenth century, everyone knew what was about to happen whenever Indians danced—they were about to go on the warpath.

Secretary of the interior Henry Teller created the Courts of Indian Offenses in 1883. These courts were presided over by American Indian judges who were under the jurisdiction of the agents on the reservations. Teller had already written to the commissioner of Indian affairs the year before to make his case:

> I desire to call your attention to what I regard as a great hindrance to the civilization of the Indians, viz, the continuance of the old heathenish dances, such as the sun-dance, scalp-dance, &c. These dances, or feasts, as they are sometimes called, ought, in my judgment, to be discontinued, and if the Indians now supported by the Government are not willing to discontinue them, the agents should be instructed to compel such discontinuance. These feasts or dances are not social gatherings for the amusement of these people, but, on the contrary, are intended and calculated to stimulate the warlike passions of the young warriors of the tribe.

This was not mere talk. The Courts of Indian Offenses had the power to investigate all Indian religious activities and to convict and punish those who did not comply. Two years later, the Office of Indian Affairs implemented regulations that called for Indians who participated in their traditional rituals to be imprisoned for thirty days.

One agent, quoted in the commissioner's report for 1885, reports that "Since the organization of the court dancing has been discontinued and plural marriages are unknown."

The Sun Dance of the Plains Indians, which had sustained Plains tribes through difficult times, was outlawed in the 1880s and Sun Dancers were imprisoned. The government's fear of the religious revival called the Ghost Dance and its determination to suppress it culminated in the massacre at Wounded Knee in 1890. Estimates of the dead range from 150 to nearly 400 men, women, and children. Congress awarded eighteen Medals of Honor to members of the Seventh Cavalry for this action. Thirty leaders of the Ghost Dance were rounded up by General Nelson Miles and imprisoned at Fort Sheridan. When William F. Cody visited him in Chicago, Miles suggested that Cody hire the ringleaders as show Indians. So twenty-three of the imprisoned Ghost Dance leaders were paroled into Buffalo Bill's Wild West show and sailed from Philadelphia on April 1, 1891. The prisoners were supposed to stay abroad for eighteen months. This tour kept them away from Pine Ridge, where it was feared they might stir up more trouble. And it wouldn"t cost the government a cent.

To dance as a religious act was illegal, but to earn money playing yourself in a lighthearted version of your own history and culture was entrepreneurial ingenuity. What could be more American than that? Buffalo Bill and the show Indians formed a touring company that recast the events of the past years into the myth of the Wild West, a myth they acted out in nearly every city in Europe.

The government was uneasy when Buffalo Bill and the show Indians, tired of the road, arrived back in Chicago in March after only eleven months. Most of the Ghost Dancers were allowed to return to Pine Ridge. But some, accused of plotting from abroad, were again incarcerated at Fort Sheridan, and one was taken on an educational tour of jails, courtrooms, and the state penitentiary at Joliet, Illinois.

In the twentieth century, war was no longer an issue. But the opposition to dancing and ceremonies continued. Not only was it pagan and heathenish, dancing sometimes went on for days, taking valuable time away from farming. And at some dances, Indians, who were poor anyway, insisted on giving away their most prized possessions. All this "dancing" went squarely against American Protestant values of thrift and industry, not to mention private property and material accumulation.

The commissioner of Indian affairs created one regulation after another to outlaw traditional customs. The "short hair order" of 1901 forbade long hair on men, paint, and traditional clothing. It authorized agents to withhold employment and supplies to force compliance and if that didn't work, "a short confinement in the guardhouse with shorn locks, at hard labor, should furnish a cure."

The regulations went on, "Indian dances and so-called feasts should be prohibited. In many cases these dances and feasts are simply subterfuges to cover degrading acts and to disguise immoral purposes. You are directed to use your best efforts in the suppression of these evils." Agents who were unwilling to comply lost their jobs, but they were urged to use tact and perseverance to avoid outright revolt.

Dancing became a bitterly controversial topic again in the 1920s. Many people agreed that American Indian policy had failed. But how should it be reformed? The largest and most zealous group of reformers were from Christian church groups. The commissioner of Indian Affairs supported the missionaries. He felt that they sought "the highest welfare of the Indians." One lurid report was circulated claiming that Pueblo dances involved sexual excesses and orgies. The head of the Indian Rights Association, a lobbying group that included many missionaries, never questioned the report. The association lobbied the government to suppress all dancing. Other government groups agreed. Indian dancing was probably immoral and at the very least, it encouraged laziness and neglect of livestock.

In 1921 the Office of Indian Affairs issued Circular 1665 to all reservation superintendents. This circular differentiated between ceremonials that brought "pleasure and relaxation" and other kinds of dances. These dangerous other dances included the Sun Dance and "so-called religious ceremonies" that involved self-torture, the reckless giving away of property, prolonged periods of celebration, the use of injurious drugs and intoxicants, or excessive performances that promoted idleness, superstitious cruelty, and dangers to health. Any dances that fit these categories were punishable by fines and imprisonment. This directive encouraged missionary activity on reservations. It also directed missionaries and government officials to turn the non-Indian public, who liked to attend Indian dances, against them.

Indian people did not stop dancing, of course, but they had to do so surreptitiously. One strategy they used was to schedule dances for American holidays like Christmas and the Fourth of July. Dances could also be held at tribal fairs and rodeos. Religious ceremonies continued secretly in remote and hard-to-monitor places.

Two years later a supplement to this circular was issued, again as a response to suggestions made by missionaries. It was known as the Dance Order. Superintendents were instructed to limit dances to one each month, in midweek, to be held at a location in the center of each district. No dances were to be held during planting and harvesting seasons and anyone under fifty years of age was prohibited from participating in any ceremony that showed immoral or degrading influences. The commissioner of Indian affairs then wrote a "Message to All Indians." He warned that he could arbitrarily end all "useless and harmful performances" but preferred that Indians give them up of their own free will. In a year, if they hadn't, another course of action would be considered.

During the same period, the early 1920s, the Bursum bill was proposed. This bill would have taken land from Pueblo people, who held it under Spanish land grants, and awarded it to non-Indians squatting on Pueblo land. The Bursum bill aroused public opposition, especially among anthropologists, writers, and artists who had been inspired by the landscape and Indian cultures of New Mexico. The most determined opponent was John Collier, an activist who lived in Taos. Collier admired the Pueblo lifestyle and felt that Pueblo cultures provided an alternative to the materialism and industrialization of American society. He received active support from an organization of public-spirited women who had powerful friends in many places, the General Federation of Women's Clubs. The Bursum bill was defeated by this coalition.

Collier fiercely opposed the missionary groups who wanted to suppress dancing. He testified before Congress in 1923 and called for laws to protect Indian religious freedom. The curator of the Museum of the American Indian became an ally. How, the curator asked, could all these white people possibly know about these degrading acts when they had never been allowed inside a kiva to witness any of the ceremonies?

The missionaries, in response, stepped up their campaign to inflame the public against tribal dances. They continued to describe Indian dances as immoral, immodest, and revolting, and to circulate reports that claimed to have witnessed sexual acts during ceremonies.

At the same time, Congress became concerned about the widespread corruption in the Office of Indian Affairs. How was it that an Indian agent, on a small salary, could retire a wealthy man after a couple of years working on a reservation? Congress commissioned an independent evaluation of the management of the Indian reservations. This report, usually called the Meriam Report, came out in 1928 and exposed the terrible conditions on many reservations and the mismanagement of the Bureau of Indian Affairs. In a dramatic turnaround from previous government policy, the Meriam Report urged tolerance for tribal customs and religions. In response, for the first time, people who were sympathetic to Indian culture were appointed to positions of power. John Collier became commissioner of Indian affairs.

Under Collier, the Indian Reorganization Act was passed in 1934. This was a turning point in American policy. The measure acknowledged that Indian culture had value and that Indian people had the right to retain their own traditions and to practice their own religions if they chose. For the first time ever, the American government acknowledged that Indian people need not give up their culture in order to have the rights and freedoms of other Americans.

Vine Deloria, Jr., who was born in 1933 on the Pine Ridge reservation, recounts that some of his earliest memories center around ceremonies and dances that were finally taking place after many years of prohibitions.

> With the passage of the Indian Reorganization Act, native ceremonies and practices were given full recognition by Federal authorities. My earliest memories are of trips along dusty roads to Kyle, a small settlement in the heart of the reservation, to attend the dances. Ancient men, veterans of battles even then considered footnotes to the settlement of the West, brought their costumes out of hiding and walked about the grounds gathering the honors they had earned half a century before. They danced as if the intervening 50 years had been a lost weekend from which they had fully recovered.

The freedom to practice Native religions continues to be an issue as Indian groups fight legal battles over eagle feathers, peyote, disruption of ceremonies, the seizure of ceremonial objects, many of which still remain in museums, and the denial of access to sacred sites.

Indian dancing, despite a century of suppression, is flourishing today. Urban Indian communities, whose members come from many different tribes, have turned to powwows as a way to express a multitribal identity. This has given dancing a prominent place in contemporary Indian culture, and the most accomplished dancers compete for large monetary prizes on the powwow circuit. Plains Indian dance and music dominate at powwows, and non-Indian people are often invited to participate. Some powwows, like the Red Earth in Oklahoma and the Gathering of Nations in Albuquerque, are large commercial performances for paying, mostly non-Indian audiences. These stress more individualistic performance dances like the Hoop Dance, the Eagle Dance, and the Spear-and-Shield Dance.

In more isolated rural communities, powwows are smaller and simpler, a group of local people gathered in a community center or at a private house—a celebration of community. They can even be organized by a single family to celebrate a family event. What both large and small powwows have in common is the notion of honoring a person or group of people.

With trademark wry humor, Vine Deloria, Jr., calls anthropologists to account for their roles as instigators of all this contemporary dancing. He says that after the Second World War, when anthropologists came to visit reservations, they were disappointed not to find people participating in the ceremonies, feasts, and giveaways they had read about. Many of these customs had been kept up, but they had "been transposed into church gatherings, participation in the county fair, and tribal celebrations, particularly fairs and rodeos."

> Suddenly the Sioux were presented with an authority figure who bemoaned the fact that whenever he visited the reservations the Sioux were not out dancing in the manner of their ancestors. In a real sense they were not real.
>
> Today the summers are taken up with one great orgy of dancing and celebrating as each small community of Indians sponsors a weekend powwow for the people in the surrounding communities. Gone are the little gardens which used to provide fresh vegetables in the summer and canned goods in the winter. Gone are the chickens which provided eggs and Sun-

day dinner. In the winter the situation becomes critical for families who spent the summer dancing.

In a curious paradox, while the government actively punished Indians who took part in ceremonies until 1934, most Americans defined Indianness by only two activities—war and dancing. War meant old-style Indian wars Hollywood and Buffalo Bill–style—wagon trains, bows and arrows, fast horses. Few people realize that ten thousand Indians volunteered to fight in World War I, although they were neither citizens nor eligible for the draft. In appreciation, the government granted citizenship to those who returned. Many Indians also fought in World War II, in Korea, in Vietnam, and in Desert Storm. In fact, the Kiowa created a new dance to honor Kiowa soldiers when they returned from Desert Storm.

The American public still loves the romance of the Indian past. Even now, when I cruise the Native American section in a good bookstore, the majority of the books are about Plains tribes and focus on the past, or on traditions that evoke the past. The Indians are the heroes and the cavalry the savages, but even so, it's the same old story. There are whole shelves bowed in the middle under the weight of New Age books that explain how to achieve wholeness through Plains Indian rituals. Little did I know, when I was given *Seven Arrows*, that producing books about Native American spirituality for non-Indians would become an industry. The bloodthirsty savage has given way to the befeathered dancer in touch with the universe, but either way, most Americans hold on to a stereotyped image of the Indian. This image is so pervasive and so resilient that even highly educated people accept it without question. A prominent Indian leader in the 1920s bemoaned the fact that Indians have to "play Indian in order to be Indian." In fact, playing Indian has become such an accepted part of both Indian and non-Indian identity that we forget that "playing Indian" is just play.

A dancing Indian chief as athletic mascot brings together the two most common types of play Indians—the warrior and the dancer. As symbol and icon, he has indisputable power. Our national attic is piled high with the leftovers from hundreds of years of playing Indian—paintings and books, reels of western movies, Scout uniforms, canvas banners from traveling Wild West shows, crepe paper costumes for Thanksgiving, headbands from summer camp. All these prop up Chief Illiniwek as he dances.

Reformers and government agents were determined to eradicate American Indian dance as an activity imbued with religious and cultural meaning and to re-create it as a commercial entertainment controlled by non-Indians. The existence of Chief Illiniwek a century after the Ghost Dancers toured Europe as both performers and prisoners is a testament to the success of this campaign. Those who have danced as Chief Illiniwek have said how heavy the buckskin is, how it weighs on you and slows you down. If Indian people are sensitive about the sight of white college students dressing as Indians and dancing at halftime, perhaps it is because, more than most of us, they feel the weight of history on their shoulders.

Scandalous and Disparaging

If we were to travel back in time and walk through the World's Fair held in St. Louis in 1904 to celebrate the centennial of the Louisiana Purchase, we could visit the large exhibition organized by the Smithsonian Institution. Here, we would see and learn about "primitive peoples." Over two thousand Eskimos, American Indians, Pygmies, and others are camped out in villages. Curious visitors like ourselves observe them as they go about their daily lives and demonstrate artisan activities. The exhibit is designed to teach us about human progress, specifically the way cultures progress from savagery to primitivism to civilization. The promenade through the fair is a bit like a board game. Start at Go near the Pygmy village, pass the American Indians and the Eskimos, avoid getting stuck on top of the Ferris wheel, and arrive successfully at Finish: the exhibits that glorify American invention and the latest technology. The American Indian schoolhouse is an important icon on this path, a transformative tunnel: American Indians enter as lazy heathens and exit as industrious Christian farmers and schoolteachers (although they might have characterized the off-reservation boarding schools as more akin to Go to Jail).

Suzan Shown Harjo has a photograph of her Cheyenne grandfather and great-grandfather. They stand in a line of American Indians outside the schoolhouse at the 1904 Fair. They are on exhibit. In the photograph, her grandfather, Chief Thunder Bird, stands beside his father, Chief Bull Bear. Both men wear feather headdresses and solemn expressions. From a narrow window above them, a white family, parents and two daughters in wide straw hats, look down on the scene. When the fair ends, the two Cheyenne men must return to the reservation in Oklahoma. They are not allowed to leave it without permission. Their children are sent away to boarding school.

At Chilocco Indian School in Oklahoma, Chief Thunder Bird's daughter, Harjo's mother, met Harjo's father, who is Hodulgee Muscogee. At the school he was regularly beaten with boards and belts. Each time he escaped to his home thirty miles away, he was returned to the school by federal agents.

Harjo, a widow and mother of two grown children, is the founder of the Morning Star Institute, a nonprofit organization dedicated to protecting American Indian culture. She is a former executive director of the National Congress of American Indians and served as a special assistant on Indian affairs to the Carter administration. Her latest struggle comes out of an exhibition of her own that she calls "the mantel of shame." This display over her fireplace contains Red Man Chewing Tobacco, a bottle of Crazy Horse Malt Liquor, Land O' Lakes butter, rubber tomahawks, and photos of Chief Illiniwek and Chief Wahoo. "It's not so much that each of these is horrible in and of itself," she says. "The problem is the cumulative effect. It suggests that Indians are dead, gone, buried, forgotten. That we are creatures of the past and not quite human."

Nearly one hundred years have passed since her grandfather and great-grandfather were exhibited as "physical types." But Harjo sees a saddening link between the "human zoo" at the St. Louis Fair and modern sports mascots. And she and other American Indians feel particular outrage that in this era, a team in the nation's capital has a racial slur against them as its name. They see it every day on the sports pages. They hear it on the radio and face it in the metro. And although when they hear "redskin," they think of human beings hunted for a bounty like wolves, no one else seems to take the slightest notice. That is why the Morning Star Institute has organized a petition of cancellation against the federally registered trademarks held by the Washington Redskins football team. Harjo and six other prominent American Indians—Raymond Apodaca, Vine Deloria, Jr., Norbert S. Hill, Jr., Mateo Romero, William Means, and Manley Begay,

Jr.—are the petitioners. Each petitioner is a federally enrolled member of a different tribe and all have been active in national organizations that represent American Indians.

Pro Football, Inc., the Washington franchise, responded that the petition infringed on its First Amendment rights. However, the regulatory body that hears trademark cases, the Trademark Trial and Appeal Board, refused to rule either way on the First Amendment, saying that it was outside its jurisdiction. Either way, freedom of speech would not be denied to anyone. The team's owners (and fans) could use the word "redskin" as much as they liked. They could continue to call the team by that name if they wished. What is in dispute is whether the word "redskin" is entitled to federal trademark protection. Harjo hopes that if they lose trademark registration, the team's owners, no longer able to collect royalties on licensed merchandise or sue the producers of knock-off merchandise, will change the name to protect their commercial interests.

The Lanham Act, passed in 1946 to expand federal trademark protection, specifies that marks that comprise or consist of immoral, deceptive, or scandalous matter cannot be registered. Nor can marks that "may disparage . . . persons living or dead . . . or may bring them into contempt or disrepute." Someone who is opposed to a mark has five years after it is registered to file a complaint. However, if there is reason to believe a mark was registered erroneously and that it never should have received federal trademark status, a petition of cancellation can be filed at any time. To employ this section of the Lanham Act is an innovative legal strategy devised by Stephen Baird. The lawyers tested it successfully against a company that wanted to market fishing tackle under the trademark "Injun Joe." The Patent and Trademark Office official who made the ruling agreed that "Injun" was a racial slur and that "a clear error was made" in publishing the mark. And when the National Basketball Association tried to reactivate the Sheboygan (Wisconsin) Redskins trademark to sell clothing, the Patent and Trademark Office refused.

But in the past, the decisions of the trademark board about what is scandalous or immoral have been erratic and contradictory. Scandalous to whom? A majority of the population? Potential purchasers of the product? The group to whom the product refers? And of course what is immoral to one generation may seem commonplace several decades later.

"Madonna" as a wine label was deemed unregistrable in the 1930s. Although its proponents pointed out that it wasn't whiskey or rum and that wine was drunk in the Bible, the judges refused registration because they felt that a majority of the public would be scandalized by the idea of the Virgin Mary on a bottle behind the bar. When a cigarette company tried to trademark a cigarette named "Senussi" in 1959, the board also refused. Senussi is the name of a Muslim sect that forbids the use of tobacco. Although most Americans might not be aware of the word's meaning, the fact that the product would offend Muslims was sufficient to prevent its registration. Similarly, "Bubby Trap" for brassieres was turned down. In the latter case, it was decided that women, the potential purchasers, would be offended. The Old Glory Condom Company was initially refused registration for a package that showed a condom with patriotic stars and stripes; it was believed that a significant portion of the American public would find this offensive in the 1990s. However, on appeal, the board reversed its decision when Old Glory's attorneys made a case for the company's seriousness of purpose in patriotically promoting safe sex. In this case, good intentions were taken into account. Two women opposed a restaurant's registration of the phrase "Only a Breast in the Mouth Is Better Than a Leg in the Hand," and their argument that this slogan brought women into contempt and disrepute was sufficient to prevent its registration.

If a trademark is considered disparaging, and this is the criterion that would apply in American Indian cases, the question arises, who decides? Does a significant portion of the public have to be offended, as was attested with wine named after Mary or red, white, and blue condoms? Or should it be the group to whom the product refers, as in the case of the cigarettes, brassieres, and chicken legs? In 1893, when Aunt Jemima first appeared, no one, black or white, spoke up publicly to say the character was disparaging to African Americans. But when Aunt Jemima advertisements appeared in national magazines, complete with incidents from the fictional character's life as a slave, African Americans began to voice their disapproval. Cyril Briggs, the editor and publisher of *Crusader* magazine, based in New York, vehemently denounced the trademark in 1918 and called upon his African American readers to boycott the brand. In 1932 a marketing survey of African American consumers in southern cities found a strong negative response to the ads. Those surveyed disliked the references to slavery, and they found particularly offensive the handkerchief on Aunt Jemima's head. To call someone an "Aunt Jemima" became an insult in the 1950s, hurled by African Americans at other African Americans, the strongest possible statement of that group's feelings. The NAACP called for a boycott of Aunt Jemima products in the 1960s. The organization's opposition centered on the local appearances by black actresses who dressed like house slaves and portrayed the smiling old cook. Many white Americans did not understand the objections. They saw Aunt Jemima as a harmless portrayal that stressed positive qualities—competence, strength, reliability, and nurturance. After all, she made the best pancakes in the land.

In response to the controversy, Quaker Oats finally altered her image in 1968, changing the handkerchief to a headband and slimming her down. This image remained until 1989 when it was again updated. The modern Aunt Jemima, an African American woman with graying hair and no headgear, can still be found on supermarket shelves. Although she is somewhat problematic, she is too profitable to relinquish. Shown the old Aunt Jemima "mammy" trademark and the ads depicting her as a loyal and contented slave, it seems probable that a large portion of the public would now find this mark disparaging and offensive. It is clear that public sensibility and sensitivity change over time.

The meanings we attach to words change, too, particularly the secondary or connotative meanings. In the contemporary marketplace, the beverage company that sought to register Madonna wine might have faced opposition from a rock and roll star who could have reasonably argued that the public associated the name with her commercial enterprise. When a word is under consideration, interpreters of the Lanham Act turn to dictionaries. As English evolves, dictionaries are reissued in new editions. New words find their way in; old words, although they often remain, may be labeled nonstandard, antiquated, or offensive. My third edition of the *American Heritage Dictionary* (1992), which I love for its easy-to-read print and its small black and white illustrations in the margins, labels "redskin" "offensive slang" "used as a disparaging term for a Native American." Its usage editor, Geoffrey Nunberg, believes that the term is correctly labeled and testified as an expert witness for the petitioners. My *Webster's New Collegiate*, published in 1980, says only "noun: American Indian," implying that the two words are synonymous. This is the position taken by two linguists who have testified as expert witnesses for Pro Football, Inc. One, Ronald Butters of Duke University, gave a paper at a meeting of the Dictionary Society of America held in May 1998. In the paper, he maintained that the word "redskin" doesn't offend American Indians and that dictionaries should stop labeling it derogatory. He cited, among other references, a 1929 song entitled "Redskin," a novel by James Fenimore Cooper, and a recent article in the *New Republic* that used "redskin" in the title. He theorizes that Americans today associate the word "redskin" with the Washington Redskins football team, giving the word a secondary meaning that has actually become its primary meaning. And he points out that the terms "redskin potato" and "redskin peanuts" are still widely used, although one no longer hears Brazil nuts called "niggertoes."

Lexicographers at the conference were taken aback when they discovered that Butters had done the research he presented as a paid consultant for Pro Football, Inc. The newsletter *Copy Editor*, which reported on the conference, pointed out that there was a disagreement between Butters's point of view and that of two contemporary usage guides, which both called "redskin" "highly offensive." What do you think? the newsletter editors asked their readers, most of whom are professional editors. The publication received thirty replies—the most ever on a single topic. Respondents concurred twenty-nine to one that "redskin" was offensive. One editor of a food magazine wrote in to point out that the preferred usage for the spuds was "red-skinned potatoes," and that the name was a description of their appearance, and had never been a reference to American Indians. All the Native Americans who wrote to *Copy Editor* were offended by the term. Only one editor disagreed, citing a poll he had conducted in his own newspaper in which several American Indians wrote in to say they were not offended.

The Washington Redskins' defense attorneys acknowledge that "redskin" is informal, like the words "cop" and "Brit." They also admit that it's dated. But they point to its usage by respected authors such as James Fenimore Cooper and Mark Twain as proof that it is a neutral term. Even James Joyce used "redskin" in the second chapter of *Ulysses*, in a passage often cited for its anti-Semitism.

Jack Kent Cooke, the former Redskins owner, vowed he'd go to his grave before he'd change the team's name. It was a vow he kept. His son John Kent Cooke, who hoped to buy the team, was equally adamant. The team's lawyers characterized the legal action against their trademark as "a way for certain fringe elements to air their political views." However, the District of Columbia City Council, hardly a fringe element in the city, had already passed a resolution asking for a name change. When the current owners bought the team, they were urged by an editorial in the *Washington Post* to do the right thing and change the name as one of the prerogatives of new ownership. They refused. The name honors Native Americans, the team insists. They also wave the banner of tradition, although professional teams frequently change both their names and locations. And fans cope. The owner of the Washington Bullets waved his wand and changed the basketball team into Wizards after the public expressed ambivalence over a name that seemed to glorify violence. And when the Houston Oilers went to Nashville, the National Football League nixed the idea of Rebels. The team became the Titans.

It is difficult to measure whether a term is considered offensive by the public. One telling piece of evidence, according to Nunberg, is that searches online do not uncover recent uses in journalism that are not about sports and that are neutral or positive. You don't find headlines like "Redskins meeting with senators over treaty rights" or "Redskin elected to city council." The term is no longer in use because a consensus has been reached that it is offensive and disparaging. In fact, "redskin" appears in the title of one reference book about ethnic slurs: *Unkind Words: Ethnic Labeling from Redskin to WASP* by Irving Lewis Allen, published in 1990.

But the petitioners also commissioned a telephone survey. Both non-Indian Americans and Native Americans were asked whether they found certain terms for Indian people offensive. Forty-six percent of the non-Indian Americans found "redskin" offensive. Among the Native Americans sampled, 37 percent objected to the term. Both groups were more offended by the word "Injun": about half of those surveyed in both groups found it offensive. And the word "squaw" was more offensive to Native Americans (47 percent) than to the general non-Indian public (36 percent).

I asked Geoffrey Nunberg if he could provide an equivalent term to "redskin." "Maybe 'darkie,'" he offered. "Or more likely 'wop.'" But he pointed out that it's impossible to consider these words equivalents "because the stereotype of one group is not exactly analogous to that of another."

Michael Lindsay and Stephen Baird, the Minneapolis lawyers who represent the petitioners pro bono, make a case in the brief that it should be the group referred to who should be the authority on what disparages or offends. Otherwise, minority groups, particularly small ones, would have no recourse in federal trademark law, since it is unlikely that members of the majority would be sensitive to their reactions. And they point out that the wording of the Lanham Act stipulates only that petitioners prove that a trademark "may disparage" or "may bring into contempt" persons living or dead. They feel they have proved not only that, but more—that the team's name does disparage Native Americans.

The petitioners received a supportive precedent in March 1999 when the Utah Supreme Court remanded to the state's tax commission a decision it had made concerning personalized license plates that spelled out "REDSKIN." Utah law does not allow personalized license plates that "express contempt, ridicule or superiority of a race, deity, ethnic heritage, gender or political affiliation." But the statute did not specify who decides whether a word or phrase expresses contempt—should it be the person offended, the general public, or the tax commissioners? The commissioners ruled that since the term was used pervasively, it probably was not offensive to the general public and the plates were permissible. The state supreme court did not uphold this criterion. It was not reasonable, the judges ruled, for any one person, whether state official or Native American, to decide. Nor was it reasonable to ask whether the general public found a word contemptuous since the public might be unaware of its meaning. They said that "the only reasonable standard was that of the objective, reasonable person" and ordered the tax commission to revisit the case. The plates, owned by Washington Redskins fans, were revoked.

On April 2, 1999, the Trademark Trial and Appeal Board ruled for the petitioners. In a 145-page ruling, the board canceled the Washington franchise's seven trademarks. It was a significant legal victory for the anti-mascot coalition. The team can keep the name, of course. The right to name your own business is protected by the First Amendment. The owners still maintain state and common law rights to trademark protection. But they have lost the commercial power that comes with owning a federally registered trademark. They can no longer call on the federal government to enforce and protect their exclusive right to profit from the registered names and marks.

In the ruling, the three administrative judges said that although "redskin" was not scandalous, it does disparage Native Americans. Although the survey had found that 46 percent of non-Indian Americans and 37 percent of Native Americans were offended by the term "redskin," not a majority, the judges found this percentage large enough to be significant. They rejected Pro Football's argument that "redskin" has a new secondary meaning and refers only to the team and no longer to American Indian people.

Pro Football, Inc. has appealed the cancellation. And as long as the case is under appeal, the company maintains its trademark rights. Licensing fees for the National Football League are pooled, so the team will continue to receive its share. In the appeal, the team's lawyers may argue that the Lanham Act itself is unconstitutional because its criteria—scandalous and disparaging—are too vague to be enforceable. They could also argue that the ruling abridges their First Amendment rights. The case could go all the way to the Supreme Court.

Although they won't comment publicly, the lawyers for the Cleveland Indians, Kansas City Chiefs, Chicago Blackhawks, and Atlanta Braves are, I would imagine, studying the ruling closely. It would be much harder to prove that any of these team names disparage Native Americans or bring them into contempt. Unlike "redskin," the words themselves are not ethnic slurs. You would have to prove that

If the decision against the Washington Redskins is upheld, high schools all over the country, like this one in Tulsa, Oklahoma, would face renewed pressure to change their names. Photograph by Stephen Holman.

Cartoon by Tony Auth, *Philadelphia Inquirer*, October 22, 1997.

they become demeaning in the context of professional sports. Sports fans who are sensitive to the mascot issue agree that the logo for the Cleveland Indians, the bright red, bucktoothed, big-nosed, befeathered, and very cartoonish Chief Wahoo, is both stereotyped and demeaning. President Clinton refused to wear a Wahoo cap when he threw out the first ball in 1994. Even some fans who believe that naming teams after Indians is an honor and want to keep the names concede that both Chief Wahoo and the tomahawk chop ought to go.

Activists Charlene Teters, Vernon Bellecourt, and Michael Haney acknowledge that fans have become habituated to protesters outside the stadiums. Although they will continue to protest, they admit that the demonstrations have had little effect. Their strategy for the future is to file complaints under both civil rights and trademark statutes. Court cases, even those that are eventually lost, serve an important function. While they are being argued, media coverage brings the debate into our public discourse. Some of the rest of us may actually do what American Indians so badly want us to. We may stop for a moment, put our assumptions aside, and consider. We might even ask ourselves whether, if they damage the self-esteem of Indian children or teach our own children that stereotypes are acceptable, the mascots are fun and games worth maintaining.

The Tribe

It is opening day 1999 at Jacobs Field, an impressive, five-year-old stadium in downtown Cleveland and the home of the Cleveland Indians baseball team. According to tradition, it always snows on opening day, but there are no snowflakes in sight. It is an ordinary chilly Monday morning in mid-April and even though the game won't start for hours, the restaurants and bars around the stadium are already filling up with fans who gather to eat Polish sausage and hash browns for breakfast while they talk over the tribe's chances for a pennant. A store that sells Indians merchandise is already open too, and doing a brisk business. The fans all wear hats and jackets decorated with the Indians' logo, a bright red cartoon Indian nicknamed Chief Wahoo who sports a single feather behind his head. He grins so expansively that his cheeks swell outward on both sides of his face as if he's a red chipmunk. His nose is large and his eyes are oddly triangular. Is he shifty, or simply surprised at how well the team is doing this year? Hard to say, but he certainly gets around. He's on every hat, the back of every jacket, on banners above the street, on garbage cans, on cars. Outlined in neon, he's also in the historical museum. One of the few concessions that team owner Richard Jacobs made to Wahoo critics, when the new stadium was built in 1994, was not to remount the thirty-foot neon Wahoo sign that has been a Cleveland landmark since the sixties. Instead, the neon monstrosity or masterpiece, depending on your point of view, graces the historical museum and museum visitors can voice their approval or criticism in a comment book placed nearby

Hours before game time, another group gathers outside the stadium. Like the fans, they have come for opening day, but they don't intend to enter Jacobs Field. They are here to take part in a protest organized by the Committee of 500

Years of Dignity and Resistance. Many wear baseball hats with the Chief Wahoo logo slashed out. They refer to Chief Wahoo as "little red sambo" and their banners show the cartoon Indian reprinted with stereotyped Asian, Hispanic, and black features. Printed underneath this series of images, which would never be seen in public any more, are the words, "This Honors Who?"

"This is not about baseball," says Juan Reyna, a Mexican Apache who heads up the group. "This is about racism." Reyna has been arrested twice at Jacobs Field for protesting, the first time at a World Series game in 1997. That time, the protesters were burning a straw effigy of Chief Wahoo when they were arrested. The case came up in April 1998, was shown on Court TV, and was thrown out after the prosecution presented its arguments. Three days later, protesters gathered outside the stadium for opening day. But when they started to burn another straw effigy, five of the demonstrators were arrested for suspicion of arson. They were held for a day and then released. They were never charged.

One of those detained was Juanita Helphrey, a Hidatsa woman from North Dakota, now the minister for racial justice of the United Church of Christ. The United Church of Christ, whose national headquarters is across the street from the stadium, has been generous with financial and organizational support for the anti-Wahoo movement. Helphrey recalls that she got through the three hours she spent in a small room under Jacobs Field by singing church hymns and powwow songs from her childhood. The following morning, at the arraignment, she learned that the complaints against her said she was violent and had resisted arrest. Actually Helphrey, a quiet woman with long gray hair, says that she went willingly and was not handcuffed.

Before the 1999 opening day demonstration begins, there is a press conference at which their lawyer announces that the five protesters who were arrested the previous year have filed a suit against the Cleveland police department for false arrest.

Another lawsuit against the baseball franchise uses Title II of the 1964 Civil Rights Act. Title II guarantees "full and equal enjoyment" of places of public accommodation to all persons regardless of race, religion, color, or national origin. The lawsuit charges that the use of Indian imagery keeps Indian people, who find the images repugnant, from enjoying equal access to the stadium, which is a public place. This is a new legal strategy advanced in a February 1999 article in the *Harvard Law Review*. It has not been tested. In order to win the case, the claimants would have to prove that the mascots, names, and logos, and the war whoops and chants that go with them, deter American Indians from attending and enjoying baseball games at Jacobs Field. Lawyers think the strategy has potential, not only in Cleveland but at stadiums across the country.

"Warriors, braves, chiefs, Indians—" says Vernon Bellecourt, the president of the National Coalition on Racism in Sports and the Media, who has been arrested twice at Jacobs Field. "These are words created for us. I don't believe that there are words for any of these things in our languages." Bellecourt's voice is distinctive, a raspy growl that comes from the back of his throat, and he has a slight accent that doesn't sound like Minnesota.

The speakers are upbeat in the wake of the Patent and Trademark Office ruling. When asked why they don't use the same legal strategy that worked against the Redskins, a trademark cancellation proceeding, Bellecourt says there's no need to repeat that legislation. He feels sure that if the Redskins lose their appeal, Cleveland will see the writing on the wall and retire Wahoo. The Cleveland team's licensed merchandise is among the most popular in major league baseball, behind that of the New York Yankees. In 1998 the team earned $1.5 million from the sale of licensed merchandise and about $15 million from its team shops in the Cleveland area. At home games, the stadium is always sold out.

"We have been dehumanized, mysticized, demonized, romanticized, and villainized," Bellecourt continues. He is Anishinabe, and has been active in the American Indian Movement since the 1970s. A thin man in his sixties, dressed

Protest on opening day 1999 at Jacobs Field, home of the Cleveland Indians. Photograph by Carol Spindel.

in black, he is wearing his trademark black hat with beadwork band; it throws his lined face into shadow and turns his mouth into a straight line that hardly seems to move when his words emerge. "You know," continues Bellecourt, who has a way of making you wait, drawing a word out in his distinctive nasal drawl, "When I stand outside stadiums, reporters are always asking me, 'Don't you have more important issues than these mascots?'" He pauses. "And you know what I say?" Another pause. "I say . . . yes, we do have other important issues." He speeds up to a rapid fire delivery, his finger coming up to punctuate his words. "I say to those reporters, 'let's talk about sovereignty, let's talk about treaty rights, let's talk about repatriation.' And you know what? Every time, they close their notebooks and walk away."

Lying in front of the steps where the speakers stand is a carved and painted wooden bas-relief of Chief Wahoo inside a plain wood coffin; the piece was created by a group of Native American artists in Athens, Ohio. Standing the coffin upright in an oil can, they set the carved Wahoo afire. Television cameras quickly encircle it. The image of the carved face in flames, with the word "Tribe" carved below it, is shown on both local and national news broadcasts.

An older man in an Indians jacket and Wahoo hat stands on the edge of the crowd, near the oil can. He has a dark creased face and short, tightly curled hair that is mostly salt with a little pepper. Whether he is there to listen to the speeches or warm his hands over the fire is unclear. But Charlene Teters walks over and quietly asks him if he knows why they are doing this. She mentions his Wahoo hat and jacket.

"I've been a fan for fifty years," he tells her. "There's nothing wrong with this." He gestures to the hat. "I'm not a prejudiced person. I love baseball."

Bruce Two Eagles joins them. He has a soft persuasive voice with a thick Massachusetts accent. "Indian people aren't against baseball," he tells the man. "We just don't want to be portrayed as a cartoon character."

"I'm not prejudiced. I'm Italian." The man says his name is Sal. He's a retired ironworker.

Bruce talks about the need to educate people. "People don't realize how images like the Wahoo logo affect our children."

"How does it affect your children?" Sal asks.

Charlene talks about the high rate of teen suicide among Indian youths, how low self-esteem is widespread.

"Italian people have been stereotyped, too," Bruce adds. "People think they're all in the Mafia." Sal nods and to their surprise, big slow tears roll down his face.

"I'm not a prejudiced person. I'm a fan," he insists.

"I can see by your tears that you didn't know," Bruce tells him. "What we need to do is educate people. That's why we're here."

"I'm not prejudiced," Sal replies, "but I love baseball." He doesn't leave. After Charlene is called away, the two men continue to stand next to the oil drum that contains the burning effigy. Bruce suggests they trade hats. He'll give Sal his hat with the Wahoo logo slashed out and Sal can give the Wahoo hat to Bruce.

"This hat cost me twenty-three dollars," Sal says.

"This one's just as good," Bruce replies.

"I'd want to keep my pins," Sal tells him. There are two pins attached to the hat. One is an angel. The other is his retirement pin from the Ironworkers' Local. Bruce was an ironworker too, and they talk pipefitting and welding.

Sal slowly takes off his hat, removes the two pins, pockets them carefully, and hands the hat to Bruce. Charlene comes back and puts her arm around him. She looks tearful, but smiles for the first time all morning. Bruce holds up Sal's old Wahoo hat and then puts it in the fire.

Reporters come over and interview Sal. But after they leave, he returns to talk to Bruce again. "I'm not going to buy another Wahoo hat," he says, "but I can't wear this." He returns the protest hat. Before he leaves he tells Charlene that he will put his jacket in the closet and that it will stay there.

Later, as the protesters march around the stadium, Bruce calls over to a young African American man who works at the stadium. "You know," he says in his thick Massachusetts accent, "when you marched for civil rights, we stood beside you. We'd like you to stand up for us now." The young man looks down. It is clear that he has heard.

As the march passes a bar whose small terrace is filled with fans, a man puts his hand to his mouth. "Woo-woooo-woo-wooo!" But when marchers turn toward him with cameras and video recorders, he retreats inside the bar.

When large numbers of fans begin to arrive, the protesters move closer to the main walkway into the stadium. The plaza in front of the stadium is alive now with the bright red Wahoo logo. It's thickly embroidered on jackets, caps, sleeves, gloves, and socks. Some people wear jackets with an older Wahoo logo—this face is light brown rather than fire-engine red and has a long hooked nose. Other fans wear blue or orange sponge feathers that rise a foot into the air above their heads. The word "Tribe" is printed vertically on each feather.

"Get a life," the fans yell as they pass the demonstration. Some smile, as if opening day wouldn't be complete without a protest. Along with the fireworks and the matching Wahoo clothing and the planes that fly over trailing messages, the demonstration is part of the spectacle. "Go Tribe!" some yell, with raised fists. Others smirk, as if the whole idea strikes them as absurd.

Two young men, their faces painted blue and red in geometric blocks, pass the protest and are razzed by Juan Reyna, who has the microphone. When I see them later outside the stadium gate, I ask if they know why the demonstrators were yelling at them. "I think some tribe doesn't like it," says one. "I didn't really listen to what they said," adds the other.

I offer that Indians are offended by the Wahoo image.

"But it doesn't look anything like an Indian," one retorts.

"Well, it's supposed to represent one," I say.

They look at me in surprise, as if this has never occurred to them.

"It's labeled in big letters." I point to the sign above the stadium, which says "Indians" in monumental cursive. The blue eyebrows of one boy rise slightly.

An older man with Cleveland pins scattered over the top of his baseball cap stands near the protest and watches with bemused interest. When I ask what he thinks of the demonstrators' message, he smiles understandingly, as if they are children who have good intentions but are confused. "The team was named to honor Indians," he says. "The team was named after an Indian."

"How do you know?" I ask him.

"I read it," he says. "It's in the paper all the time. They had a contest to name the team and one fan suggested Indians—because of this ball player . . . Sockalexis." He says the unusual name precisely, as if it's a trump card, the history card. "He was their star player."

"It's not true," I reply.

"What do you mean?"

"It's made up," I say. "The sportswriters repeat that story all the time. But there was no contest, there was no fan." It's my turn to shrug. "Sports journalism. You can't believe everything you read."

He turns to his middle-aged son. "Time to go in."

Louis Francis Sockalexis was a Penobscot from Old Town, Maine, who was recruited by the Cleveland Spiders, a National League team. He played for only three seasons, from 1897 to 1899. He batted .444 in college and when recruited to play for Cleveland, he seemed destined for a great career as a slugger. One legendary manager from that era said that Sockalexis was the greatest natural athlete he had ever seen in baseball. In his first major league game, Sockalexis hit home runs the first two times he batted.

Sportswriters and fans quickly picked up on the team's new player; he was nicknamed "Chief" by sportswriters; his own fans saluted him with honorary "war dances" and whoops. Opposing fans called for his scalp. The team quickly realized that "the Indian" was perhaps even more useful as a promotional tool than he was as a hitter.

Verbal abuse was one of the arts of the game in that era, and opposing players taunted "the Indian" mercilessly. His fall from grace is a baseball parable. He broke his leg in a literal fall from the second story of a brothel and was arrested for disorderly conduct in front of a bar. His alcoholism worsened and his ability to play declined. The newspapers held him up as a warning about the evils of drink. Unfortunately, his tragic life confirmed the stereotype of the drunken Indian in many people's minds. Fired at the end of the 1899 season, he played briefly in the minors in Connecticut and Massachusetts. He was an unemployed drifter when he died at the age of forty-two in Maine.

The story of Louis Sockalexis is a tragic one of a talented athlete who was unable to fulfill his potential because of emotional instability, alcoholism, and prejudice. If they didn't need to justify their name and logo against the charge of racism, it seems unlikely that the Cleveland Indians baseball team would choose to embrace him as an icon.

Before the team was renamed in 1915, they were the Naps, named after Napoleon Lajoie, their popular star player and manager. But when Nap was traded in 1914, the team's owner had to find a new name. Sportswriters were disappointed with Naps, anyway. What could they call them when the team was winning—the Napless Naps?

The story of how the team became the Indians is repeated over and over in promotional literature. It goes like this: a contest was run in a local newspaper and the winning entry, Indians, was suggested by a fan in honor of Sockalexis.

Ellen Staurowsky, a sociologist who studies sports in society, asked the team which newspaper sponsored the contest. There were four in Cleveland at the time. It seemed odd to Staurowsky that the team would risk alienating the sportswriters of the other three dailies by holding a contest that involved only one newspaper. She also asked the team the fan's name and what he won.

The team's public relations staff replied that they had no idea; they had never looked any of this up. Ironic, given the wording of a 1995 press release about the name and logo issue, which reminds readers that the name has "historical significance" and offers, as a first step to understanding the complexities of the name issue, "a history lesson."

Staurowsky went to the Cleveland archives herself. What she found was that the team's owner, faced with Nap's departure, announced that a committee of baseball writers would meet in nine days to choose a new name. In the interval, sportswriters bantered about possible names and one sports editor did solicit suggestions from fans. Fifty-seven people sent in ideas, but three articles about their suggestions never mention Indians as one of them. When the baseball writers held their meeting and announced that they had chosen Indians, there was widespread approval. Clevelanders saw the name's potential immediately—a team that could go on the warpath and scalp rival teams was just what they'd had in mind, especially after enduring Naps and Spiders (commonly found in basements). There is no mention of Louis Sockalexis in 1915. Why would a baseball player who never lived up to his potential, even if he did play briefly in Cleveland, have been honored by having a team named after him? The idea that he may well have been the first American Indian to play major league baseball and should be honored as a pioneer sounds like a 1990s point of view applied retrospectively. The most prominent Native American athlete of that era, Jim Thorpe, had, just two years earlier in 1913, been stripped of his two Olympic gold medals for having played minor league baseball. His name was stricken from the Olympic records. Baseball writers and team owners were not interested in the complexities of the lives of Indian athletes like Thorpe and Sockalexis. What they wanted was to assume the identity of fictional Indians—those war-whoopin', scalp-huntin', drum-playin' guys in paint and feathers who are always on the warpath. The Wild West shows were in their heyday, so to make an emotional connection between baseball and show Indians was a win-win promotional strategy. It had worked wonders in Boston—the Boston Braves had moved up from last place to win the World Series!

In Cleveland, as in other cities and on campuses, people who wonder whether Indian mascots honor or demean Indians often come away, after reading about the issue, confused by the way history is presented. In Cleveland, the official team history about the anonymous fan who writes in because of a desire to remember and honor Sockalexis creates a cloud of good intentions around the company. Not only does the story make it seem that one of the goals in naming the team was to honor Indians, it implies that fans have a real influence on the baseball franchise's decisions, an impression the team wants to foster.

In reality, professional sports teams are multimillion-dollar entertainment corporations that are managed by CEOs for profit. A team, like any other product, must create and maintain brand name loyalty. But public relations managers and sports journalists work to keep alive the mythology of American sports—that each team is unique with its own colorful history and traditions, that each team is an integral part of the city where it is currently based, and that each team gives the city, no matter what it costs taxpayers, something priceless. In other words, it's not about money, but something more valuable and more American, something intangible that we should be ashamed of questioning. Cleveland owner Richard Jacobs sold the Indians in 1999 for $323 million to a member of the powerful Dolan family, who made their millions at Cablevision. The amount set a record for the sale of a baseball franchise. The new owner Lawrence Dolan announced he would keep the name and Chief Wahoo, despite the controversy. American Indians joked about buying the team themselves and renaming it the Cleveland White People with a hillbilly who plays the banjo for a mascot. This is obviously more than a joke; it's a desire born out of frustration. They are tired of standing outside stadiums with bullhorns, tired of requesting meetings with owners at which the owners never appear. They are tired of being asked by security to leave the stadium because their banners are "offensive" to the Cleveland fans. (This happened to two members of Florida AIM when they unrolled a banner behind home plate at a Cleveland–Devil Rays game in Tampa. The banner said, "American Indians Are Human Beings Not Mascots For America's Fun and Games.") They are tired of being told to lighten up. They would like, for

Advertising that uses Chief Wahoo to market Miller beer is no longer produced. The change was due to pressure from an organization of religious institutional investors, the Interfaith Center for Corporate Responsibility. Photograph by Carol Spindel.

once, to have a seat at the sports table for a serious discussion, but since that isn't happening, their only recourse is the courts.

But legal procedures take years. In the meantime, the Interfaith Center for Corporate Responsibility, an organization of Catholic, Jewish, and Protestant institutional investors, whose members' portfolios total over $100 billion, has had some success convincing companies to take Wahoo off their ads. Miller, Anheuser-Busch, and Coca-Cola have agreed, and Denny's does not allow its employees to wear Wahoo clothing at work.

Do you or do you not Wahoo? In Cleveland, this question is not taken lightly. The public library and some religious organizations and local businesses have tried to ban Wahoo from their buildings. They are attacked for having no sense of humor. Local religious groups often deviate from national policy when it comes to the little red logo. Although the United Methodist Church has passed a national resolution against the mascots, when the East Ohio Conference voted on an anti-Wahoo resolution, one woman said that she'd give up being Methodist before she'd quit wearing Wahoo. The resolution was defeated.

"Racism never wins," is one of the activists' slogans. If Cleveland wants to be not just a contender, but a champion, the real Indians have a suggestion. Forget firing the manager. Fire the mascot, change the name, and remove all associations to Indian people. The real Indians promise to be on the field the next day with drums, tobacco, and feathers to offer up real thanks and real blessings.

A Young Child Speaking

Debbie Reese grew up in northern New Mexico in Nambé Pueblo, a community of six hundred people, divided into an upper and lower village by families, a place where everyone knows everyone else and most people are related. Her grandmother's house adjoined theirs, and as a child she roamed the hills with her grandmother, collecting herbs and scavenging for bits and pieces like discarded wire spools, which they fashioned into fences and gates. In the kiva she was taught to dance and she and the other children of the pueblo danced in ceremonies on the annual Feast Day, which takes place on October 4. On these occasions she wore traditional clothing sewn for her by her grandmother. "It's this Sunday," Debbie says wistfully, "and three of my nieces will dance for the first time."

Her father worked at the nearby Los Alamos lab and in addition to work, family, and the obligations of the pueblo, took courses at night to get a bachelor's degree in engineering. In May 1984 Debbie and her father graduated from the University of New Mexico in the same commencement exercises. She received a master's degree from the University of Oklahoma at Norman. In Oklahoma, she also taught at an off-reservation government boarding school for American Indian children. Most of the children were wards of the court and the youngest were in the second grade. This school gave her a harsher perspective on Native life than anything she had known.

After she graduated from the University of Oklahoma, she returned to Santa Fe, where she taught in another Indian boarding school, one at the opposite extreme, an elite preparatory school. She met her husband, George, a white teacher from Pennsylvania, there. They have one daughter, Elizabeth. The three lived at Nambé as part of Debbie's extended family.

The young couple became friends with a professor from the University of Illinois who was doing research in New Mexico. When they mentioned that Ph.D.'s in education were part of their long-term plans, he urged them to apply to Illinois. The professor had explained the controversy over Chief Illiniwek, but Debbie didn't see stereotypes as a serious problem. Debbie's main concern was that, away from Nambé, her daughter's Pueblo identity be affirmed and nurtured. Elizabeth was three and had just danced for the first time.

"When I arrived here, I often brought up my heritage and my experiences growing up Pueblo. I'm very proud of it and I talk about it easily. And when I started doing that, right away, ears perked up." She laughs. "I could see the gears turning and people thinking, oh, I can ask this person. Tell me about Native Americans. What do you think about the way Thanksgiving is taught in the schools? Should Native Americans be introduced into the curriculum at Thanksgiving? And of course . . ." She pauses. "What do you think about the chief? There was a big lack of knowledge and an intense desire to know. I was pleased to be able to help with that."

But Debbie was also surprised at the level of ignorance. She remembers going into Elizabeth's preschool at snack time. A little girl asked her, "How come your skin is brown?"

Debbie replied that she was an Indian person, a Pueblo Indian.

"But Indians aren't real, they're all dead," the child answered. Of many similar encounters with both children and adults, this one stands out in Debbie's memory because it was a young child speaking and because she was so aware that her daughter was sitting next to her, listening.

The following year, the Disney animated film *Pocahontas* was released and on the playground, the four-year-old girls fought over who would play Pocahontas. Elizabeth said it should be her, because she was Native American. You can't be Native American because your skin's not brown and your hair's not black like Pocahontas, the others retorted. This infuriated Elizabeth, who favors her father.

One day the teacher told Debbie that her daughter didn't seem to be ready for kindergarten. Elizabeth had been throwing tantrums and sometimes she hid under the table. During a conference, as the teacher described the outbursts, Debbie said that bells went off in her head. She realized that each one had occurred after a wrangle over Pocahontas or in one case, when the teacher read a book about Chief Seattle. In this best-selling book, the Indians, in Plains Indian dress although they lived on the West Coast, were depicted as mythical beings who lived in the clouds, beautifully and evocatively drawn, but transparent, so that grass and trees showed through their bodies. The white people in the book were opaque and wore ordinary, contemporary clothing. The book reproduces a moving speech about respect for the earth attributed to Chief Seattle that has been widely reprinted on posters and calendars. It was written by a white writer in the 1970s for a documentary on the environment.

"That's not right about my people," Elizabeth insisted.

"But Elizabeth, this book is not about your people," the teacher replied. "You're Pueblo Indian. This is about a different tribe."

Aware that her daughter's sense of self was at stake, Debbie began to look more closely at how Indians were depicted in children's books. She was invited to many elementary classrooms as a speaker. Most of the children she met thought of Indians as very exotic or as extinct. One typical exchange with a child went like this:

"How did you get here?"

Debbie didn't answer right away.

"Do you have a car?"

"Yes, it's a red one."

"But Indians don't have cars, they have horses."

This happened over and over. The schools she had attended in New Mexico were approximately a third Native American, a third Hispanic, and a third white. Her own experiences had convinced her that stereotypes, although they are everywhere in the media, did not seriously affect children's perceptions. She had never believed they were a serious problem. The children she knew in New Mexico and Oklahoma, whether Indian or white, counterbalanced stereotypes with their own day-to-day interactions. In Illinois, however, the children she met had only stereotypes to go on. And their teachers, although aware that these stereotypes were misleading, did not have the confidence in their own knowledge about American Indian culture to correct them. More and more teachers contacted her. Which books were accurate? How should they teach young children about Native Americans? Debbie decided to write her dissertation about American Indian stereotypes in literature for young children. She reviews books for publications like *Horn Book* and gives frequent presentations to teachers and education students. Although she agrees that children see stereotypes in television and in the movies, she decided to focus on books because we accord to books "a greater level of authenticity." She wonders if that doesn't make the inaccuracies in books even more damaging.

Debbie finds herself giving a presentation on stereotypes to teachers or educators at least once a month. The first transparency she shows is of three-year-old Elizabeth standing with her older cousins in front of the kiva, dressed in traditional clothing to dance in a ceremony. "I show this one to let people know why I care about this, what motivates me." The second transparency shows a book called *Five Chinese Brothers*. The cover is a drawing of Asian men with slanted eyes and black hats. "I understand people's fear of making mistakes based on lack of knowledge because I've made those same mistakes. I used to love this book, but now I can see that it stereotypes Chinese people. I've put it aside."

She believes that young children need to see more visual images of contemporary Native Americans and she is particularly pleased when she finds a book that shows Native American children doing everyday things to which other children can relate. In one book an Indian child brings a pair of handmade moccasins to show-and-tell. "Every child can relate to show-and-tell," she says warmly. Another begins with a scene of an Indian family in an ordinary-looking living room; they gather around an older relative in an armchair to hear the folk-tale that makes up the rest of the book.

But many children's books, no matter how beautifully illustrated, how elegantly designed, or how recently published, pass on misleading images to children. One visually stunning book has Squamish from the West Coast dressed in Plains style. Another book with a poetic text shows Hopi dancers at a horse race ("as if we're exotic people who dress like this to go everywhere"). In the crowd of people in jeans and flannel shirts, the Hopi dancer in a horned headdress, tanned deerskin, moccasins, and elaborate face paint does look otherworldly. And yet I have read this book to my children many times and never wondered what he's doing there. Another award-winning book is about a boy who goes down into a kiva to fight a battle. "A kiva is a spiritual and educational place," she says calmly. "It has nothing to do with battles."

In a survey she did on the Internet, Debbie found that in general, editors, publishers, reviewers, and authors objected to her reviewing a book based on sociopolitical concerns. They thought she should stop worrying about stereotypes and read the book as a work of literature. Librarians and teachers, in general, felt the opposite. With limited money to spend, they want the reviewer to point out potential problems. They tend to see children's books, even fiction, as both literary and educational.

Someday Debbie would like to do a large-scale research project about the effects stereotypes in the media have on American Indian children and on all children. She'd like to talk to children in Illinois and in the East, in places where there are few Native Americans, and in other places where there are many. Then she'd have numbers to back up the anecdotal research. But that's a long-term goal, she admits. For now she wants to finish her Ph.D. and get a job teaching in a university.

In one study children were asked, "How would you know if an Indian walked into the room?" The responses, not surprisingly, were familiar. They would ride horses, they would wear feathers. They would carry a bow and arrow.

"That's why I feel so strongly that every time children study Indians, there should be a contemporary part of the unit. Ideally, the unit should start with the present, with modern-day Indian people who do ordinary American things." Debbie pauses. "People ask me all the time if we need to have a unit on Native Americans. I think that right now, we do—to counter the miseducation. Maybe in several generations we won't need to."

A Racially Hostile Environment?

When I catch up with Principal Chief Joyce Dugan of the Eastern Band Chero-kee, she is at the front of a crowded elementary school gymnasium in Chero-kee, North Carolina. The graduating sixth-graders, in their best clothes, are seated in front of her on chairs arranged in neat long rows. Most, but not all, have shiny black hair. Their parents and grandparents fill the bleachers, trying to keep younger brothers and sisters settled and cameras held ready at the same time. Chief Dugan, a motherly woman with curly brown hair, is chal-lenging the sixth-graders, every single one of them, to be on the stage six years from now when their class graduates from high school. "It has never hap-pened," she tells them honestly. "It would be a wonderful thing to see ninety-two seniors on that stage." She sounds like the schoolteacher she was before she returned to the reservation and tribal politics. She urges the young gradu-ates to have pride, and no matter where they go, to remember who they are and where they come from. After the special awards and all the certificates have been handed out, the sixth-grade chorus sings an "American Medley." They wend their way from "My Country 'tis of Thee" through one classic after another and end with the words from the Statue of Liberty: "Send them, your homeless, tempest-tossed to me, I lift my lamp beside the golden door." They repeat the chorus, drawing out the notes. There is no hint of irony in this scene, only sincere goodwill.

Back at the tribal council house, an emergency meeting about funding for the hospital, or rather a shortage of it, is going on in the council chambers. The hospital has received only 50 percent of the funding it needs for the com-ing year; treatment programs for diabetes and substance abuse are vital necessities. People gather on the porch, helping themselves to coffee from an automatic coffee machine in the front hall. A crew is readying the ceremonial grounds for a Memorial Day powwow. The Eastern Band is the smallest of three groups of Cherokee and the only one left on their ancestral land in the mountains of North Carolina. Most tribal members saw Chief Dugan's election as progress since it ended years of corrupt leadership by a chief who lined his own pockets and has been indicted for tax evasion. In the Qualla Boundary, as on most Indian reservations, stereotypes and sports mascots are not a concern for most people. Most Cherokee residents root for the Atlanta Braves baseball team. But in the world of American Indian activism beyond this enclave, Chief Joyce Dugan has just achieved instant infamy. Indian activists see her as a sellout who briefly held the future of the anti-mascot movement in her hands and refused to take a stand.

The controversy Chief Dugan got caught up in began as a local dispute in the Asheville area, but received national attention after the U.S. Department of Justice responded to a complaint about the school. The complaint, filed by a parent, was about Indian mascots, or more specifically, about the team names at Clyde A. Erwin High School, a large modern school set on a hilltop in what used to be the rural community of Erwin, now just at the edge of Asheville's suburban sprawl. Outside the school is a twenty-five-foot statue of an Indian man in a loincloth, one hand raised as if to say, "How." A sign painted on the gymnasium reads, "Home of the Warriors and Squaws."

When the team from the high school at Cherokee, the Lady Braves, played at Erwin in January 1997, Cherokee elders who went along were taken aback to hear "Go Squaws!" At first they thought their players were being insulted. But they soon realized that it was the Erwin fans cheering their own team.

One of these elders wrote a letter to the principal of Erwin. She sent a copy to Chief Dugan, who also wrote to Principal Malcolm Brown. Chief Dugan's letter said in part,

I personally feel this symbol is detrimental to young people in an educational setting where the images they become accustomed to remain with them throughout their lives. As a former educator, I have witnessed, with great sadness, the images our young people must contend with while searching for their identity. The use of these types of mascots has never before become an issue because our own community has learned to accept them rather than create further conflict and division between our community and the non-Indian world.

She ended her letter, "Please consider my feelings as you ponder the future of your school and the youth in your care. What may seem insignificant to many will characterize the future in ways we only now are understanding."

The principal replied to Chief Dugan that the high school did not intend the mascot to be detrimental. Warrior and Squaw, he assured her, were used with great pride. However, he was concerned about the term Squaws, and hoped to resolve the issue quickly.

Chief Dugan and the Cherokee elder were not the first people to bring up the issue. Three months earlier, in October 1996, when Charlene Teters was interviewed by Peter Jennings, Pat and Don Merzlak of Erwin happened to be watching. Pat, a retired nurse, went on the Internet and realized that people all over the country were objecting to American Indian mascots. This mattered to Pat. Although she is not Indian, she has five adopted American Indian children—three older sons and two little girls. Two of the boys had already graduated from Erwin and one was currently a student there. The girls came to them as babies, but the boys ranged from eight to fourteen when Pat and Don adopted them and clearly remember reservation life. They are Sisseton and Rosebud Sioux. Regulations make it difficult to adopt children away from their tribe, but the combination of Don's Blackfoot blood and the couple's commitment to nurturing the children's Indian culture enabled them to meet the adoption requirements.

This twenty-five-foot statue of an Indian man in a loincloth looms over Clyde A. Erwin High School outside Asheville, North Carolina. The Department of Justice investigated whether teams named Warriors and Squaws and displays of Indian imagery created a racially hostile environment for American Indian students. Photograph by Carol Spindel.

"I had never liked the mascot," Pat says in her down-to-earth voice. "But I always figured you had to grin and bear it." Their son Rayne had been uneasy that year about going to pep rallies or games. And while he was at Erwin, his older brother Richard had briefly tried to come to terms with the Indian theme by offering to be the mascot and ride his own horse onto the football field. "He tried to do it respectfully," says Don. But he gave it up, discouraged by the other students' reaction. They wanted a turn to be the mascot, too, not understanding that for Richard it was a statement of cultural identity. Pat thinks that more than anything her boys just tried to fit in. "They either had to go along with it or speak up and be harassed." This all came back to Pat when she discovered a world of anti-mascot activism on the Web. "I thought, well, why couldn't we protest, too?" Pat and Don talked to all three Indian sons. She showed them the school system's nondiscrimination policy, which obligates staff to establish and maintain a learning environment that respects "cultural differences" and the rights of students "to seek and maintain their own identities." Richard wadded the piece of paper up and threw it on the floor, saying, "They don't respect Indians!"

Indian friends in the community, including Bruce Two Eagles, who is originally from Massachusetts but retired to Asheville nine years ago, supported the idea of a complaint. Bruce, Don, and Pat met with the superintendent of schools and explained why they disliked the term "squaw" in particular. The superintendent listened sympathetically; he seemed confident that by the time school started the following year, the word would no longer be in use. But when the school year ended in May, they were informed there would be no change. Privately, administrators told the Merzlaks and Bruce that they wanted to change Squaws and had the authority, but preferred to initiate an educational process. They wanted the students to see that it was the right thing to do, rather than something imposed on them. Bruce, Don, and Pat took their concerns to the Asheville newspaper, which published a front-page article. Reaction in the community was immediate; there were cries of wasting time on a trivial issue and political correctness gone berserk. "I thought at my age that I wasn't naive anymore, but I was," Pat says. "I thought if I brought it to people's attention that this hurt my children and their children, too, that they'd change it."

Pat says that people asked her about the mascot of a rival team. "What about the War Horses? And I told them, when a little War Horse has to come home and ask, why are they using us as mascots?"—she laughs—"well, then I'll worry about it."

"I don't have to take my children to a Cleveland Indians game," adds Don. "But I have to take them to school."

For the educational unit on mascots, school officials videotaped speakers from different points of view. Bruce was not invited to speak in the video; they thought his remarks might be inflammatory. Pat spoke briefly. The cultural affairs director for the Eastern Band Cherokee, Lynne Harlan, presented an Indian point of view. The school officials also provided two articles, both explaining American Indian objections to mascots. And female athletes from Erwin visited Cherokee to tour the museum and meet with Chief Dugan. All sides, in rare agreement, feel that this trip was a success and that in the role of educator, Chief Dugan was wonderful. The girls came back and began to talk to other students about the word "squaw."

Most dictionaries define "squaw" as a Native American woman or wife. Only one of the dictionaries I surveyed failed to label it either disparaging or offensive. Many people feel that "prostitute" is a more accurate synonym. "Floozy," "hussy," and "harlot" are often given as synonyms. Although all parties agree that it is derogatory, the etymology of the word is a hot debate in certain circles. From what language did it originate and what did it originally mean? The dictionaries I looked in said either Massachuset, Narragansett, or Algonquian, a large language family that covers most Indian groups along the Atlantic coast. Recently, the theory that it derives from a Mohawk word meaning female genitalia has gained widespread acceptance. Suzan Shown Harjo, speaking on Oprah Winfrey's show to millions of viewers, gave this definition, and many activists disseminate this derivation as if it is certain.

On the Internet you can find long debates among linguists about the word's etymology. The largest group argues for the Massachuset derivation. They believe that "squaw" is derived from a word ending in the Massachuset language, *squa*. It was neutral and could be added to any word to make it female. Female deer, female person. There are seventeenth-century uses by English settlers who use the word in a nonpejorative way to refer to Indian women. Over time, the connotation of the word changed and it became an insult. Although "squaw" sounds like one of the syllables in the Mohawk word, that is not in itself proof that it derives from it. All the linguists who argue about "squaw" agree that it is now a term that is always demeaning to women. That is not in question. Where the word came from and what its original meaning was may never be resolved.

Many Indians refuse to pronounce "squaw," calling it the "s-word." There is a nationwide movement to change the names of geographical features that include "squaw." Once people heard that the word was not simply disparaging, but vulgar, the renaming movement picked up steam. The state of Minnesota has recommended changing all names with "squaw" in them. The Colorado squaw-fish has already been changed by an official biological naming commission to the pikeminnow.

Bruce Two Eagles and the Merzlaks found an ally in Monroe Gilmour, a community organizer whose awkwardly named Western North Carolina Citizens to End Institutional Bigotry works against racism in the area. WNCCEIB is mainly Monroe, but what he lacks in staff and funding he makes up for in energy and determination. His office is in the small house he shares with his wife and four children, perched on a fern-covered hillside outside Asheville. "You can't live on scenery, but we're making a stab at it," says Monroe, gesturing to the mountains around him. His office consists of a desk in the bedroom, with the fax, computer, scanner, and laser printer all crammed into the adjacent bathroom. A steady stream of faxes, all written with passionate care, emanates from Monroe's bathroom and rises over the hills, headed for the world beyond.

Monroe is angry and disappointed about the role the school board played. He thinks the board should have enforced its own policy when the issue was brought to its attention. School officials decided that after the educational unit, the students would vote on the mascots. "You don't let high school kids vote on racism," says Monroe in frustration. "Did kids vote on integration?"

When the one thousand Erwin students voted in May 1998, 41 percent wanted to keep the team names, 33 percent wanted change, and the rest either were "unconcerned" or opted not to vote. The school board announced that the students' decision was binding and that the team names would stay.

Shocked and disappointed, Bruce Two Eagles and the Merzlaks, along with supporters, held a news conference outside Erwin High School on the first day of school the following August. They received widespread local coverage and a six-minute story on National Public Radio. Pat also started a letter-writing campaign to state and national officials. One person she contacted was a senior attorney at the U.S. Department of Justice, Lawrence Baca. Baca, a Harvard-trained lawyer who is Pawnee, has litigated a number of landmark cases involving Indian civil rights, successfully stopping banks and finance companies from redlining reservations and automatically refusing credit to Indian applicants. Baca agreed to look into Pat Merzlak's complaint.

In February 1999 the Justice Department announced that it was investigating whether Erwin High School's mascots were a violation of federal antidiscrimination laws. If the school district were found to be in violation, its eight million dollars of federal funding could be in jeopardy. In addition, if the school district decided to contest a Justice Department lawsuit, it could spend a sizeable proportion of its budget on legal fees.

Once the federal government stepped in, people's backs went up. North Carolina mountain people have a long tradition of southern highland independence, some would say stubbornness. Many resented government interference. Some students and community members even reversed direction. A poll showed that student support for changing the name dropped to 24 percent after the Justice Department announced its investigation. Some people felt that Erwin had been unfairly targeted. After all, schools all over the country had Indian mascots. Why weren't they also under investigation? Jesse Helms complained about the Justice Department "abusing their school system in this fashion." There was a great deal of anger at Bruce, Don, and Pat for going to the Justice Department. In an eerie echo of sixties civil rights struggles, the debate seemed to be more about local control than about Indian mascots.

"I could see how people could take the word "squaw" to be demeaning or offensive. I was in favor of removing it," says Mal Brown, the principal of Erwin. Among the high school students, he looks gentlemanly in his khaki pants, crisp white shirt, and narrow leather suspenders. "I have a wife and daughter and I wouldn't want them called that. But offensive or demeaning is not racially hostile. When it was alleged that a racially hostile environment existed at my school . . ." Brown cannot say the phrase in the civil rights statute without his soft southern voice rising emotionally. "I resented that immensely." He is taking me on a tour of the school, showing me the painted murals with Indian themes and the glass case of old bead-decorated articles that someone donated to the school years ago. Students greet him affectionately in the halls and he jokes easily with them as he passes. Brown explains that as he saw it, he had two problems to face: the mascot issue and the resentment from the Erwin community about changing their tradition.

In fact, the Erwin teams have not always been the Warriors. When the school opened in the fifties, students chose the name Demons. Certain religious people in the community were offended. Columnist Perry Young, writing in the *Asheville Citizen-Times,* remembers, "We thought they were very silly to take offense. But our principal told us we must respect their feelings and we had no right to offend anyone in our community. . . . Our principal said choose a new mascot and we cheerfully did it." He recalls that the matter was resolved in a few days. And at the middle school next door to Erwin High, the principal simply changed Squaws to Lady Warriors over the summer after the first complaint. No discussion, no democratic process. Of course he was leaving for another post and didn't have to face the backlash. But when school reopened in the fall, there wasn't any.

There has been a lot of talk about mascots, but Erwin hasn't had one for years. Willy the Warrior, a big-headed character with a stereotyped Indian face, was retired about five years before the investigation without any fanfare. The students, having heard that Willy was in a closet somewhere, mounted a "Free Willy" campaign in jest. For a brief period in 1991, the Merzlaks' middle son, Richard, rode out onto the field on a horse and carried a flaming lance like Osceola at Florida State.

The Justice Department investigation was covered by CNN and ABC as well as the *Washington Post* and the *Philadelphia Inquirer.* Anti-mascot activists were watching closely. If the Department of Justice ruled that Indian mascots violate the civil rights of American Indian students, then every school district with Indian mascots would be in violation of the federal code and at risk of losing federal funding. The hopes of anti-mascot activists all over the country were high.

At its March 1999 meeting, the school board voted on the issue. Its compromise was to cease using Squaws. The Justice Department immediately closed its investigation and allowed the school to retain the Warriors name. The Justice Department's letter to the school board also stipulates that Chief Dugan or her representative should tour the school to identify any religious symbols that may be on display and that these should be removed; and that a qualified educational consultant should verify that the school district has adequate materials about American Indian history and culture. The letter from the Justice Department says that the Indian statue and two totem poles may stay.

Erwin held a Field Day in April. At the Field Day the school announced a new name for the female athletes, the Lady Warriors. The T-shirts printed for the occasion show Willy the Warrior in a badly drawn caricature, bare-chested, leaning on his lance and holding a hot dog. His long feather bonnet trails behind him like a tail; it makes him look like an alligator in feathers. Monroe has faxed me a copy of the T-shirt, and I ask Principal Brown about it. "There was no agreement about images in the Justice Department's letter," he replies smoothly. "Of course I approved that. Willy the Warrior has had a difficult year, now he's kicking back and relaxing." Brown has received e-mails from around the country criticizing the T-shirt after it was posted on WNCCEIB's Web page. "Let me ask you this. Who do I get permission from?"

I suggest that it might be simpler to have an animal mascot that the students could have fun with. "That might be easier," he says with a strong, slow emphasis on the last word. "But sometimes you can't take the easy way."

In the hall outside his office, Mal Brown gestures to the entryway of the school. "They said we were racially hostile." He shakes his head in disbelief. "That anyone could think that someone would come in here, a student, and because of their race, who they are, I would be . . ." His voice rises in indignation. ". . . hostile. That I would . . ." He pauses as if it's unthinkable, what he must say. ". . . that I would be rude." Unconsciously he touches his chest, as if wounded. "I can't think of anything worse."

Bruce Two Eagles says the Justice Department wanted to wrap the case up quickly so as not to distract from confirmation hearings. He doesn't understand why Department of Justice negotiators backed down so easily nor why Chief Dugan had the final say. "The Eastern Band sell tomahawks to the Atlanta Braves, so how could they make a decision on mascots without having a direct conflict of interest?" He points out that there are fifty five thousand Indian people in North Carolina, that the Eastern Band do not represent them, and that the Asheville organization to which he and the Merzlaks belong, the Intertribal Association, was not consulted about the resolution although they had been involved from the beginning.

David Voyles, who teaches English at Erwin, recalls the night he sat down to read the materials provided for the educational unit on mascots. One handout, put together by Barbara Munson, who chairs the Mascot and Logo Taskforce of the Wisconsin Indian Education Association, was written in an informative and matter-of-fact question-and-answer format. "When I read it, that's when I realized, we're not just talking about "squaw." We're talking about using Indians as mascots. The light went on for me."

Voyles is not only a teacher at Erwin but the father of a student there. "This is an educational issue," he says earnestly in slow, soft North Carolina tones. "If people really knew the history, they wouldn't want to use Indians as mascots." He believes in the possibility of enacting change through education, although it's a slow process, but he's not sure the vote was appropriate in a high school setting. "Maybe next they'll want to vote on smoking in the hall or beer in the cafeteria. . . . Sometimes you just have to say to kids, this is what we're going to do because it's the right thing to do." But he also concedes that knowing that the school board wasn't going to act, he and others went along with the student vote because it was the only option they had.

"It sounded like a good idea and maybe if our educational process had been better . . . I'm generally kind of idealistic, but that is maybe just too idealistic. If you're in a policy-making position, sometimes you have to take responsibility and dictate a change."

In the town of Cherokee, strung out along the mountain highway, everywhere you turn there are images of Indians wearing Plains Indian garb and headdresses. There is even a Redskin Motel. Lynne Harlan acknowledges that Cherokee people have not only taken on the Plains image, but have fostered it. In the crowd of parents leaving the graduation ceremony, she points out one woman wearing a Seminoles T-shirt and a man in a Redskins cap. "People want an image of themselves. They want to think of themselves positively. There are no images of Cherokees being mass-produced by a major corporation. Even the Cherokee clothing company uses a Plains Indian image. That's the majority culture's idea about Indians. People here identify with that because they want some image of themselves."

Lynne Harlan grew up on the Qualla Boundary. She is a sturdy-looking woman with long black hair and an open, energetic manner. A historian, she went into museum work to do what she calls public history. At the National Museum of the American Indian, she specialized in the traditional care and handling of American Indian ceremonial objects in museum collections. She came home to work for the tribe a few years ago. "Most of us who are educated want to contribute something to our own people. It just has more meaning."

The elementary school we are standing in had a cartoon Indian painted on the gym floor much like Chief Wahoo when Lynne was a student there. We go over to look, but it has been changed to a letter *C* adorned with feathers. "Well, that's good," she says with a pleased laugh. "Shows you how long it's been since I've come in here." The high school teams are still the Braves and Lady Braves. "I think it's a whole different situation if we call ourselves that. But we didn't make up the names anyway. It was the BIA who ran the schools. All the schools have the same names and the same colors. Warriors. Braves. They liked maroon and gold." She chuckles. "And red, of course."

The tribe has had a special relationship with the Atlanta Braves baseball team for as long as she can remember. "They're our local team and our kids are the Braves, too. Of course, that's not our image they're selling. Again it's Plains Indians and that gives us an out."

She grins, aware that she's contradicting herself, and says Indians have to have a sense of humor to survive. She and a Winnebago friend have a long-standing joke in which Lynne says, "My grandma's a Jeep." He replies, "Mine's an RV."

The tribe doesn't get any benefits from Jeep's use of the name. "They did give us one free. But that was years ago. It was good public relations for them."

As for making tomahawks for the Braves, Lynne is quick to acknowledge that they do. "It's not under Cherokee ownership and it's not a big source of income for us. But it does mean jobs. About fifty people work there."

An impressive-looking Harrah's casino stands in gleaming contrast to the other businesses that line the road to Smoky Mountains National Park. The other shops all have that tourist Indian trading post look—wooden posts and porch, dyed feathers and painted wooden spears for sale. The Redskin Motel, she tells me, is not under Indian ownership and it's on deeded land, so they have no influence. Lynne says that for years one shop was called the Buck and Squaw Gift Shop, but Chief Dugan talked to them and it's now the B and S.

Lynne remembers that when she was growing up in Cherokee, "squaw" was a bad word she wasn't supposed to say. She wasn't sure exactly what it meant. But when she got older, she came to understand that it referred to men's private parts.

When Chief Dugan comes out of the sixth-grade graduation ceremony, I ask her if she considered, when the Department of Justice turned to her, making a more sweeping indictment of mascots. "No, I never did," she replies. "I think you have to start by educating young people, changing textbooks, giving them more accurate information." She says she is not aware of any legal proceedings against companies that use the name Cherokee. Would she consider being a party to a lawsuit to regain control of the name? She says she would.

After I leave the elementary school I visit the Museum of the Cherokee Indian, just across the powwow grounds from the tribal council house. It has recently been renovated and is state-of-the-art. Recorded voices read from old texts; holograph storytellers and medicine men appear in flickering light. The stories draw me in, as they do the other visitors. A Cherokee house just before removal looks like any other settler's cabin, with silver candlesticks on the table and woolen clothing with pewter buttons. At a scene of a camp during the Trail of Tears, a recorded voice reads from a soldier's journal. One burial after another. One more child lost to disease. The images of eighteenth-century Cherokee leaders are arresting in their uniqueness—there are no feather war bonnets, no beaded, fringed buckskin. The men wear cotton tunics, decorated leggings, and cloaks made of European cloth. Their heads are shaved except for one lock of hair that is drawn up.

Most compelling for me is the story of Sequoyah, one of the few human beings to ever wholly invent a syllabary. He spent so many hours alone in the fields that his family thought he had gone mad. But Sequoyah emerged with a workable system for writing the Cherokee language. As I stand in front of a realistic-looking reproduction of a stone tablet with the letters "carved" on it, a voice intones each syllable and the corresponding symbol lights up. I picture my own personal system of visual symbols, most learned, some invented. Now that I understand the hegemony of the pretend Indian image, is it possible that when I hear "Indian," the Cherokee men with shaved heads will light up in the carved tablet of my mind? Or Debbie Reese talking seriously about children's books? Or Bruce Two Eagles trading hats with the retired ironworker?

Back in Lynne Harlan's office, she hands me the fax she has received from Monroe of the Erwin High Field Day T-shirt. She shakes her head. "Guess my educational efforts were a failure."

Mascots, she thinks, are a result of the dominant American culture's obsession with private property and ownership. "Ever since Columbus came here," she says, "Americans have thought they owned everything here, including the human beings. Just like they owned blacks as slaves." She intends to keep pushing for more accurate, less demeaning images of Indians, but only through educational efforts. The way activists seek out the media makes her uncomfortable. This is a split I've encountered everywhere I've gone. When activists hear a dramatic or persuasive line, they repeat it through a bullhorn. Educators try to confirm whether it's true, then they write articles.

Lynne remembers the day the athletes from Erwin came to Cherokee. They were suprised to see, on the bulletin board near the coffee machine, a cartoon from the Asheville paper that depicted Erwin people as stupid rednecks. "I told the girls, we have an image of you, too."

•　　•　　•

The factory is located on a side road just off the highway. The buildings are long and low, faded blue. The trucks backed up to the bays could all use a paint job but on the side each one says, "The Cherokees, Largest Workshop of American Indian Craftsmen." The name of the company reminds me of an African trickster tale in which a hare says his name is The Guests so he can get all the food. Or Odysseus. Who put out your eye? Nobody. Who is this feast for? The Guests. Who made these tomahawks? The Cherokees.

The management are all gone for lunch. In the buildings a few workers lounge near the workbenches drinking sodas. The detritus of Indian tourist paraphernalia—brightly dyed gull and chicken feathers and leather thongs—lies in heaps on the floor. Stacked against the walls are hundreds of spears, made of sticks painted red and white. In another building an old man works at slingshots, although everyone else is taking a break. I ask him about the work. "Puts bread on the table," he replies.

Each product that leaves this workshop has a little yellowish tag shaped like an animal hide. It says, "Made by The Cherokees, Qualla Reservation, Cherokee, N.C." The reverse says, "Made in America by Native Americans." This is true, although the Native Americans are minimum-wage workers and the profits go to the non-Indian owners, not to the tribe. A Cherokee man I talk to tells me his parents worked there in the late 1950s for twenty dollars a week.

As I drive away, I pass a man in a brilliant yellow powwow costume standing outside a small shopping center. "Take your picture with an Indian chief— $1.00," says a hand-lettered sign. A woman sits on the little platform next to the basket of dollar bills; she is making beadwork cases for disposable lighters. The photo chief is surprisingly young. When I ask if anyone on the reservation ever gives him a hard time about what he does, he shakes his head, causing the fluffy yellow feathers to billow and wave. "I know most people here and if they pass by, they stop and chat."

Pat and Don Merzlak haven't given up. Pat has recently been to an ACLU workshop on religious freedom and has learned that even if you aren't forced to pray, but there is an atmosphere of coercion, that can be a violation of an individual's right to freedom of religion. To her, that sounds awfully close to what her sons experienced at Erwin, hiding their beliefs so they could fit in.

Monroe Gilmour's file cabinet and computer in the corner of his bathroom have become a resource center for people who want to change Indian mascots in their public schools. Grimly, he shows me a fax of a school gymnasium in Tennessee. The "scalps" of opposing teams hang from the gym rafters. Monroe's letter to the principal was both polite and passionate, a plea not to stereotype Indians as warlike and savage. Letters, e-mails, and faxes arrive in Monroe's office from people all over the country. "They are going through exactly what we are going through. The language their opponents and school officials use is so similar. It feels like all these people are reading from the same script."

Homecoming

The leaves are already turning red and orange-yellow, and the wind blows hard, but it is a soft, warm wind, the last breath of summer. Indian summer. Why we call it that I don't know. At Memorial Stadium, it is homecoming. There have already been parties, dinners honoring alumni, a parade with blue and orange floats. But this warm windy Saturday morning is the football game. Illinois vs. Wisconsin. The Fighting Illini don't stand a chance.

At the center of campus, a drum beats softly and steadily. Protesters assemble, mostly students, a few older people, a boy. This week there are guest speakers—Michael Haney, a Seminole from Oklahoma, Tim Giago, a well-known Oglala journalist and until recently the publisher of *Indian Country Today*, Charlene Teters, a Spokane alumna. Other Native Americans have traveled from Louisville and Chicago. They have brought a large round drum and tobacco, which they offer to the four directions.

The group of perhaps 250 people marches behind the drum to the stadium. As the group approaches a fraternity, the frat boys run for their Chief Illiniwek flag. They plant the pole behind their stone balustrade and gather around, as if making their last stand.

"What a joke!" they say to each other loudly. "Protesting the chief!" They laugh bitterly.

As the demonstration passes a field of people picnicking at card tables, a woman I know from youth soccer, the wife of a campus minister, steps out from among the tailgaters. She stands alone and applauds. No one joins her. The atmosphere is icy.

Vernon Bellecourt, of the National Coalition Against Racism in Sports and the Media, outside Memorial Stadium, University of Illinois, on October 16, 1999. Photograph by Tom Bassett.

"Don't you have anything better to do? Get a job!" This comes from a group of older people sitting around their van in folding chairs, tailgaters.

The demonstrators are not supposed to reply. But I can't keep quiet. I say, "I have a job. I teach these students."

We walk right down the central alley between the orange and blue tents set up outside the stadium. Each college is staging a comeback party, welcoming alumni with hot dogs and soda, hoping they'll feel a sense of loyalty and send a contribution. College of Communications, College of Commerce. The tent people turn and shout, "Yea chief!" and laugh, certain that they are in the majority, certain that we are few and kooky. But one African American woman sticks her head and fist out of a tent, smiles, and yells, "Right on! Right on! Right on!" until the entire procession has passed by.

The marchers climb the steps and line up three and four deep outside the brick stadium. Their signs blow wildly. The signs read, "Racism Is Never Dignified"; "BIG 10 = BIGOTRY"; and "Is Your Halftime Entertainment Worth the Dignity of a People?" Students try to hand out small orange squares of paper with information, but there are few takers. A grandfatherly man in an orange cap pauses to look the marchers over, then gives them the finger and walks into the stadium.

Real Indians in the heart of Illini territory make the fans uncomfortable. When real Indians beat a drum and sing outside the stadium it is difficult to maintain the fiction that they are long gone and would want to be remembered as a football team.

A little old lady, nattily dressed in orange sweater with appliquéd Indians, navy pleated skirt, orange tights, and bright orange leather high-tops, walks toward the stadium with a firm step. She has a round friendly face and light hair that makes a soft halo around her head. She takes in the protesters, stops. "That's ridiculous," she says. She starts to walk into the stadium, then turns back and throws up her hands. "Why don't you just go someplace else?"

"You want to destroy everything I fought for!" an older man yells. It is a curious accusation. In response, unable to reply, the protesters hold out their signs. A young man walks by and says angrily, "Why don't you find a real cause? The chief! Why don't you save real people?"

Glancing up, I see one of the few Native members of the local community. An expression of pain crosses his face. He is quiet, gray-haired, a family counselor by profession, and also an artist who exhibits locally. I don't know him well, but we have spoken; his voice always holds both warmth and irony. Instantly he composes his face again, presses his lips together. The moment is gone, but I have seen it.

"If it's trivial, as you say, if it's not important, then why not just change it?" Charlene Teters asks the crowd through a bullhorn. They ignore her.

"You should be working on alcoholism and illiteracy. You should do something constructive," someone tells us. We are lined up now, waiting to leave the stadium. From the top of the steps, a woman looks at me questioningly. She is slightly older than I am, well-coiffed, dressed in expensive sportswear. In response to the question in her eyes, I point to my button. Over a slashed-out Indian profile is printed the phrase "No Stereotypes in Our Schools." To my surprise, the woman walks down the steps toward me.

"Well, I can agree with that," she says, after she reads the button.

"But there are children here at the game," I say. "And this *is* a school. I teach here."

She nods toward the Native American speakers. "They should worry about educating their children, not about this."

"But that's why they've come. For their children. Native Americans have the highest teenage suicide rate of any group in the country."

"Then they should educate them better," she says and turns away to climb the stairs to her friends.

Fans in orange and blue are still filing past us, going toward the stadium, as we march away. We pass an African American family who look at us with troubled eyes. They make no sign of recognition.

"Go home! Get a life!" the fans yell. "Go home!"

Michael Haney, who towers over the other marchers in a multicolored Seminole jacket, does not believe in turning the other cheek, nor in silent protest. And he has the bullhorn. "Go home?" he replies. "This was my home until you took it away. You're the immigrants. And ignorant immigrants, too. White trash, that's what you are. I know you're slow learners, but five hundred years is a long time!" I cringe every time he yells. And silently root for him to keep on yelling.

The next day, the local paper has a color picture of the demonstration on the front page. "A group of anti-chief protesters bang a drum," the caption begins. This photo is next to one of the homecoming court on the football field. After last year's protest, when the king and queen opened their coats to display anti-chief T-shirts, the coronation of a king and queen has been discontinued. Nevertheless, one of my students tells me that again this year, tensions over the mascot divided the homecoming court. Half pinned their orange ribbons to their chests with the Chief Illiniwek buttons provided. The other half used identical buttons, but with the image slashed out. The two groups refused to speak to each other as they stood on the sidelines. The students in the newspaper photo are all pro-chief. Carnation boutonnieres and corsages, and buttons with the chief logo are pinned to the lapels of their suits. In the photo, they stand with their arms crossed in front of them, their elbows stuck out, their chins raised high in imitation of their chief.

Video Letters

I am sitting in a studio at our public television station as people tape "video letters" in response to Jay Rosenstein's documentary *In Whose Honor?* which was shown the night before on public television. The video letters, created by viewers in response to the films shown, are a regular feature of the program *POV*. Most of those who come in to speak before the camera are motivated not by the documentary itself but by the comments of Susan Gravenhorst, the chairwoman of the board of trustees. She took part in a panel discussion that was broadcast locally after the documentary. Gravenhorst is firmly convinced that only a very strange person could dislike a mascot she adores. One after another, the speakers address the camera in passionate voices, determined to get through to her. "What if you loaned out your favorite sweater, Mrs. Gravenhorst, and it came back to you all covered with big tomato stains?" asks one woman. Gravenhorst has not been in the studio since the panel discussion and will never see these tapes, but she inspires a strong reaction.

The exception is a retired couple who have often been guests at a Hopi pueblo. He is wearing a beautiful silver bolero and says forcefully, "When we go to Second Mesa, we don't always understand everything about the kachinas and their religion, but we are respectful of their traditions. I wish the Native Americans who come here would be equally respectful of our traditions."

A short, plump woman in khaki shorts comes in. Her white hair is braided into two long thin braids that give her the look of a German matron and she is carrying a bike helmet. She sits, watching the others speak their piece, but doesn't sign up to do so herself. When I ask why not, she says she realizes now that she isn't prepared. I ask what she wanted to say. "Oh, I wanted to talk about playing Indian." Her voice is very quiet. "It gave me so much pleasure when I was young. I loved the out of doors and I was a Girl Scout. It's only now that I see what we were doing: playacting at being Indians. And I see now that it isn't right. And yet . . ." Her voice turns wistful. "When I was young, I got so much satisfaction out of that."

The story of Chief Illiniwek is a microcosmic history of white American attitudes toward American Indians in this century. The students in the tribe of Illini have seen the photographs of Edward Curtis and any number of western movies. They have accepted these depictions as accurate portrayals of the American past. Their high school history textbooks provide only the barest outlines of the interactions between whites and Indians. With very few Native people on their campus to dispute the notion, students accept the popular myth that Indians have, for a variety of reasons, mostly perished. In response to criticism and to their increased awareness about cultural sensitivity, students have given up the Indian blankets and peace pipes they have worn playing Indian since the 1920s. The athletic program regulates the reproductions so that there are no more caricatures or toilet paper, and Chief Illiniwek has evolved from a halftime stunt into an icon. But the tribe of Illini stubbornly hold on to their right to this one ceremony—the halftime dance and song leading of Chief Illiniwek. The depth of their attachment to him and the deference they show in his presence are confused with respect and deference toward real American Indians. They genuinely feel that to admire and adore an imaginary Indian is to honor Indians. Is it racism?

"To me, something that makes you cry and gives you chills and good feelings I don't feel is racist or bad," says an alumnus. Most of us connect racism with negative thoughts and oppressive actions, or the belief that members of another group are untrustworthy, incapable, and innately inferior. For a writer, "racism" is a maddeningly imprecise word, no matter how real the disease to which it refers. How can one word possibly render extremes from the lynching of blacks by whites to the assumption by a black teacher that an Asian kid will be inherently good at math?

Illini, Seminole, and Redskin fans, who picture American Indian warriors as brave and dignified and who aspire to be like Indian chiefs themselves, are shocked and offended when they are called racist for admiring and identifying with American Indian icons. Most fans have no intention of supporting a racist practice, but intentionally or not, they do perpetuate a romantic stereotype in which Indians are always war-bonneted warriors, living in an imaginary Wild West, galloping fast ponies, sleeping in tepees, and going on the warpath against enemy tribes. It sounds like great fun, much more appealing than working nine to five in a beige cubicle. And add to this carefree and colorful life the multiple bonus of supernatural powers, a strong connection to the natural world, the moral superiority of underdog status, and a sure sense of identity and belonging. No wonder contemporary Americans want to join the tribe they have created in their imaginations. It beats real life by a mile.

Most white Americans feel shame about racism, either about their feelings, about what our country has done collectively to people of color, or about their own reluctance to relinquish the comforts and advantages they enjoy. As soon as the word "racism" is spoken, people of color perk up, ready to talk about one of their major concerns. But most white Americans turn away or become defensive. We want to avoid confronting one of our worst fears: that we ourselves will be found out, that our thoughts will be exposed as racist. Therefore, we often picture racism as remote and extreme. Many white people have told me that when they picture racism they see a lynching years ago in a southern town or the recent terrible murder of a black man who was dragged to death behind a truck. They don't consider the daily disadvantages/advantages inherent in our society racism because they don't notice them. Similarly, although African American sports fans realize that the daily indignities of racism cause real harm, they find it hard to imagine that their positive feelings about baseball and Chief Wahoo, or football and the Redskins, expressed by wearing a hat or T-shirt, could result in negative consequences for real Native people. It seems too positive, too trivial, to count as real racism.

Most of us would agree that racism flourishes on a foundation of stereotypes and prejudices and that when people treat each other as individuals and seek information about each other, racism diminishes. Our attitudes toward Indians have been complex and contradictory, a blend of both positive and negative desires and stereotypes, a "wistful reservoir" that reflects our own longings more than any reality. And many of these stereotypes have been positive, even filled with adulation.

The strongest proof of how positively Americans feel about what American Indians represent to them is that many claim to have Indian blood themselves. A person has, of course, a fair number of great and great-great-grandmothers, but Indian ones, both real and imaginary, are claimed more loudly and more proudly by most Americans than other sorts. A French or Russian or German great-grandmother simply does not have the same cachet. For all we know, she may have been a peasant or a washerwoman. And I have never heard a white American boast about a slave foremother, although this is certainly possible. But for both white and black Americans, a Cherokee great-grandmother is a different story, one already well-developed in our fantasies: an Indian princess—graceful yet tough, wild-spirited and freedom-loving.

These positive attitudes about American Indians have always been mixed with other, more negative ones. Essentially, when it comes to Indians, we feel ambivalent. We have demanded that American Indians give up Indian ways and become more like us. We have enforced this policy legislatively, economically, and militarily. And yet once they do, America loses all interest in them and turns to fictional Indian characters instead. During a Wild West show, Sitting Bull spoke about education for Indian children and his words were translated, without his knowledge, into gory tales of ambush. When the Society of American Indians met in Chicago in 1923, there was little interest in their policy meetings but thousands of people traveled outside the city to watch their dances. When a highly regarded Native theater group, Spiderwoman Theater, visited the University of Illinois in 1996 to perform their original works, they received a call asking if they could "dress up and dance" for schoolchildren. This fascination is a refusal to see American Indians as human beings, as people who have the potential to change and develop. Irish Americans are not expected to live on potatoes and to dance jigs for our entertainment. African Americans are not expected to sleep in grass-roofed huts or reenact the story of their enslavement as a pageant. White Americans are never called inauthentic because they have electric lights instead of the kerosene lanterns of their great-grandparents.

It shouldn't surprise us that American Indians feel smothered by this fantasy of Indian life. It is inescapable and all-pervasive. It forces them to live in two worlds, that of their reality and our fantasy simultaneously, passing back and forth the way Houdini walked through brick walls. Dave Narcomey, a retired navy commander who is Seminole from Oklahoma and has retired to Florida, recounts an exchange in a supermarket one day. A boy, noticing his long black hair and Indian looks, came up to him. "Excuse me, can I ask you something?" the boy asked politely. Dave said sure.

"What nation are you?"

"I'm Seminole," Dave answered, pleased at the way the question was phrased.

"Oh," said the boy. "Sorry. I'm a Gators fan."

Which side of the wall are they standing on? The reality side or the fantasy side? Or are they stuck somewhere in the sticky mortar of good intentions? Those who named the Florida State team after the Seminoles had only good intentions. But they never asked either the Florida or the Oklahoma Seminole tribe for permission. Theirs was not an act of borrowing, but one of theft. In addition to the name Seminole, they have taken one of the tribe's he-

Osceola, the mascot of Florida State University's powerhouse football team, opens every game by throwing a flaming lance. Osceola was a historical figure who opposed American expansion into Indian land in Florida. Courtesy of Florida State University.

roes, Osceola, out of the historical record. In reality Osceola was violently opposed to American expansion and land sales. He once drove his hunting knife through a treaty to make this point. He favored beautiful clothing and elaborate ornaments. He violently resisted removal. When he came to talk peace with the Americans under a white flag in 1837, he was surrounded and put in a federal prison. After he died there, the attending doctor cut off Osceola's head. Rather than giving his clothing and possessions to his two wives, who had come to his deathbed, the doctor kept them for trophies. Osceola's head was displayed in a medical college.

Mascots were not created with the intent of demeaning American Indians. White college students thought that Indians were gone forever. Those who had the chance to study with Indians in Boy Scout camps or hobby gatherings admired them as teachers. They assumed that the dances and stories they learned were the last transmissions from a culture that would soon be completely extinct. But Indian society and Indian culture were more resilient than college students, Boy Scout leaders, or museum curators expected. Indian groups combined, adapted, and survived. Some Native students have turned up at the University of Illinois, where there have heretofore been, in the words of the poet Michael Holloway, "too many chiefs and not enough Indians." Although they are not Illinois descendants, their Indian identity catalyzes them to speak up, to insist that the non-Indian students of the University of Illinois have no right to appropriate their image. We are still here, they insist. We are alive and we do not want to be your mascot.

When I read the *Jesuit Relations* or colonial accounts of the Mississippi Valley, I glimpse a world that never appeared in my history textbooks, a New World dominated by Indian leaders to whom Europeans gave gifts and with whom they made alliances. Both groups adapted; each tried to gain advantage from the other's presence. And yet Indians often are depicted as if they were marginal figures in American history, a pantomime between the important acts in which the speaking parts are all held by European explorers and settlers or by early American leaders. This is simply not true. Every history is an interpretation of the past and everyone is entitled to their own interpretation. But I would argue that a more inclusive and encompassing history is essential in a multicultural community. This is why the mascot question is not trivial, and why resistance to changing the mascots is so fierce and so emotionally charged. What is being decided outside the stadiums and in the school board meetings is which version of history we will pass on to the next generation. Only a history that encompasses multiple viewpoints can include Osceola as an American hero. Otherwise, he must be an Indian hero or be reduced to a mascot, a Wild West actor on the football field.

At Ole Miss in Oxford, Mississippi, the president of the university has called for a dialogue on the appropriateness of their mascot, Ole Reb, a caricature of a pre–Civil War plantation owner. Their southern heritage and the values of chivalry and bravery associated with the mythical land of Dixie are important to many Ole Miss students and alumni. But the Ole Miss community is no longer an exclusive club of descendants of slave owners who want to paint the antebellum South as a happy, harmonious place. When the football coach found himself unable to recruit black players, the Confederate flag waving in the stands was outlawed. If the college wants to take its place in the modern world, it has to find some compromise between the myth of Dixie and the realities of Mississippi history.

Like the Indians he was modeled on, the Indian chief who was invented in the 1920s by the Marching Illini as a motivational figure, a uniquely midwestern version of the ideal Greek youth, strong in mind and body, has survived longer, I'm sure, than any of those present at his creation could have imagined. No longer simply a figure to be alluded to in pregame pep talks, he is the logo of an athletic corporation that promotes and merchandises college sports as televised entertainment. American Indians have come to the university and have asked that he be retired, so that non-Indians can see them as they are, without the "white noise" stereotypes generate. Of course what they are asking is more complex than that, for they want to be simultaneously recognized as Indians, members of a specific tribe, survivors of a particularly difficult history, and fellow human beings. They ask that the weight of history be acknowledged, and that non-Indians refrain from appropriating their images for commercial or entertainment purposes. Given the past we all inherit, it seems like a reasonable request.

"In our country, if you want to honor someone," Charlene Teters says evenly, "you name a building after them or put up a statue of them. You don't dress up like them and dance around." Her art and her life have been changed by her encounter with Chief Illiniwek. The soft, harmonious paintings she created before coming to the University of Illinois have given way to large installations that incorporate and critique popular culture. She now travels around the country, speaking about stereotypes of Indians and protesting mascots. During baseball season you may meet her outside the stadium in Atlanta or in Cleveland, holding a sign or a bullhorn, looking serious, seeming on the verge of tears. In football season she is outside the stadium in Washington, D.C., or Kansas City, bundled up warmly, hands in her pockets. She says now that if she'd known that the photo of her holding that first sign would be so widely reproduced, she would have done more than write "Indians Are Human Beings Not Mascots" on white posterboard with black marker. "I would have made it more artistic," she says, smiling. Not that it would have mattered. In a recent protest she held only a piece of paper that said, "We are human beings." When I was a girl in Memphis, striking garbage workers marched with signs that read, "I am a man."

And the woman in the white braids, what of her? Her feelings are genuine, her confusion is real. I sympathize with her. The longing for a closer connection to nature, the desire to belong unequivocally to a particular place, to a community are real human feelings, ones I have shared. American Indians have paid a price because they must either conform to the fantasy of what an Indian is like or remain invisible. But other Americans have also lost something by basing their identity on a mythic sense of self.

James Baldwin, always a perceptive observer, says that what passes for identity in America are a series of myths about heroic ancestors. In order to create heroic settlers and founders, we must also create heroic Indians to greet them.

Charlene Teters surrounded by Native American children at a rally in Urbana, Illinois on October 16, 1999. Photograph by Brent McDonald.

Most of the encounters between Americans and Indians in our past have been forgotten. Among the thousands of significant moments in hundreds of years of white-Indian contact, there are only two that we have retained, replayed, and committed to our national memory.

The most important of these, although it lasted for years rather than minutes, is the military defeat of the Plains Indians. The Battle of Little Bighorn is a centerfold in this glossy special section of our memories. Why does Little Bighorn fascinate us so? Our myth about the battle justifies our notion that we had no choice but to use military force against the Plains Indians. Had we not, the Little Bighorn myth goes, we would all have ended up like Custer.

The other moment we remember is the moment of arrival, the experience that Marquette describes, of stepping ashore and being welcomed. We wish we had not betrayed our role as guests at the feast. For more than anything we want to be at home in our own land, but we are painfully aware that we came to this place as intruders. This is why we sustain the myth of the Indians who welcomed us, fought nobly, and then were destined to perish, conveniently leaving a vast expanse of wilderness at our disposal. Dressed as an Indian who fought at Little Bighorn, Chief Illiniwek pantomimes at every halftime this charade of welcome to his followers, the modern tribe of Illini.

Walt Disney's animated *Pocahontas* carries the same message. John Smith, presented as a good colonist who treats Indians fairly, is wounded near the end of the film. The historical John Smith was wounded when his powder horn exploded, but in the movie he throws himself in front of Powhatan, the father of Pocahontas, in a heroic effort to save the chief's life.

In both accounts Smith is taken by ship back to England. In the Disney version, as Pocahontas bids him a romantic farewell, Powhatan approaches, and removing his own blanket of animal skins from around his shoulders, he covers Smith with it. Solemnly he says, "You are always welcome among our people. Thank you, my brother." This blessing is the movie's resolution. How satisfying for us, the white descendants of Smith and his fellow colonizers, to have earned our place in the New World through our ancestor's good deeds, to have such a noble figure proclaim his gratitude and pronounce us kin.

An extra helping of irony is heaped on the Disney film because of the identity of the performer who speaks Powhatan's lines with such authority. He is Russell Means, one of the founders of the American Indian Movement, the highly visible group of militant young activists who in the late 1960s and early 1970s occupied at various times the *Mayflower II*, Mount Rushmore, and most significantly, the village of Wounded Knee for over two months. It was Russell Means who launched the first legal salvo in the fight by Indian activists to reclaim their images when he threatened to sue the Cleveland Indians and Atlanta Braves baseball teams in 1972.

Myth, according to Barthes, is "speech *stolen and restored.* Only, speech which is stolen is no longer quite that which was stolen: when it was brought back, it was not put quite in its place." The real Powhatan's words would have been full of anxiety for the future. The real Illiniwek Indians were forcibly deported from Illinois. But the animated Disney Powhatan grants a lifelong welcome to the good Englishman. And the mythic Illinois chief, stolen and returned to this usurped turf, dances happily. He gives his blessing to the way it all turned out.

We can accept this blessing only if we remain ignorant of our own history. Pontiac, the Ottawa war leader who captured British forts and pushed for a spiritual revival of Indian values, came to Illinois to recruit allies and died there. Tecumseh, a Shawnee leader, tried to unite all the Indian tribes and create an independent Indian nation. It was a brilliant idea, and had he succeeded, it would have changed the course of American history. He also recruited allies among the Illinois tribes. Shabbona, a young Potawatomi chief, left his village in Illinois and accompanied Tecumseh until his death. But we know nothing of this. Pontiac is a car and Tecumseh a summer camp. And we cannot name Shabbona or Black Hawk, who fought to retain Sauk and Fox land in northern Illinois in the 1820s. Nor have we heard of Marie Rouensa. Carlos Montezuma, who fought for citizenship and rights for his people until his death in 1923, is forgotten, and modern-day Indians remain invisible to us.

And yet we are not satisfied by blank spaces, nor do we want a past composed of them. As Marina Warner writes, "But the imagination doesn't blank out; its characteristic movement tends to write graffiti on any empty space. Without telling the particular story, a generic one will expand to fill the gap." The particular Indian leaders who lived in Illinois and passed through there— Marie Rouensa, Pontiac, Tecumseh, Shabbona, Black Hawk, and Carlos Montezuma—have been forgotten; it is the generic chief who is celebrated and honored, the graffiti story that is retold. What is startling is the power that a character like Chief Illiniwek accrues over time. What is disturbing is how very easily we are convinced by our own mythology.

The Native American writer Paula Gunn Allen has written that "In short, Indians think it is important to remember, while Americans believe it is important to forget." If this is so, this is a curious and complicated pattern of forgetfulness we practice. Our rivers, mountains, and cities are named in Indian languages and our identity is founded on the myth of their demise. So thoroughly have we documented this demise that we often fail to see or recognize contemporary Native Americans, even when they speak to us. But are we really forgetful, or do we make a choice, albeit unconsciously, for a generic myth over the gritty ambiguities, the sandy starts and stops, and the unresolved questions that make up this particular story? In our desire to belong on these prairies, we identify with a symbol that is, as Barthes says, "deprived of memory." But by doing so, we forfeit a genuine knowledge of who we are and a genuine connection to this place where we live.

In an elegant metaphor, Virginia Woolf describes how women have served for centuries as a looking glass to magnify men at twice their normal size. American Indians have served other Americans in much the same way, as the still surface of a wistful reservoir that casts back at us, not a true reflection, but one that shows us the way we wish to be.

While writing about Chief Illiniwek and reading about the Illinois Indians, I found myself also reading about my mother's mother's family, who were some of the earliest settlers in Arkansas. I had heard about one ancestor, a French-Canadian voyageur who came down the Mississippi River as a paddler for a French priest when he was fourteen. In his old age he played host to the naturalist Thomas Nuttall and is described in the account of Nuttall's travels. But what I never knew was that my great-great-great-grandfather did not go directly down the Mississippi from Canada to Arkansas. The priest was assigned to the "pays des Illinois" and my forebear Joseph Baugis spent twenty-three years in the French village of Kaskaskia before migrating south to Arkansas Post. He traded with the same Indians whose lives I have been reading about. He probably spoke

Kaskaskia. He was married and served as a churchwarden at the church in Kaskaskia. On microfilm in the University of Illinois library I found a copy of his marriage certificate, written in antiquated French. Although his wife was able to write her name, he could only make a cross. Some of his business transactions were also there, not simply difficult to decipher, but painful to read, for he bought and sold slaves, both black and Indian.

Before setting out on this inquiry, I felt that I had no connection to this place, that I ended up here at random, the victim of the Harpies of Geographic Dislocation, mythological figures I imagined to embody the incessant mobility and uprootedness of modern life. But learning its history has changed how I see this piece of prairie, and for the first time, I feel as if I might belong here, not because I have a great-great-great-grandfather who lived in Illinois in colonial times, but because I have come to know the story of this place.

As I write this, the 1999 World Series has just ended. During the playoffs, the newspapers were filled with accounts of Indians and Braves, chopping and chanting, winning and losing, scalping their rivals, and always and forever, on the warpath. Every time a Cleveland player came to bat, Chief Wahoo grinned idiotically in the corner of the television screen. During the World Series the screen was filled with thousands of Atlanta fans, chanting "war chants" and waving foam tomahawks. In fact, the Braves met with American Indian leaders during the playoffs. They were asked once again to change their name. For the moment, the activists asked the team to request that fans refrain from doing the tomahawk chop and the war chants. Time Warner, which owns the Braves, offered free public service announcements about real Indians instead. And when the Braves played the Yankees in the World Series a month later, they were still chopping and chanting as crazily as ever.

Football season is also under way. At Florida State University in Tallahassee, home of the Florida State Seminoles, Osceola rides into the stadium on Renegade, a black and white Appaloosa. He throws a flaming lance to open the game and the Seminoles cheer. Osceola has appeared on their football field for twenty years, but the Seminoles insist he is not a mascot either, but a symbol they "respect and prize," who reminds them that although they cannot always win, they can remain brave, dignified, and proud. This pageant has the support of the flamboyant Seminole leader James Billie, who was tribal chairman for twenty-two years. The first tribal leader to introduce Indian gaming, Billie is a performer who has his own rock band and an alligator wrestler who recently lost part of a finger. He has created tribal enterprises, many based on tourism, that made $300 million last year for the Florida Seminoles, who number less than three thousand. He was stripped of power in May 2001 by the tribal council. He has been accused of sexual harassment, tax evasion, and skimming millions of dollars off tribal funds.

Before writing this, I assumed that an awareness about stereotypes belonged to our post–civil rights movement era. But the hours I've spent reading old newspapers have convinced me that in the past, people were more image-conscious than I had imagined. In the *Champaign Daily Gazette* for August 15, 1907, next to a story about Buffalo Bill's Wild West, I happened upon this article:

> Two negroes created a diversion on a Champaign-Decatur interurban car Wednesday evening in putting a stop to the singing of "Old Black Joe" by a number of young white men who live east of Urbana. It is said the negroes became offended by the song soon after they got on the car and finally asked the men to cease singing that song. The request was not granted and finally a demand was made that the song be stopped. This led to trouble in which one of the negroes drew a revolver and shot a hole in the car floor. This was a signal which passengers understood as that for getting out of the car, and the singers were the first to leave, being in such a hurry that they went through the windows instead of taking the longer route to the door. Other passengers followed their example and before the

car could be stopped at the Dallenbach crossing west of the city, only the crew was left.

No attempt was made to capture the man who did the shooting and it is said no one knew him. This is the story given by one of the department heads of the road as reported to him, and does not agree with the rumors that an attempt had been made by a negro to kill a white man.

I find it interesting that two black men, although outnumbered in the car, spoke up when offended by a song almost one hundred years ago. Of course the hidden revolver had something to do with their boldness. It's likely the song was a provocation, a musical taunt, likely that the young white men shuffled and mimed a minstrel show as they crooned. I can't help it, my imagination is off and running and I picture the man with the revolver on trains all over the country, a mysterious crusader for the right to be depicted with respect, who shoots toward the floor whenever his people are belittled. Then moves on. But I realize this is a curious fantasy—a combination of *Have Gun Will Travel* and Rosa Parks. What strikes me most about the story is how long ago it took place. Long before the NAACP boycotted Quaker Oats for their Aunt Jemima advertisements, long before civil rights or political correctness, long before our contemporary debate over public symbols like Indian mascots and the Confederate flag, this man spoke up because he was offended. At a time when minstrel shows were popular and slaves were often described as living happily on the plantations, the man on the interurban car insisted otherwise.

Sixty-eight years later, in 1975, Vernon Bellecourt's brother Clyde came to the University of Illinois as a member of AIM and said that the halftime performance in which a student pretended to be an Indian offended him. In response, a former chief replied that Chief Illiniwek portrays Indians the way they want to be portrayed. Would the former chief have made a similar statement to a black leader speaking about Aunt Jemima? It seems unlikely, but what makes the difference? Is it because African Americans are a larger group and have more political power? Is it because the identity of American blacks, defined by the one-drop rule, is not tangled in the ambiguities that make American Indian identity so complicated, and that can be used to dismiss Native spokespeople?

Bellecourt and the armed man on the interurban car spoke up not only for respect but for truthful history. The myth of contented slaves may assuage our guilt about slavery but it denies the suffering of slave descendants and postpones our coming to terms with our past. The white woman who places a mammy doll in her kitchen may feel genuine affection for it, but her fondness is for an idealized past, not for African American women. Quaker Oats has not retired Aunt Jemima, but in 1968 the company did retire her slave clothing and slave cabin. It ceased to print ads recounting her happy memories of working as a cook on a fictional plantation. In one of these ads, Aunt Jemima saved her master from northern soldiers by distracting them with pancakes. In another, she sheltered and fed two southern officers hiding from northern troops.

At the beginning of the twenty-first century, most of us no longer sustain the myth of contented slaves, loyal to their benevolent masters, who stay on by choice after emancipation. However, we are still unwilling to relinquish a version of our history that demands mythic settlers, a mythic frontier, and mythic Indian warriors—warriors who forced us to fight them because they were innately warlike by nature, warriors who were honorably vanquished in a fair fight, warriors who have no descendants to tell their side of the tale. Like the mammy dolls and Aunt Jemima ads, Indian mascots present a mythic past that is simpler and sweeter, a mythic history that absolves much. The sports fan who wears a Chief Wahoo hat may feel genuine affection for the Wahoo character, but his fondness is for a romanticized illusory past that never was, not for contemporary Native American people or culture. The mascots have only one twisted connection to contemporary Native Americans: they deny the Native view of our shared past.

In an essay about the West, the writer Marilynne Robinson reminds us that "myths are complex narratives in which human cultures stabilize and encode their deepest ambivalences." There is no deeper American ambivalence than our feelings about how we acquired the land we love. "The power of myth," she continues, "lies in the fact that it arrests ambivalence." Ambivalent about the truth, we turn to myths like Starved Rock and mascots like Osceola and Chief Illiniwek to reconcile the contradiction between our aspirations and our history.

Barbara Munson is cautiously hopeful about the role history can play in resolving mascot issues. A former art teacher and counselor, she is a member of the Oneida nation and she chairs the Indian Mascot and Logo Taskforce of the Wisconsin Indian Education Association. When the Wisconsin superintendent of public instruction wrote a letter requesting schools to change Indian-based names and logos, Barbara and her daughter offered to help with the transition at the local high school in Mosinee. Students at the high school, from which her daughter had recently graduated, call themselves the Indians. The arrival of the letter seemed to offer the right moment for Barbara and her daughter to finally speak up. After they spoke, the school board voted to keep the name. "I felt like the original invisible Indian," she says, "despite the fact that we had been active, positive members of the community for many years." People cited the area's Indian heritage; there was a portrait of Chief Mosinee in every phone book and in the public library. Barbara did some research and found that the beautiful portrait of an elderly man with a lined face was not a portrait of a local chief, but of Ka-be-nug-way, a leader of the Cass Lake Chippewa in Minnesota. The portrait was used by the Mosinee Paper Company to market its paper towels with the slogan "tough as an Indian." This advertising campaign had turned the image into a local icon and inspired the high school to change their teams from Papermakers to Indians. But even learning this did not inspire a change back to Papermakers or to something new. The Indian logo remains.

But Munson remains hopeful about what happens in a community when Indian people and teachers advocate for change. "Many community members," she tells me, "might prefer the fabrications and myth. But whether they want it or not, they get a gift of history." As she found herself offering an unwelcome education, she observed, "Every community that gives up one of these logos has some sacrifice to make. That goes with change. So what are they getting?" As an Indian educator, she knew the change benefited Indian people, but what happened to the community itself when the logo was replaced with something more positive?

Munson believes that non-Indian community members receive a more complex view of their own ancestors, that they come to see them as ordinary human people. It may be some time before a community appreciates this. "Even if some people don't see it as positive now, I know that eventually, this gift of a more complex and truthful history will change something in the community. This makes me feel hopeful."

When I started writing this book, I knew only that Chief Illiniwek's halftime dancing made me uneasy. That the marching band was being criticized for inventing a fictional character also made me uneasy. When the university announced that this character was "authentic," my unease grew. I set out to write this book in order to make sense of my own confusion.

At some point along the way I became convinced that the American Indians I interviewed were right. I learned the history behind their anger. How they were perceived as doomed, how they were denigrated, studied as objects, and then romanticized, and how, finally, those cultural traits that appealed to other Americans, particularly the dancing and the dramatic regalia, were not borrowed, but taken, without any ethic at all. Some of those acts and items have religious value for Indian people, and after years of intense suppression of their religious beliefs by a country that prides itself on religious freedom, they resent their display for commercial entertainment. Having struggled to hold on to each marker of their culture, they have no wish to loan out what remains to those who have never acknowledged or appreciated its intrinsic value. Again and again, I witnessed what happened when they stepped up to speak as contemporary Indian people. They were discounted, ignored, or angrily attacked.

Edward Curtis, who used Indians to create his own photographic artworks, said it was "true that advancement demands the extermination of these wild, care-free, picturesque Indians, and in the language of our President, we cannot keep them or their lands for bric-a-brac." Curtis, who was referring to a remark by Teddy Roosevelt, meant that we could not afford to keep the Indians the way we now keep bison, in parks, to observe and admire, as souvenirs. Bric-a-brac is a collection of small objects of ornamental or sentimental value. But this is precisely what we have done. We have pretended that real Indian people no longer exist and we have kept the picturesque fantasy Indians of the Wild West shows and western movies and the environmental movement Indians who remain forever in touch with the earth, kept the feather headdresses and tepees, the drumming and dancing, for American bric-a-brac. We keep them because they ornament our landscape and because we are sentimental about the romantic version of our past their images suggest to us. Had Indian leaders been asked, in Teddy Roosevelt's day, whether they wanted to be bric-a-brac, I suspect they would have answered, just as the Illini answered Marquette, "We are people." And they might have continued, "We are human beings, not bric-a-brac."

The skeletons I saw at Chucalissa when I was a child are no longer on display. The Choctaw say that they are not their ancestors and they cannot properly bury them, so they remain in storage. The old "mammy" Aunt Jemima has become the province of collectors, museums, and postmodern theorists. The music for the halftime show is duplicated by a photocopy machine rather than by a student with pen and ink at a nickel a page. But an American Indian identity is still a commodity that can be taken on, as if it belonged to everyone.

When I began writing I assumed that the history of Indian-white relations took place far west of central Illinois. It concerned those people, way over there. And those people way back then. Now I realize that it is taking place here and concerns these people. And that these people are my people, whether I have an ancestor among them or not. Us. In the here and now.

Finally I think I have come to understand that American history and Native American history are not a sheet that we, like a divorcing couple, can rip down the middle so that we can hang on to our own ripped halves, to our familiar faded mythologies and our percale heroes, wash them, wear them, and hang them up to dry with clothespins on separate lines. You get Tecumseh and we get George Washington. You take Osceola and we'll keep Stonewall Jackson. There is only one faded cloth, woven as a single piece, a white and blue star coverlet decorated with beadwork, spotted with blood. Somehow we each have to find a corner to hold while it flaps in the wind.

Addendum from Grand Forks, North Dakota

He seems like a character who stepped out of an academic spoof—a Las Vegas casino owner who wanders into academia with an open palm of million dollar bills that he wants to give away. Let's name our character Ralph and make him not only a hard-nosed businessman but a former hockey goalie who wants to give his alma mater the best hockey arena in the world, bar none. Let's add that he's reclusive and lives in one of the towers of his own Imperial Palace, a gigantic hotel and casino on the Las Vegas strip. And then, in a flashback to the 1980s, we'll include a scene of our donor at a lavish party he threw to celebrate Hitler's birthday. We won't leave out the sheet cakes with swastikas, the beer hall music, the matching portraits of Ralph and Adolph in uniform, or the bartenders wearing T-shirts printed with "Adolf Hitler European Tour—1939–1945."

By this time, you're probably thinking our plot is implausible. Even though people like Ralph probably do exist, they don't donate large sums to public universities. But at the University of North Dakota, Ralph is for real. In the same month in which the Las Vegas press broke the story of his Nazi-themed parties, alumnus Ralph Engelstad offered $5 million to UND to repair its hockey rink. The university sent a group to Las Vegas. Their tour of the Imperial Palace Casino included the "war room," decorated with murals of Nazi leaders and filled with a collection of Third Reich banners and weapons. They spoke briefly with Engelstad. After their return, the parties and the displays of Nazi memorabilia were described as "bad taste" and the gift was accepted. The Nevada Gaming Control Board took a harder line, fining Engelstad 1.5 million dollars for the "embarrassment" he caused the state.

The campus hoped for more largesse, but people in Grand Forks believe that Engelstad made it clear that he wasn't happy with either the athletic director or the president. In a coincidence, both resigned in the fall of 1998 and in December of that year Ralph Engelstad announced a $100 million donation. For a small state-funded school with a budget of $250 million, it was an extraordinary moment. In fact, it was one of the ten largest gifts ever given to an American university.

But Engelstad is not the kind of donor who hands over a check and then reappears for a ribbon-cutting ceremony and a banquet. What he offered was to build a state-of-the art arena for the powerhouse North Dakota hockey team, the Fighting Sioux. The arena would cost about $50 million. What was left the school could spend as it wished.

One other thing seems to have been on our donor's mind: symbols. North Dakota teams no longer played under the old Fighting Sioux logo, a realistic profile of an Indian warrior which looked very much like the logo of the Chicago Blackhawks. The new logo, designed to reduce tensions with Native Americans, was also a warrior's head in profile, but the face and feathers were highly stylized and it was printed in green on white, the school colors. Engelstad had led a petition drive to bring back the old logo but had not succeeded.

Native Americans are North Dakota's largest minority and the nickname Fighting Sioux, which dates to the 1930s, has been problematic since the early 1970s when a fraternity created an obscene ice sculpture of an Indian woman. The Sioux Nation surrounds the campus and UND has responded to their objections by retiring caricatured or disrespectful images. But they have held onto the Fighting Sioux name. An earlier president said about the nickname, "When the leaders of the Sioux Nation come and tell me they don't want it, I'll respect that."

In recent years, most of the tribes that make up the Sioux nation in North and South Dakota have said just that. Despite the ongoing tensions, a new logo just for the hockey team was unveiled in 1999, a gift from the alumni association. This one was commissioned from a Native artist and, not too surprisingly, turned out to be a modernized version of the old logo that Ralph Engelstad liked. The Sioux warrior in the new logo is drawn with strong black outlines and a fierce expression in the style of a comic book superhero. Many faculty, students, and tribal members were outraged when it was unveiled. Harking back to an age of more explicit stereotypes, the new logo seemed to them a provocative act.

Charles Kupchella, who had just been installed as president of the university, may not have realized how combustible this issue was. When the new logo was introduced in Grand Forks in November 1999, it was as if someone had taken a bellows to the glowing controversy. It re-ignited. Anti-Indian graffiti appeared on campus buildings and Native students reported incidents of harassment.

Following a time-honored academic recipe for cooling combustibles, Kupchella formed a committee to examine the issue. He seemed to be about to announce a change when he sent an e-mail on December 18, 2000, to the State Board of Higher Education. He wrote that he saw no choice but to respect the request of the state's tribal councils. It must be noted that the University of North Dakota is one of the leading schools in the country when it comes to recruitment and retention of Native students. UND has a respected Department of Indian Studies as well as programs for Native nurses, doctors, teachers, journalists, lawyers, and educators.

Two days later, Engelstad sent President Kupchella a letter that contained none of the niceties of campus-speak. Change the name, the letter said, and you can forget the arena. Although it was partially built and he had already spent $35 million, if the team were not the Fighting Sioux, Engelstad threatened to walk away, turning off the heat as he went out the door. He was counting on the North Dakota winter to do the rest.

The next day, the State Board of Higher Education held an unscheduled teleconference and voted 8-0 to keep both the Fighting Sioux name and the new logo. Construction resumed.

The arena was dedicated in October 2001. In the days before the opening, Ralph Engelstad threw three separate parties for the elementary, middle school, and high school students of Grand Forks. Outside the stadium sat some sort of statue completely covered with plywood.

"It's Ralph," some Grand Forks residents said knowingly.

"No, Sitting Bull," others replied.

On the cold windy morning of October 5, the statue was unveiled. Native Americans were showcased at the ceremony. One spoke, and two young men in brightly colored feathers danced. As the last cloths came off the statue, one of the dancers played haunting flute music. The statue turned out to be Sitting Bull on a horse carrying a prayer circle. A family of approving descendants of Sitting Bull, including an elderly woman in a wheelchair, were pointed out, thanked, and applauded. Other Native Americans stood at a distance, watching in disapproval.

Ralph and Betty Engelstad cut the green ribbon imprinted with the Fighting Sioux hockey logo to officially open the luxurious little stadium. Bright green blazers were a fashion staple at the ceremony. Engelstad and his grandson, however, wore matching black leather bomber jackets with the Fighting Sioux hockey logo appliqued on the back.

In the large Sioux Merchandise shop inside, the warrior's head appeared on pencils and pucks, on leather jackets like Ralph Engelstad's, and on luggage sets. The bottles of water were labeled H-Sioux-O. The crowd moved into the lobby for the unveiling of a second statue, and this time it was Ralph Engelstad. The statue had been donated by appreciative alumni. As they praised his generosity, the university officials watched their donor warily. Engelstad has a reputation for unpredictability and had not committed to any particular role in these ceremonies. The officials breathed visible sighs of relief when he agreed to stand next to his statue for a photograph.

The arena itself is a marvel. The rink's boards contain a state-of-the-art sound system that amplifies the sound every time a player crashes into them. Another sound system amplifies the swoosh of the puck into the net. The electronic scoreboards, video boards, and laser light system cost millions. The bathrooms, tiled in granite, have closed-circuit televisions so fans don't miss a single minute of the action if they leave their seats, which have leather cushions and cherry wood armrests. There are forty-eight luxury suites that rent for up to $40,000 each, and all are rented through the 2003 season.

For the players, there is a 10,000-square-foot exercise room built on a spring-mounted wooden floor, a sauna and a jacuzzi large enough to hold twenty-four hockey players at once, and an underwater treadmill equipped with cameras. The home team's lockers are cherry and oak. On every possible surface is inlaid or printed or inscribed the words Fighting Sioux or the logo of the warrior's head with the four eagle feathers. There are 4,500 of the logos in the arena, many of them made of highly permanent materials like granite or brass. The largest is inlaid in the lobby floor in white, green, and black granite. Between Sitting Bull and the electronic advertising kiosk on the street is a four-hundred-foot hedge that looks a bit uneven from the ground. When viewed from above, even these bushes spell out FIGHTING SIOUX.

As you leave the arena, you walk under Ralph Engelstad's sayings in bronze above the lintels: "No dream comes true until you wake up and go to work." Or "The harder I work, the luckier I get." In the only interview he has ever granted, to his hometown newspaper in Thief River Falls, Minnesota, Engelstad said these mottoes are the secrets to his rags-to-riches success. He also admitted that he is angry over the rise of gambling casinos on Indian reservations and resents the tax advantages Indian-owned casinos enjoy.

According to Engelstad, the arena ate up the entire 100 million dollars. There won't be any left over for other programs. Nor has he handed over his gift. It still belongs to him and is being run by one of his management companies. After the ceremonies, Engelstad did say a few words to the press. Whether he handed over the arena, he said, would depend on how the university was managed.

That same day a conference about the issue of team names and logos based on American Indians took place in the student union a short walk away. After an opening speech by Winona LaDuke, the topics ranged from the legalities of trademarks to spiritual loss to harassment of Indian students. Another descendant of Sitting Bull decried the university's appropriation of his ancestor. As he spoke, a T-shirt that was being sold in a bar near campus was passed around. The following day the Fighting Sioux football team would play their arch rivals, the North Dakota State Bison. "Buck the Bison Under," the green letters said. The crude image showed an Indian, pants down, behind a bison. When many of the Native people at the conference saw the T-shirt, their eyes filled with tears. President Kupchella quickly issued a statement condemning the shirts and stating that anyone wearing one would not be allowed into the game. However, a new version of this theme is printed every year. As long as the teams remain the Fighting Sioux, it seems unlikely this will change.

The conference ended with a march to the arena. The protestors carried green balloons. At a rally in the parking lot of the arena they attached white prayer flags to a makeshift fence. Many faculty members who joined the march agreed with a colleague whose letter to the *Grand Forks Herald* thanked Ralph Engelstad for making it clear that "we place more importance on money than on integrity, that we prefer 'tradition' to justice, that we honor sports over education, and that expediency and convenience carry more weight among us than do ethics and morality."

Before the game that night, there was another brief ceremony. Ralph and Betty Engelstad and their grandson walked to center ice on a green carpet and received a standing ovation so loud Betty Engelstad covered her ears. The arena was filled to capacity. Ralph Engelstad's two hundred guests from Las Vegas wore matching jerseys with the new logo and the number twenty-three, his number when he was a backup goalie at North Dakota. Again Engelstad said only a few words. He ended: "May the Fighting Sioux and the Fighting Sioux logo stand forever." His grandson dropped the ceremonial first puck.

At intermission, a laser light show flashed green lights and glowing images of the logo. The North Dakota Fighting Sioux lost to the Minnesota Gophers.

How will this story end? The cost of keeping the brass polished and the underwater camera running at the Ralph Engelstad Arena is estimated at three million dollars per year. The bushes have to be trimmed so the aerial typography stays sharp. Profits are expected to reach four million this year and the university will receive the difference. But a gift with cables attached has other costs that are harder to calculate.

When the Fighting Sioux went on the road this year, they were greeted with protests. At home, the arena has created tensions between business leaders who have embraced it and members of the campus community who view it with ambivalence.

The NCAA, which regulates all college sports, has agreed to look at the Indian name and mascot issue. An NCAA ruling that bans team names and logos based on Indians may be UND's only hope to extricate their reputation and get their hands on the deed to the imperial ice palace.

There is definite potential for a sequel, even a series of campus whodunits. Who is sending threatening faxes to faculty members who speak against the logo? And even if our seventy-year-old character meets his demise, there's always the question of exactly what is in Ralph Engelstad's will.

Afterword

Leaving pretend Indians out of sports may be more gesture than substantive change in American attitudes, but it is the gesture that Native people want from the rest of us, a kind of symbolic reparation, an act of acknowledgment.

Native America received a powerful message of support in April 2001 when the United States Commission on Civil Rights, at the urging of the only Native American commissioner, Elsie Meeks, issued a statement on the subject. This advisory body to the U.S. government has no enforcement authority, but its serious studies of discriminatory practices often lead to legislation. The statement is addressed to non-Native schools and says that "the use of the imagery and traditions, no matter how popular, should end when they are offensive." Thirty years had passed since the Red Power movement first spoke out against mascots, thirty years since Native students at Oklahoma and Stanford agitated for change, only twelve years since a Native student stood outside the basketball arena at Illinois holding a poster board sign. In this relatively short time, the movement to retire Indian-based imagery from schools has been recognized as a legitimate struggle for American civil rights.

Suzan Shown Harjo, who has lobbied for and worked on legislation to preserve Indian culture since the 1970s, says that she has never seen an issue galvanize so many people in Indian Country. "Repatriation? Most Native people didn't know or understand or care about it at the time. But mascots—these are public slurs, easy to understand. Thousands of Native people have done something about the problem in their own schools and communities." Remarkably, people working against mascots in Maryland and Texas, California, and Vermont communicate with each other through the internet. As I write this, activists all over the country are following a bill in the California legislature that would ban mascots in California schools.

Roy Saigo, the president of St. Cloud State University in Minnesota, asked the National Collegiate Athletic Association to consider a resolution stating that the NCAA does not condone the logos and nicknames. President Saigo said that his own experience as a Japanese-American who was sent to an internment camp during World War II taught him that ethnic stereotyping is a serious matter. A precedent was set when the NCAA threatened not to schedule championship events in states that did not take action to retire the Confederate flag. The statement on that subject said in part, "The NCAA wishes to express its continuing concern over any official symbol that conveys discrimination and racism."

NCAA-affiliated schools include not only the Utah Runnin' Utes, the Florida State Seminoles, the Illinois Fighting Illini, the Arkansas State Indians, and the North Dakota Fighting Sioux, but also the Southeastern Oklahoma State Savages and Lady Savages. We could probably argue that we're all savages at heart, but S.O.S.U. doesn't let us. Their logo of two feathers is a clear reference to American Indians.

Administrators at colleges and universities who are caught between their own non-discrimination policies and demands from alumni and boosters would be off the hook if the NCAA were to ban the Indian imagery. They could throw up their hands and tell their alumni and boosters, "We had to do it!" and the NCAA would be the bad guy who spoiled everyone's fun. Even Ralph Engelstad would have to accept the authority of the NCAA if the North Dakota hockey team is to compete. However, a policy that bans certain team names might well be challenged in court on the grounds that it seeks to limit free speech.

Meanwhile, back at Illinois, in order to satisfy the conditions of the association that accredits the university, the trustees had called for a "dialogue." Anyone, anywhere could express an opinion about Chief Illiniwek. A retired judge was retained to sift through the testimony and produce a report.

For the one day of public testimony, Native Americans converged on the Illinois campus from Minnesota, Mississippi, North Carolina, and New Mexico. They erected a lodge on the grass in front of the auditorium and lined up for a chance to speak.

The youngest Native speaker was Wayne Crue. Wayne is an adopted Shoshone-Bannock boy whose family came to Champaign-Urbana so that his adoptive mother Cyd could attend graduate school at the University of Illinois. Wayne looked Indian, wore his hair long, and was a champion grass dancer. Although she had never been politically active before, his mother Cyd became involved in the anti-chief movement. She served as the head of the Illinois chapter of the National Coalition on Racism in Sports and the Media and was often quoted in the local press. At the dialogue, she stood behind Wayne, who was thirteen, while he read a statement that said in part, "Eagle feathers and paint are spiritual items I must earn and take care of in a prayerful way. You don't just buy them, you don't just decide to wear them, you must earn them. My regalia is sacred. I don't wear it down the street or to a sporting event. I only wear my regalia in a circle that has been blessed by a medicine man."

But when the other Native people had gone home, Wayne still had to go to middle school in Champaign. Seeing the anger directed at Wayne, his shop teacher, after attending a diversity workshop, declared the shop a "stereotype-free zone" and asked students to turn their Chief Illiniwek T-shirts inside out when they entered. The shop teacher was disciplined for taking this step. The Crue family accused another popular teacher of racism for comments she made to Wayne in the classroom. Eventually, Wayne's family, in order to protect him, sent him away to stay with friends and attend a reservation school for one semester.

After Wayne left town, I was at a luncheon for Illinois writers and someone mentioned the chief and my book. "It's a shame," one woman said to me, "that a family would use a child that way." I looked at her blankly. "Oh, you know," she said, "that family that adopted that Indian boy just so they could get rid of the chief. That just undermines the whole movement." When I was finally able to close my mouth and form words with my tongue, I told her that I knew the family, that they had adopted the boy long before they ever heard of Chief Illiniwek and that they were not involved in politics before moving to Illinois. But it was clear my words made no impression. The debate had become so bitter that each side thought the worst of the other. And as in other places, Native people who spoke out paid a higher price for their visibility than others.

In addition to the four-minute speeches, the dialogue received some 18,000 written comments. These included letters from Native organizations and civil rights organizations like the Southern Poverty Law Center. But the majority came from alumni and boosters and said, "Don't give in to the vocal minority. Keep the chief!" Some of these people claimed they had an Indian ancestor, although they were not sure to which tribe their ancestor had belonged. The report classified these letter writers as Native Americans in favor of the chief. The final bill for this charade was over $300,000. When the judge issued his report in September of 2000, both sides, in rare agreement, agreed that the exercise had been a waste of time and money.

Fed up with the university's refusal to act, professor Stephen Kaufman mentioned to the *Chicago Sun-Times* that the next step might be to contact potential athletic recruits to make sure they knew that the university was ignoring civil rights organizations like the NAACP. Although Kaufman had yelled "racism" at the university for years, now, when he whispered "might contact recruits," the roof blew sky-high. The chancellor sent a mass email to every member of the campus community, over 30,000 people, informing them that because of NCAA rules, they could not contact athletic recruits without first getting clearance from the division of intercollegiate athletics. When the chancellor refused to retract his gag order, the American Civil Liberties Union sued. The judge issued a temporary restraining order to the university. After the chancellor sent out a second e-mail that was a partial retraction, the university filed a motion to dismiss the suit, arguing that the problem had been resolved. But the ACLU felt the second e-mail did not go far enough to ensure free speech and the ACLU lawyers filed additional claims, including damages.

A new chancellor arrived and pledged to increase diversity at Illinois. When a protestor was arrested at a basketball game, she publicly articulated her commitment to free speech and said that the security guards had likely not followed university policy. She was viciously attacked in the local press for months afterward. The letter writers made it clear they would gladly forego their rights to free speech if they could be sure there would be no more protestors at basketball games.

In March 2002, the only African-American trustee, who had been charged with investigating whether a compromise was feasible, declared that it was not. After yet another year of study, he declared that either the university should retire the chief suitably or keep him and reinvigorate the tradition. As anti-climatic as it sounds, this was a small victory for the anti-chief forces, as they were the ones who had insisted that a compromise was unacceptable.

It was hardly a newsworthy pronouncement and yet Indian mascots were discussed on every sports program and every major network that week in mid-March 2002. The reason? A group of American Indians, Latinos, and white guys at the University of North Colorado decided to dub their intramural basketball team the Fightin' Whites. Their mascot was a 1950s-looking white guy in a suit and tie.

The media loved the idea. Sports columnists were off and running. The team hand motion, one suggested, could be reaching in a back pocket for a wallet. Orders for team T-shirts poured in. Actually, the Fightin' Whites had taken their name to make a point. A high school near Greeley called its teams the Reds. Its mascot was a caricature of a big-nosed Indian in buckskin pants and moccasins. But when Solomon Little Owl and other team members went to the high school to discuss the mascot, the administrators refused to hear their concerns.

Of course, making a 1950s white guy into a mascot is not the same as adopting an Indian warrior. White guys were running things in the 1950s and they still are. Their image dominates the media, their opinions are the ones we hear, their version of history is the one we are likely to learn. We are never in doubt that there are lots of kinds of white guys because we see them everywhere. Some people argued that the whole thing missed the point: white guys were thrilled to be mascots for a change, but they still didn't have a clue how Indians felt.

The Fightin' Whites provided some welcome comic relief. Native people were particularly incensed in March 2002 about a poll released by *Sports Illustrated*. The poll asked 351 Native Americans about Indian mascots and names and found that 80 percent did not think teams should stop using them. This poll's results were exactly opposite of a poll conducted by the Native newspaper *Indian Country Today*. Sports pages all across the country featured the *Sports Illustrated* poll and drew the conclusion that activists, despite their successes, did not represent most Native Americans. How do they know these 351 people really are Native? Native people asked angrily. And why can't they just accept what our organizations have said?

The conversations in the media provoked by the poll and the white guy mascot repeated many of the same old arguments. But what about the Florida State Seminoles? Florida State pays royalties. What's wrong with a contractual agreement that works? Actually both Florida State and the Seminole Tribe insist that they have never paid or received any royalties. Neither the school nor the tribe would spell out the agreement they share, nor would they say how long it has been in place. It seems to be an informal association that has come about fairly recently in response to criticism from other Native groups. Many of the tribe's enterprises are based on tourism and the connection with a popular team is good publicity. James Billie, who endorsed the performance and team name while tribal chairman, was stripped of power in May 2001. However, the man who ushered in the era of Indian gaming by introducing high stakes bingo on the Seminole reservation is still a popular figure in the state. The three-thousand member tribe would have little to gain and much to lose if they initiated a bitter battle with Florida State and its alumni.

What about the Fighting Irish of Notre Dame? was invariably the next question. Isn't it the same thing? But it isn't quite because the Fighting Irish are the team name at a school where the Irish have played a significant role, and Irish-Americans have been important in Notre Dame athletics. They are using their own identity, not taking someone else's. In most cases where teams are named after groups of humans, they are not contemporary ethnic groups like American Indians. Families do not check off Pirates, Trojans, Spartans, Vikings, or Padres on census forms. As far as I know there are no Viking children trying to explain to their friends that they are proud of their Viking culture but their dad doesn't dress or act like the comic strip character Hagar the Horrible.

I know of only one non-Indian team name that has been charged with being offensive on ethnic and religious grounds—the Sonoma State Cossacks. In a curious parallel to the way American Indian mascots are presented as noble warriors, Cossacks were originally introduced to Sonoma State students as "Russian gentleman adventurers." There was no mention of pogroms. Objections from a Jewish student and the local Jewish community were taken seriously and soon followed by a vote to change. In fall 2002 Sonoma State teams will compete as the Seawolves.

From reading the work of Claude Steele, a Stanford psychologist, I learned about what he calls "stereotype threat." Stereotypes are damaging, his research shows, when they touch on an area where we do not feel secure, where we are threatened. Stereotypes won't hurt an African-American boy who wants to play professional basketball, but they may affect his performance when he sits down to take a standardized test. Stereotypes will not adversely affect a woman who wants to be a nurse or a teacher, but they may undermine her when she decides whether to pursue a career in engineering. Native Americans are vulnerable in a number of areas. Many Native students are likely to feel stereotype threat in academic settings. In addition, Native people often say they feel invisible and forgotten relative to other minority groups. Their cultural and religious beliefs are misunderstood and misrepresented. This means that their very identity is under threat. Since mascots strike at identity, I can only conclude that these stereotypes are likely to adversely affect Native students.

In every debate over team names and logos, it is the accusation of racism that sparks the strongest feelings and the most vociferous counter-attacks. When fans go to great lengths to justify their team name, they are also battling to prove that, "We are not racists." White Americans desperately want to think of themselves as fair and egalitarian.

Social psychologists point out that blatant racism is rarely expressed anymore because it is no longer socially acceptable. Racism still exists, but it has become more subtle. Modern racism is often expressed indirectly through a strong desire to hold onto traditional values which disadvantage non-whites. If the social psychologists are right, defending mascot traditions is an acceptable way to publicly express anti-Indian sentiment.

Students who want to keep Chief Illiniwek are accused, sometimes angrily, of racism, and they respond defensively. They have never seen a "No Indians" sign and would probably not patronize a restaurant that placed one in its window. They oppose overt discrimination. But they miss the point because what they are being accused of is more widespread and more subtle. They are being accused of taking part in a pervasive societal network of belief that disadvantages Native Americans as students because it "celebrates" and "honors" them as school sports icons. Unfortunately, local battles like the one in my town become so heated that repressed hostility toward Native students and families rises to the surface. This is why state legislatures or regulatory organizations like the NCAA can play an important role in expediting change.

As a writer, I have had the experience, since *Dancing at Halftime* was published, of coming out from behind my desk to try to change my community and beyond. This book often focuses on dramatic moments outside stadiums, but change also happens because a legion of quietly determined people just keep writing letters and just keep showing up to state their case at meetings. Their optimism and determination are remarkable. Twenty years ago high school students not far from where I live cheered on their team, the Pekin Chinks. When Asian Americans objected, they adamantly defended their team name. Someday, American Indian mascots will seem just as outdated.

Acknowledgments

I am grateful to every one of the many people who talked to me about their own experiences with Indian mascots, as well as each student who posed questions. Many others passed on references, articles, names, or stories. Although I can't thank every single person with whom I've conversed on this subject, those conversations have been an important part of writing this book. I'd especially like to thank Clyde Bellecourt, Vernon Bellecourt, Jon Blume, Scott Brackenridge, Dee Brown, Malcolm Brown, Keith Coughlin, Michael Haney, Hugh Danforth, Chris Davis, Jack Davis, Joyce Dugan, William Engelbrecht, Brenda Farnell, Tim Giago, Monroe Gilmour, Bruce Hannon, Lynne Harlan, Pat Hofmann, William Hug, Seely Johnston, Ed Kalb, Stephen Kaufman, Michael Lindsay, Claude Meillasoux, Pat and Don Merzlak, Joe Miller, Barbara Munson, Dave Narcomey, Geoffrey Nunberg, Debbie Reese, Jay Rosenstein, Gary Smith, Ned Swanson, Karen Roberts Strong, Charlene Teters, Dennis Tibbetts, Bruce Two Eagles, David Voyles, Nell Jessup Newton, and John White for their generosity in sharing their memories and thoughts with me. I am grateful to Terry Dismuke for hospitality in Asheville. I am also appreciative of help from librarians in every library I visited or contacted.

Many people read portions of the book, in one of its many incarnations, and their responses helped me immeasurably. This final version owes its existence to the insistence of Eric Zinner. Frederick Hoxie read an earlier draft and offered suggestions. Karen Winter Nelson, Norma Marder, and Herbert Marder read drafts; their responses to the work greatly improved it. My book club—Nancy Abelmann, Karen Winter-Nelson, Marilyn Booth, Bea Nettles, Jeanie Taylor, Jo Kibbee, Sally McMahan, and Frances Jacobson—were indispensable, as always. Sharon Irish, Murray Spindel, Chris Spindel, Monty Hunter, Hannah Hunter, Caroline Heller, Alice Deck, and Tom Turino provided ideas, support, and newspaper clippings. The women of Women Against Racism stood beside me. Nick Bassett helped research merchandise in campus stores; Becca Bassett accompanied me to demonstrations, sometimes in the pouring rain. Tom Bassett lent his expertise as a researcher, as well as much practical and moral support. When I ran into obstacles publishing this book, many friends rallied around me. I would particularly like to thank Peter Dimock.

I am also grateful to the many other people who helped me with the photographs that illustrate the book. Brad Hudson provided advice, Brent McDonald took photos around Memorial Stadium, and Bea Nettles offered support, advice, and the still life of souvenirs. Ann Brandenburg generously lent me photographs from her family's collection. Roger Botte and Annick LePape found the postcard of Buffalo Bill in France. Tom Bassett took photos and helped with the selection of images.

An earlier essay entitled "Chief Illiniwek: Vanishing Chief of the Halftime Illini" appeared in the fall–winter 1997 issue of *Crab Orchard Review*. Finally, it was the words of Michael Dorris, encountered in the newspaper, that first set me on this path. Although I never met him, I imagined sending him a copy of this book when it was complete as a way of expressing my gratitude. Now that is no longer possible. Instead, I can only recall readers to his work and send thanks to his memory.

Bibliographic Essay

Teachers at many levels tell me that the subject of mascots works well as a way to introduce students to many issues. Teachers will find that Jay Rosenstein's film *In Whose Honor* complements this book well and is accessible for diverse ages and groups. A Native point of view about mascots can be easily found in many columns published in *Indian Country Today*, the nation's largest native newspaper (www.indiancountry.com). Another valuable resource is the American Indian Sports Team Mascots webpage edited by Robert Eurich (members.tripod .com/earnestman/1indexpage.htm).

For a general introduction to this topic, I recommend first turning to two encyclopedias. The *Encyclopedia of North American Indians*, edited by Frederick Hoxie, has entries that range from "mascots" and "Meriam Report" to "pow-wows" and "Illinois Indians." The encyclopedia's introduction, written by Hoxie, provides useful guidelines for thinking about American Indian issues. Another essential text is the Smithsonian Institution's *Handbook of North American Indians*. Volume 4, *History of Indian-White Relations,* edited by Wilcomb Washburn, contains detailed articles by scholars, many of which are relevant to this story. Volume 15, *The Northeast,* edited by Bruce Trigger, contains an entry on the Illinois Indians.

For examining white images of Indians, I have been guided by Robert Berkhofer's comprehensive study, *The White Man's Indian*, which is widely available in paperback. A summary of his work can also be found in volume 4 of the Smithsonian *Handbook of North American Indians*. Brian Dippie's book *The Vanishing American* examines the misconception that American Indians are disappearing from American life. Philip Deloria's insightful and evenhanded *Playing*

Indian would have answered many of my questions had it been published when I began.

For the history of football and student life at Illinois, I sorted through documents from the university archives, mostly football programs, yearbooks, and articles in alumni publications, but also some newspaper clippings. In antiques shops I found student handbooks and songbooks from the 1920s.

The section on Boy Scouting relies on handbooks from 1914 and 1942, and a Cub Scout handbook from 1943, as well as a recent book about the meaning of Scouting by the historian Robert MacDonald called *Sons of the Empire*. The information on Ralph Hubbard was taken from a biography called *A Man as Big as the West,* by Nellie Snyder Yost. It is a curious mixture of biography, dictated memoir, and testimonial.

To comprehend the U.S. government's American Indian policy in the 1920s and to understand the decade itself, I highly recommend Hazel Hertzberg's *Search for an American Indian Identity.* Other books that provided a context for the debates over dance in the 1920s were Kenneth Philp's *John Collier's Crusade for Indian Reform*, John Collier's *Indians of the Americas*, and Brian Dippie's *Vanishing American*. Some of the regulations themselves can be found in Wilcomb Washburn's *American Indian and the United States: A Documentary History*.

I have turned to Vine Deloria, Jr.'s work, especially his book *Custer Died for Your Sins*, again and again. Each time I have been inspired by his knowledge and his wry, humorous style. The story he recounts about dancing at Pine Ridge is reprinted in *Red Power*, by Alvin Josephy.

A great deal has been written by art historians about images of the frontier and about Edward Curtis. I relied on the book *The Vanishing Race and Other Illusions*, by Christopher Lyman. It includes an introduction by Vine Deloria, Jr., from whom I have borrowed the eloquent idea of the "wistful reservoir."

I opened the leather bindings of the *Jesuit Relations* for the first time in the reading room at the Bibliothèque Nationale in Paris. I've since read them in less elegant surroundings and the contents were just as interesting. If a reader wants to experience New France in the seventeenth and eighteenth centuries, these documents convey life lived on the ground in a way that scholarly texts written much later simply don't. There are seventy-three volumes in all and the last two are the index. The Illinois are mentioned in nearly every volume from 51 to 71. Marquette's voyages can be found in volume 59. Another contemporary account of the Illinois was written by the nephew of Henri Tonti, Pierre de Liette (or Delliette), who spent many years in the Illinois country and knew many Illini Indians well. Delliette's memoir is reprinted in *The French Foundations* and in a volume edited by Milo Quaife. For images of this period—portraits, maps, signatures, and sketches—a rich source is the catalog entitled *French Peoria and the Illinois Country*, by Judith Franke.

And for filling in the American history I never learned in school, I found Richard White's *Middle Ground* and Eric Wolf's *Europe and the People without History* particularly helpful and fascinating. Fergus Bordewich's *Killing the White Man's Indian* takes the reader on a tour of Indian reservations today. The discussions with contemporary tribal leaders provide a clear contrast to romanticized fictional Indians. He ends this book with an eloquent plea to end the distortions of myth.

The section on the Redskins trademark case is based on the Trademark Trial and Appeal Board ruling, *Harjo v. Pro Football, Inc.*, as well as on the petitioners' brief and articles written about the case.

In those places in the book where I am speaking with people, either face to face or on the phone, I have tried to make that clear. Otherwise their remarks were taken from newspaper interviews or other published sources.

Selected Bibliography

Allen, Paula Gunn. "Who Is Your Mother? Red Roots of Feminism." In *The Sacred Hoop: Recovering the Feminine in American Indian Traditions*. Boston: Beacon, 1986.

Baldwin, James. "A Talk to Teachers." In *The Price of the Ticket*. New York: St. Martin's, 1985.

Barthes, Roland. "Myth Today." In *Mythologies*. New York: Farrar, Straus and Giroux, 1972.

Bataille, Gretchen, and Charles Silet, eds. *The Pretend Indians: Images of Native Americans in the Movies*. Ames: Iowa State University Press, 1980.

Berkhofer, Robert, Jr. *The White Man's Indian*. New York: Vintage, 1978.

Bolotin, Norman, and Christine Laing. *The World's Columbian Exposition*. Washington, DC: Preservation Press, 1992.

Bordewich, Fergus. *Killing the White Man's Indian: Reinventing Native Americans at the End of the Twentieth Century*. New York: Anchor Books, 1996.

Brown, Margaret Kimball. *Cultural Transformations among the Illinois*. East Lansing: Michigan State University Museum Publications, 1979.

Burford, Clive. *"We're Loyal to You, Illinois": The Story of the University of Illinois Bands under Albert Austin Harding for Forty-three Years*. Danville: Interstate Press, 1952.

Colangelo, Aaron Strider. "Note: A Public Accommodations Challenge to the Use of Indian Team Names and Sports Mascots in Professional Sports." *Harvard Law Review* 112, no. 4 (February 1999).

Coleman, Nick. "Jerking the Strings." *Minnesota Monthly*, October 2001, 44–48.

Collier, John. *The Indians of the Americas*. New York: Norton, 1947.

Culhane, John. *The American Circus*. New York: Henry Holt, 1990.

Custer, Elizabeth. *Boots and Saddles*. Norman: University of Oklahoma Press, 1961.

Davis, Duane, and A. Damani Harris. Program for *They Landed at Plymouth*, performed at Lincoln Hall Theater, University of Illinois, April 29, 30, and May 1, 1995.

Davis, Theodore. "Registration of Scandalous, Immoral, and Disparaging Matter under Section 2(a) of the Lanham Act: Can One Man's Vulgarity Be Another's Registered Trademark?" *Ohio State Law Journal* 54 (1993): 331-401. Reprinted in *The Trademark Reporter* 83 (1993).

Deloria, Philip. *Playing Indian*. New Haven: Yale University Press, 1998.

Deloria, Vine, Jr. *Custer Died for Your Sins*. New York: Macmillan, 1969.

Dippie, Brian. *The Vanishing American*. Lawrence: University Press of Kansas, 1982.

Dohrmann, George. "Face-Off." *Sports Illustrated*, October 8, 2001, 45–49.

Dorris, Michael. *Paper Trail*. New York: HarperPerennial, 1995.

Eurich, Robert. "American Indian Sports Team Mascots." Web page, http://members.tripod.com/earnestman/1indexpage.htm.

Farnham, Eliza. *Life in Prairie Land*. Urbana: University of Illinois Press, 1988.

Fiske, Susan. "Stereotyping, Prejudice, and Discrimination." In *Handbook of Social Psychology*, 4th ed., edited by Daniel Gilbert, Susan Fiske, and Gardner Lindzey. Vol 2, ch. 25. Boston: McGraw-Hill, 1998.

Franke, Judith. *French Peoria and the Illinois Country*. Springfield: Illinois State Museum, 1995.

Gorn, Elliott, and Warren Goldstein. *A Brief History of American Sports*. New York: Hill and Wang, 1993.

Griffin, Susan. *The Eros of Everyday Life*. New York: Doubleday, 1995.

Harjo v. Pro Football, Inc. *United States Patent Quarterly*, series 2, Bureau of National Affairs, TTAB, June 14, 1999.

Hauser, Raymond. *An Ethnohistory of the Illinois Indian Tribe, 1673-1832*. Ann Arbor: University Microfilms, 1973.

Hertzberg, Hazel. *The Search for an American Indian Identity*. Syracuse: Syracuse University Press, 1971.

Heth, Charlotte, ed. *Native American Dance: Ceremonies and Social Traditions*. Washington, DC: Smithsonian Institution, 1992.

Holloway, Michael. "Too Many Chiefs and Not Enough Indians (A Brief History of the University of Illinois)." In *The Rocking House: Selected Poems, 1996-1998*. Urbana: Non Sequitur Press, 1998.

Hoxie, Frederick. *A Final Promise: The Campaign to Assimilate the Indians, 1880-1920*. Lincoln: University of Nebraska Press, 1984.

———, ed. *Encyclopedia of North American Indians*. Boston: Houghton Mifflin, 1996.

Hurt, James. *Writing Illinois*. Urbana: University of Illinois Press, 1992.

Iverson, Peter. *Carlos Montezuma and the Changing World of American Indians*. University of New Mexico Press, 1982.

Jackson, Donald, ed. *Black Hawk: An Autobiography*. Urbana: University of Illinois Press, 1964.

Johnson, Judi. *The Illiniwek*. American Indian Pamphlet Series, no. 2. Springfield: Illinois State Museum, n.d.

Josephy, Alvin. *Red Power*. Lincoln: University of Nebraska Press, 1999.

Lawrence, Elizabeth Atwood. *Rodeo: An Anthropologist Looks at the Tame and the Wild*. Knoxville: University of Tennessee Press, 1982.

Lippard, Lucy, ed. *Partial Recall: Photographs of Native North Americans*. New York: New Press, 1992.

Loewen, James. *Lies My Teacher Told Me*. New York: Touchstone-Simon and Schuster, 1995.

Lyman, Christopher. *The Vanishing Race and Other Illusions: Photographs of Indians by Edward S. Curtis*. Introduction by Vine Deloria, Jr. New York: Pantheon, 1982.

MacDonald, Robert H. *Sons of the Empire*. Toronto: University of Toronto Press, 1993.

Mails, Thomas. *Fools Crow*. New York: Doubleday, 1979.

Manring, M.M., *Slave in a Box: The Strange Career of Aunt Jemima*. Charlottesville: University Press of Virginia, 1998.

Matson, N. *Memories of Shabbona*. Chicago: Donnelley, Gassette and Loyd, 1880.

Maxwell, William. *The Folded Leaf*. New York: Vintage, 1996.

Merz, Charles. *The Great American Band Wagon*. New York: John Day, 1928.

Midway Types: *A Book of Illustrated Lessons about the People of the Midway Plaisance, World's Fair, 1893*. Chicago: American Engraving Co., 1894.

Mitten, Lisa. "The Mascot Issue." Web page, http://www.pitt.edu/~lmitten/mascots.html.

Moses, L. G. *Wild West Shows and the Images of American Indians*. Albuquerque: University of New Mexico Press, 1996.

Munson, Barbara. "Not for Sport," *Teaching Tolerance*. No. 15 (Spring 1999).

Myers, Albert Cook, ed. *Narratives of Early Pennsylvania, West New Jersey, and Delaware, 1630-1707*. New York: Scribner's, 1912.

Pease, Calvin T., and Raymond C. Werner, eds. *The French Foundations, 1680-1693*. Vol. 23. Collections of the Illinois State Historical Library, 1934.

Philp, Kenneth. *John Collier's Crusade for Indian Reform*. Tucson: University of Arizona Press, 1977.

Quaife, Milo, ed. *The Western Country in the Seventeenth Century: The Memoirs of Lamothe Cadillac and Pierre Liette*. Chicago: Lakeside Press, 1947.

Reese, Debbie. "Mom, Look! It's George, and He's a TV Indian!" *Horn Book Magazine*, September–October 1998.

Reynolds, John. *Pioneer History of Illinois*. Ann Arbor: University Microfilms, 1968.

Robinson, Marilynne. "Hearing Silence: Western Myth Reconsidered." In *The True Subject*, ed. Kurt Brown. St. Paul: Graywolf, 1993.

Roosevelt, Theodore. *The Winning of the West*. New York: Scribner, 1926.

Rosenstein, Jay. *In Whose Honor? American Indian Mascots in Sports*. Documentary film. New Day Films, 22D Hollywood Ave., Hohokus, NJ 07423.

Scott, James. *The Illinois Nation*. 2 vols. Streator: Streator Historical Society, 1973, 1976.

Solberg, Winton. *The University of Illinois, 1867-1894*. Urbana: University of Illinois Press, 1968.

Staurowsky, Ellen. "An Act of Honor or Exploitation? The Cleveland Indians' Use of the Louis Francis Sockalexis Story." *Sociology of Sport Journal* 15 (1998): 299-316.

Steele, Claude M. "A Threat in the Air: Stereotypes Shape Intellectual Identity and Performance." *American Psychologist* 52 (6) (1997): 613–629.

Temple, Wayne. *Indian Villages of the Illinois Country, Historic Tribes*. Illinois State Museum Scientific Papers, vol. 2, pt. 2. Springfield: Illinois State Museum, 1966.

Thwaites, Reuben Gold, ed. *The Jesuit Relations and Allied Documents: Travel and Explorations of the Jesuit Missionaries in New France*. New York: Pageant, 1959.

Tibbetts, Dennis. "Minstrel Show." Unpublished poem.

Trigger, Bruce, ed. *Handbook of North American Indians*. Vol. 15, *The Northeast*. Washington, DC: Smithsonian Institution, 1978.

Utley, Robert M. *The Lance and the Shield: The Life and Times of Sitting Bull*. New York: Henry Holt, 1993.

Vecsey, Christopher, ed. *Handbook of American Indian Religious Freedom*. New York: Crossroad, 1991.

Warner, Marina. *Six Myths of Our Time*. New York: Vintage, 1995.

Washburn, Wilcomb. *The American Indian and the United States: A Documentary History*. Westport: Greenwood Press, 1979.

———, ed. *Handbook of North American Indians*. Vol. 4, *History of Indian-White Relations*. Washington, DC: Smithsonian Institution, 1988.

White, Richard. *The Middle Ground*. New York: Cambridge University Press, 1991.

Wolf, Eric. *Europe and the People without History*. Berkeley: University of California Press, 1982.

Yost, Nellie Snyder. *A Man as Big as the West*. Boulder: Pruett, 1979.

Young, Linda. *Hail to the Orange and Blue!* Champaign: Sagamore Publishing, 1990.

Ziff, Bruce, and Pratima V. Rao. *Borrowed Power: Essays on Cultural Appropriation*. New Brunswick: Rutgers University Press, 1997.

Zlotchew, Ethan. "'Scandalous' or 'Disparaging'? It *Should* Make a Difference in Opposition and Cancellation Actions: Views on the Lanham Act's Section 2(a) Prohibitions Using the Example of Native American Symbolism in Athletics." *Columbia-VLA Journal of Law and the Arts*. 22, no. 2 (1998): 217-46.

ABOUT THE AUTHOR

Carol Spindel teaches creative nonfiction writing at the University of Illinois in Urbana-Champaign. Her first book, *In the Shadow of the Sacred Grove*, was a memoir of living in a West African village. Published by Vintage Books in 1989, it was named a Notable Book of the Year by the *New York Times Book Review*.

She has published articles and essays in magazines that range from *Magic* to *Horticulture* to *African Arts*. Her essays have appeared in literary journals and have been heard on National Public Ratio. She has taught workshops in nonfiction and the personal essay at many places including the *Iowa Summer Writing Festival* and the *Paris Writers' Workshop*. A native of Memphis, Tennesee, she now lives in Urbana, Illinois, with her husband and two children. They maintain a second home in a village in Ivory Coast, West Africa.